Writing Baseball

THE SOUTHERN ILLINOIS UNIVERSITY PRESS SERIES

Series Editor's Note

In 1943, G. P. Putnam's Sons began a series of major league team histories with the publication of Frank Graham's history of the New York Yankees. From 1943 to 1954, Putnam published histories for fifteen of the sixteen major league teams. The Philadelphia Athletics ball club was the only one not included in the series, though Putnam did publish a biography of Connie Mack in 1945. Of the fifteen team histories, only one, the St. Louis Cardinals history, originally published in 1944, was expanded for a later edition.

Thirteen of the fifteen team histories in the Putnam series were contributed by sportswriters who were eventually honored by the Hall of Fame with the J. G. Taylor Spink Award "for meritorious contributions to baseball writing." Three Spink recipients actually wrote eleven of the team histories for the series. The famed New York columnist Frank Graham, after launching the series with the Yankees history, added team histories for the Brooklyn Dodgers and the New York Giants. Chicago sports editor and journalist Warren Brown, once dubbed the Mencken of the sports page, wrote both the Chicago Cubs and the White Sox team histories. Legendary Fred Lieb, who, at the time of his death in 1980 at the age of ninety-two, held the lowest numbered membership card in the Baseball Writers Association, contributed six team histories to the Putnam series. He also wrote the Connie Mack biography for Putnam.

For our reprints of the Putnam series, we add a foreword for each team history by one of today's most renowned baseball writers. The bibliography committee of the Society for American Baseball Research has also provided an index for each team history. Other than these additions and a few minor alterations, we have preserved the original state of the books, including any possible historical inaccuracies.

The Putnam team histories have been described as the "Cadillacs" of the team history genre. With their colorful prose and their delightful narratives of baseball history as the game moved into its postwar golden age, the Putnam books have also become among the most prized collectibles for baseball historians.

Richard Peterson

THE BOSTON RED SOX

Two of Boston's Greats—Ted Williams and Babe Ruth

THE BOSTON
RED SOX

FREDERICK G. LIEB

With a New Foreword by Al Silverman

Southern Illinois University Press
Carbondale and Edwardsville

First published 1947 by G. P. Putnam's Sons. Copyright © 1947 Frederick G.
  Lieb.
Writing Baseball series edition published 2003 by Southern Illinois
  University Press. Reprinted by arrangement with G. P. Putnam's Sons, a
  member of Penguin Putnam Inc.
Series editor's note copyright © 2001 and foreword copyright © 2003 by the
  Board of Trustees, Southern Illinois University
All rights reserved
Printed in the United States of America
06 05 04 03   4 3 2 1

Library of Congress Cataloging-in-Publication Data

Lieb, Fred, b. 1888.
  The Boston Red Sox / Frederick G. Lieb ; with a new foreword by
  Al Silverman.— Writing baseball series ed.
      p. cm. — (Writing baseball)
  Originally published: New York : G.P. Putnam's Sons, 1947.
  Includes index.
      1. Boston Red Sox (Baseball team). I. Title. II. Series.
  GV875.B62 L5 2003
  796.357'64'0974461—dc21
  ISBN 0-8093-2493-8 (pbk. : alk. paper)   2002030653

Reprinted from the original 1947 edition published by G. P. Putnam's Sons.

Printed on recycled paper. ♻

The paper used in this publication meets the minimum requirements of
American National Standard for Information Sciences—Permanence of Paper
for Printed Library Materials, ANSI Z39.48-1992. ∞

To James V. Malloy

Son of a Red Sox fan; a Red Sox fan;
and father of a Red Sox fan

CONTENTS

⊖

List of Illustrations		xi
Foreword by *Al Silverman*		xiii
Preface		xix

1.	A Distinguished Pedigree	3
2.	Ban Decides to Take In Boston	8
3.	Collins' Team an Early Contender	19
4.	Pilgrims Sink Pirate Craft	33
5.	John I. Taylor Enters the Scene	49
6.	An Awful Letdown	63
7.	Red Sox Rope a Texas Cowboy	76
8.	Everything Happens in 1912	90
9.	Snodgrass Makes His $30,000 Muff	95
10.	Along Came Ruth!	114
11.	Bill Carrigan Wins Three 2-to-1 Games	124
12.	Speakerless Red Sox Still Are Good	139
13.	Evil Genie from Peoria Enters Picture	154
14.	Barrow Wins World War I Title	163
15.	The Rape of the Red Sox	178
16.	Bob Quinn Flounders in the Cellar	193

17. Rescuer Yawkey Spends His Millions   203
18. Terrible Ted Snared in San Diego   214
19. Hopes and Disappointments   224
20. Back in the Pennant Swim Again   237
21. Looking Forward   255

Index   259

ILLUSTRATIONS

☒

Two of Boston's Greats—Ted Williams and Babe Ruth *Frontispiece*

Cy Young	Facing page	66
Jimmy Collins		66
Bill Dinneen		67
John I. Taylor		67
George "Duffy" Lewis		82
Tris Speaker		82
Harry Hooper		82
"Old Rough" Bill Carrigan		83
"Smoky Joe" Wood		83
Everett Scott		130
Larry Gardner		130
Hubert "Dutch" Leonard		131
Carl Mays		131
Signing Contracts in 1918		146
Herb Pennock		147
"Sad" Sam Jones		147
Bobbie Doerr		216
Ted Williams, "The Kid"		216
Cecil "Tex" Hughson		217
Dom DiMaggio		217
Dave Ferriss, His Sister, Ann, and Mother, Mrs. W. P. Ferriss		226
Johnny Pesky		227
Rudy York		227
1946 Red Sox American League Champions		242
Thomas Austin Yawkey		243
Joe Cronin, Manager 1946 Champions		243

FOREWORD

I DON'T know why, when I was growing up in Lynn, Massachusetts, fifteen miles north of Boston, that it was the Boston Braves who captured my heart, not the Boston Red Sox. All my friends in those years—from the late 1930s until we went off to war—loved the Red Sox—not me. I think it was because, at a tender age, I was developing contrarian tendencies. Also, the Red Sox of that period, and earlier, always seemed to have a robust and exciting hitting team. Yet they always ended up breaking your heart. In the five years from 1938 through 1942, they tied for fifth once and finished second four times. The Braves had no pretensions whatsoever; you always knew where you stood with them—in seventh place mostly. But they did have Casey Stengel as their manager and infielders named Bama Rowell, Sibby Sisti, and Tony "poosh-'em-up" Cuccinello, plus a center fielder named DiMaggio—Vince, that is, the least of the brothers. I found them all irresistible.

Reading Frederick G. Lieb's intimate and informative history of the Red Sox from its birth in 1901 as the Boston Pilgrims through the 1946 season—a season that Lieb had much to write about—brought my childhood back to life. I remember in the summer of 1942 spending most afternoons on a friend's porch, weaving leather thongs together for his father's factory while we listened to the Red Sox games on the radio. As usual, the Red Sox, for a time, were challenging the Yankees, but what we were eager to keep up on were the shenanigans of Ted Williams. Of course, we wanted to know how he handled each at bat because he was having one of his greatest years. He would end up with the Triple Crown—leading the American League in batting (.356), home runs (36), and runs batted in (137). Yet the sportswriters refused to vote for him as the American League's Most Valuable Player. Instead, they gave it to Joe Gordon of the Yankees, who led the league in strikeouts, errors by a second baseman, and grounders that turned into double plays. It had to do with Williams's attitude. You never knew from day to day when "the splendid splinter" would explode, stage a sulk on the field, shoot out Fenway Park's scoreboard lights, or announce his determination to switch occupations—from baseball player to fireman. "The young Ted Williams," Lieb writes, was "irascible, hot-tempered, unsocial and easily offended." And the Red Sox, for two decades, couldn't live without him.

The franchise in almost every one of its eras, as Lieb shows us over and over in his richly documented narrative, relied on one magical ballplayer who would rise above all others, flourish for a time, and then, for one reason or another—money being the usual reason—be discarded. A prime example is Cy Young, who was the star pitcher for the Boston Pilgrims in the ball club's first eight years of life. It was Young, winning thirty-three games in 1901, thirty-two in 1902, twenty-eight in 1903, when the Pilgrims won the first modern World Series, who led the way. He won 192 of his lifetime record of 511 victories (a figure that has never been topped) in his Boston years. Then, in 1909, two years after the Pilgrims were renamed the Red Sox, Young was banished to Cleveland. He was forty-two years old.

The next Red Sox dynasty—from 1912 through 1918—resulted in four world championships. And it was Tris Speaker, establishing himself as the greatest center fielder of his day, who became the cornerstone of the team. "Everything happened in 1912!" Lieb writes. "They acquired a new park; they got a new set of owners, a new manager, a new pennant, and, of course, a new world championship." And Tris Speaker was voted the American League's Most Valuable Player. The "Grey Eagle," as he came to be called, played for the Sox through the 1915 championship season and then was traded to Cleveland. It wasn't that he had peaked as a ballplayer—he played another fantastic thirteen years in the American League—but because the Red Sox would not give him the salary increase he wanted. With the Indians in 1916, he hit a league-leading .386.

But along came the miracle-maker of them all, Babe Ruth, to become America's sweetheart. Ruth was a pitching marvel his first three years with the Red Sox, winning eighteen games in 1915, twenty-three in 1916, twenty-four in 1917. In 1918, when he began to get serious as a hitter, he won only thirteen games but batted .300 and led the league in home runs with eleven. He also pitched two vital victories against the Chicago Cubs in the World Series that enabled the Red Sox to win one more—one last, it seems—world championship. And then Harry Frazee, who bought the Red Sox in 1916, needed money.

Fred Lieb titles two of the book's chapters as follows: "Evil Genie from Peoria Enters Picture" and "The Rape of the Red Sox." Both, as you probably have already guessed, concerned Harry Frazee. One engaging revelation from Lieb about Frazee is that he started out in life as a bellhop. He could only go up from there and later became a major producer of Broadway musicals. Many of his shows were hits, some were not. And when he had a flop, the only way he could recoup was to sell one of the better Red Sox ballplayers. After a 1919 season in which Ruth hit twenty-nine home runs, astounding for its time, Frazee, desperate for capital, gave away Ruth to the New York Yankees in exchange for $100,000 in cash and a $350,000 mortgage on Fenway Park. It bailed out "the evil genie" but caused a fissure that, for the Red Sox fans, has never healed.

The worst of times for the Red Sox were the years from 1922 through 1932, when, without a savior like Cy Young or Tris Speaker or the Babe, they finished in the cellar in all but one of those years. "It was the distressful period," Lieb writes, "when the Red Sox were out at their toes and had ghastly holes in their heels."

The distressful period ended in 1933 when a nonplaying savior bought the Red Sox. Tom Yawkey was a young multimillionaire who loved baseball and wanted to win. He wasted no time. In 1934, he bought the Philadelphia Athletics' star pitcher Lefty Grove. In 1936, he went to the A's again and took from them the slugging first baseman Jimmy Foxx. In between Grove and Foxx, in 1935, Yawkey made what Lieb calls "his most sensational deal." Joe Cronin of the Washington Senators was the best shortstop in the league at that time. In 1934, at the age of twenty-eight, he became player-manager of the Senators. He also married the boss's daughter. Clark Griffith, the owner of the Senators, gave a boost to his son-in-law's career in 1935 when he sent Cronin to the Red Sox for $250,000. That prompted a sports columnist, unnamed by Lieb, to comment: "I'd be happy to sell my son-in-law for $250,000."

The Red Sox now became known as "Yawkey's Millionaires," but the money didn't seem to help his team. In 1936, after a sixth-place finish, Yawkey decided that buying players didn't work; the Red Sox would have to build a real farm system. In 1938, however, with six of its veterans batting over .300—Jimmy Foxx led the league in batting with a .349 average and 175 runs batted in; he also hit fifty home runs—the Red Sox finished in second place, nine and a half games behind the Yankees.

Then the farm system began kicking in: Ted Williams in left field, second baseman Bobby Doerr, center fielder Dom DiMaggio, shortstop Johnny Pesky, third baseman Jim Tabor—and a surprise. All through its history the Red Sox never seemed to be able to develop real major league pitchers. All of a sudden, they came up with a brace of young, fresh, and formidable arms in Tex Hughson, Mickey Harris, and Dave "Boo" Ferris. World War II took away everyone's best and brightest. But the established stars and the budding players came back in top form, and 1946 was a glo-

rious season for the Red Sox, and the perfect ending to Fred Lieb's absorb-
ing history.

What sparked the Red Sox rush to the 1946 pennant—they pulled away
early, won 104 games, and finished seventeen games ahead of their hated
rivals, the Yankees—was the unaccustomed superb pitching from Dave
"Boo" Ferris, who won twenty-five games, Tex Hughson, who won twenty,
Mickey Harris, who won seventeen, and Joe Dobson, who won thirteen
games, including some fine relief stints. But the World Series against the
St. Louis Cardinals provided the team's first hints of their fate, defined by
Boston Globe columnist Dan Shaughnessy in his 1990 book *The Curse of
the Bambino*. It had come down to the seventh game at St. Louis, the score
was tied at 1-1, when Enos Slaughter opened the bottom of the eighth with
a single. The next two Cardinal batters were retired, but then Harry Walker
singled over the shortstop and Slaughter never stopped running. Shortstop
Johnny Pesky had taken the relay and held the ball in his glove, sure that
Slaughter would hold on third base. Uh-uh. As Pesky delayed the throw to
the plate, Slaughter streaked home with the winning run. The Cardinals
were world champions.

When I learned that Fred Lieb had died in 1980 at the age of ninety-two,
it made me recall my one meeting with him, in 1951, when I was in my first
year as an apprentice editor of *Sport* magazine. Lieb came up to our office
to deliver a manuscript and say hello. I remember shaking his hand and
thinking, wow, what a life this old guy must have had. Old guy? Then in his
early sixties, the story he brought to us we titled "Was This the Greatest
Game Ever Played?" The game was the 1908 New York Giants–Chicago
Cubs one-game play-off to decide the National League champion. In the
story, he tells about how the play-off had come about. The two teams, fighting for the pennant, had met three weeks earlier and Christy Mathewson
had "beaten" the Cubs, 2-1. The "winning" run was about to cross the plate
in the bottom of the ninth, except that the nineteen-year-old Fred Merkle,
who was on first base, decided he didn't have to touch second base, since
the winning run was in. Instead, he headed for the clubhouse. The winning run was not allowed, the Merkle "boner" became instantly infamous,
and since both teams were tied at season's end, they would have to meet
one more time. Christy Mathewson gave it the old college try but he had
pitched 290 innings in the season and was arm weary. The Cubs won 4-2.

In Fred Lieb's story for *Sport*, he discloses that that game caused the
formation of the Baseball Writers Association of America. What happened
was that when the reporters went to their seats in the press box, they found
they had been usurped; the seats had been given to actors and other New

York "swells." "Get the hell out of there," Hugh Fullerton of the *Chicago Examiner* told the actor Louis Mann, who occupied his seat. Mann refused, so, as Lieb tells it, Fullerton sat on the actor's lap "and dictated 5,000 words of the soul-stirring baseball drama from this upholstered seat." Two months later, the baseball writers organized and Fred Lieb, at his death, held the lowest numbered membership card.

In the last paragraph of this book, Lieb writes, "There has been a glorious past for the Red Sox, some cruel intervening years, a satisfying present, but the greatest Red Sox years are still ahead." Well, Red Sox fans are still waiting. Wouldn't it be grand if the republication of this book might serve as the magic wand that, after eighty-four years, would break the curse of the Bambino forever?

Al Silverman
April 2002

PREFACE

WHEN Ban Johnson, brash young president of the American League, decided to toss the gauntlet to the National League and invade the east in 1901, the inclusion of Boston, an early National League stronghold, was an afterthought. Johnson jumped into Boston when he heard a revamped major American Association was planning to put a club into the Hub.

It was a stroke of genius, as from the very first Boston welcomed the new club with open arms. Led by Jimmy Collins, greatest of third basemen, the early Boston Americans, then called the Pilgrims and Puritans, were contenders from the start and won early championships in 1903 and 1904, the second flag on the last day of the season, when Jack Chesbro let fly his historic ninth-inning wild pitch. On his team Jimmy had such early Boston greats as the incomparable Cy Young; his catcher, Lou Criger; Bill Dinneen, Chick Stahl, Pat Dougherty, Freddy Parent, Buck Freeman, and Hobe Ferris.

Two years after the club's second pennant, it suffered a losing streak of twenty straight and slipped to the bottom, but the early owner, John I. Taylor, was no last-place magnate, and the club was built up again to a point where it won four pennants and as many world championships from 1912 to 1918, the golden era in Boston American League baseball.

As early as 1907 Taylor had a happy idea and decided to call his team the Red Sox, borrowing the name from the fabulous Boston Red Stockings of the seventies and eighties, and it quickly won favor. There was something gripping, red-blooded about those words, the Boston Red Sox. A member of the Red Sox felt he was a somebody, like Jim Mutrie's early New York Giants, who had a slogan, "We are the people."

The words took on an early significance for Boston fans; the name and fame of the Red Sox quickly spread through all New

England and eventually became country-wide. From Calais, Maine, on the St. Croix River, across from New Brunswick, to the Connecticut–New York state line at Fairfield and Portchester, New York, there are colonies of Red Sox fans that root as loyally for the "Crimson Socks" as those within the sacred precincts of Back Bay.

And what athletes had their spike-scarred calves encased in the red hosiery in those halcyon years—the one and only Tris Speaker, the peerless center fielder; Babe Ruth, who won his first home-run crown in a Red Sox uniform; Duffy Lewis, the alpine goat of "Duffy's Cliff"; Harry Hooper, king of right fielders; "Rough" Carrigan, who blocked them off at the plate; "Smoky Joe" Wood, who won thirty-four league and three World Series games in 1912; Everett Scott, the durable shortstop; Larry Gardner, Hugh Bedient, Jack Barry, Stuffy McInnis, Joe Bush, Sam Jones, Wally Schang, Carl Mays, and countless others.

Following the World War I world championship of 1918 came the unhappy years when the red socks of Boston were out at the toes and had ghastly holes at the heels. Even the tidiest New England housewife would have shrunk from tackling such a darning job. It was the distressful period known as the rape of the Red Sox, when Harry Frazee, the New York theatrical man, made some of the Yankees' greatest teams possible by selling the cream of the Red Sox players to the wealthy Yankee colonels, Ruppert and Huston.

Boston fans felt a sigh of relief when Bob Quinn purchased the club in 1923, but Bobbie's wealthy backer, Palmer Winslow, died soon after the purchase, and the Quinn teams were even worse than the wrecked Frazee aggregations.

The eventual savior of the Red Sox from the ruck and muck of years of second-division baseball was the wealthy Tom Yawkey, foster son and nephew of Bill Yawkey, legendary early owner of the Detroit Tigers. Through the expenditure of several million dollars for new talent and a revamped plant, Tom put the club back into the first division, but he couldn't buy a pennant, even though he spent a quarter of a million for Clark Griffith's son-in-law, Joe Cronin, whom Tom made his manager, and other fancy figures for Lefty Grove, Jimmy Foxx, Wes Ferrell, and lesser lights. The club was good, but not quite good enough to win. Four times the Red Sox ran second to great Yankee teams, but runner-up didn't satisfy Boston's pennant-hungry fans.

Yawkey, Eddie Collins, and Cronin then decided to emulate the Yankees and Cardinals and raise their own. The Red Sox developed a far-flung farm system, and early fruits were the man of many moods, Ted Williams; Dom DiMaggio, Bobbie Doerr, Johnny Pesky, Tex Hughson, Mickey Harris, Boo Ferriss, and other worthies.

Most of these bright young men marched off to war, and when they returned in 1946, the Red Sox emerged from their twenty-eight years of travail in the wilderness and won Boston's seventh American League pennant. After the long hiatus, the flag came with almost ridiculous ease, as the other two contenders, the Tigers and the once famed Yankees, were left far behind as the Red Sox ran off spring streaks of fifteen and twelve straight and were well-nigh unbeatable at Fenway Park.

And how Fenway Park fans ate up their winning dish! No appetizing plate of Boston beans went down with greater relish. Despite the limited 35,000 capacity of the attractive, well-kept park, they almost doubled Tom Yawkey's previous turnstile high—from 730,340 to 1,416,944. From all over New England, they merged on Fenway Park, and for most of the season it was great fun.

Those intrepid St. Louis Cardinals took a little of the joy out of life for Massachusetts fandom in the late season, when the Missouri upstarts, underdogs in the betting all through the 1946 World Series, nosed out the proud Red Sox, by this time frequently dubbed the Millionaires, in a tight seven-game series, with the seventh game so close that the "tying" Boston run crossed the plate as the last put-out was being made.

But the law of averages was running against the Red Sox. They already had won five World Series against no defeats, and it just couldn't go on indefinitely. There had to be an end sometime, and the season was 1946. But 1947 is another year, and there is a new goal to shoot for.

There were laughs and tears in this story of the ups, downs, and ups of Red Sox baseball, as club owners, managers, players passed through the Fens' baseball kaleidoscope. I have endeavored to portray the Red Sox picture, give the nation an authentic tale of one of its most publicized and interesting ball clubs, with a few peeps behind the curtain.

Even though the Red Sox never were my home team, perhaps a sports writer who wrote for twenty-five years in New York will be pardoned for writing a book on a Boston ball club. Boston never seemed far away on the New Haven, and the World Series that stand out most vividly in my mind were 1912, my second as a big league reporter, and 1915 and 1916. Also, a number of well-known Red Sox figures in this book, Joe Lannin, Harry Frazee, Ed Barrow, and Tom Yawkey, lived or made their headquarters in New York.

Jim Price, the Red Sox secretary under Bob Quinn, was my particular tin god—my first sports editor, and during his lifetime he gave me the inside story of many of these happenings in Boston and American League baseball.

I also wish to express my thanks for the help given me by such baseball men as Eddie Collins, Red Sox vice-president; Joe Cronin, the club's aggressive but affable manager; Tris Speaker, the famous Gray Eagle and the Red Sox's great center fielder; Duffy Lewis, Brave secretary, who played left field alongside of "Spoke"; Bob Quinn, former president of both Boston clubs; Bill Carrigan, manager of the Red Sox world champions; Ed Barrow, manager of the 1918 titleholders; Billy Evans, executive vice-president of the Detroit Tigers and former Red Sox farm superintendent; Ed Doherty, Red Sox publicity director; Dick Reichle, former Red Sox outfielder, now a St. Louis businessman; Wm. Green, Boston trainer; Ernie Lanigan, director of the National Baseball Museum; and Earl Hilligan, American League publicity chief.

The entire Boston press box has been wonderful. They couldn't have treated me better if my baseball card was marked Boston, instead of New York and St. Louis. For the early history of the Red Sox, I am especially indebted to Steve Mahoney, of the Boston *Globe*, possessor of one of the finest sports libraries in New England.

Others that were kind enough to give me valuable assists comprise almost the entire membership of the Boston chapter: Mel Webb, Gene Mack, Hy Hurwitz, and Roger Birtwell of the *Globe;* Burt Whitman of the *Herald*, Johnny Drohan and George Carnes of the *Traveler*, Jack Malaney of the *Post*, Joe Cashman and Dave Egan of the *Record*, Herb Finnegan and Austen Lake of the *American*, and Joe McGlone of the Providence *Journal*.

And stored away in memory's storehouse were Red Sox amusing incidents and tales told me by the late Paul Shannon, a lifetime friend and former fellow winter resident of St. Petersburg, Florida. I also express appreciation to J. Taylor Spink, publisher of the *Sporting News*, for permission to avail myself of the back numbers, files, and clippings of his baseball bible.

THE BOSTON RED SOX

1

⊖

A DISTINGUISHED PEDIGREE

I

THERE have been Boston Red Stockings almost since the day the national game discarded diapers. Despite Cooperstown's claims, Boston calls itself the Cradle of Baseball, as well as the Cradle of Liberty. It surely is a fact that the squalling infant, Boston baseball, which was rocked in the cradle half a decade after the close of the Civil War, wore socks of red.

However, in a way the original venerable Reds of Cincinnati gave the colors of their hose to the teams of Boston. Cincinnati had the first professional team, the Reds or Red Stockings of 1869 and 1870. The club went through the season of 1869 without a defeat, and nobody pinned their shoulders to the turf until June 14, 1870, when the Brooklyn Atlantics sent an early species of Flatbush rooters into a delirium of joy by defeating the Red Stockings, 8 to 7, in eleven innings. For many years thereafter that was a historic date, fittingly celebrated on the banks of the Gowanus Canal.

The leading spirits of that Cincinnati team were the Wright brothers—Harry and George, who played with sideboards without getting grounders tangled up in their whiskers. They were sons of a well-known English cricketer; in fact, the Wright boys learned to play cricket before they were initiated into baseball. Harry was the captain and center fielder of the Cincinnati Reds and drew $1,200. Brother George was the shortstop and at $1,400 was the highest-salaried player on the team. The Wright boys were almost as famous pioneers in baseball as were Wilbur and Orville Wright in the field

3

of aviation, but for some reason or other George Wright has a plaque at the Cooperstown Hall of Fame, while Harry, who managed early teams in Cincinnati, Boston, and Providence, seems to have got lost in the shuffle. Maybe the honor went to George because he drew $200 more on that early Cincinnati contract.

Some of the sports of the game first conceived the idea of having a league in 1871, and the National Association, the parent of the present-day National League—and of all leagues, came into being on March 4 of that year. The first clubs were the Bostons of Boston, the Athletics of Philadelphia, the Mutuals of New York, the White Stockings of Chicago, the Olympics of Washington, the Eckfords of Brooklyn, the Haymakers of Troy, New York, the Forest Citys of Cleveland, the Forest Citys of Rockford, Illinois, and the Kekiongas of Fort Wayne.

Cincinnati wasn't in this new setup, but the stars of the original Reds, the Wright brothers, catcher-outfielder Cal McVey, and Charley Gould, a first baseman, formed the nucleus of the first league club in Boston. Harry Wright was the manager, and it was perfectly natural that he should take his famous red stockings from Cincinnati to Boston. So the original club from the Hub immediately became known throughout the land as the Boston Red Stockings.

The early success that went with the red hosiery in the unorganized baseball of the late sixties followed the bright-hued stockings to Massachusetts. Harry Wright's club did not hide its light under a bushel; the Red Stockings were the super-duper club of early baseball. In fact, this early version of the Red Sox became too expert for its own good, and they wrecked the National Association by their prowess in the field and with their bats. After running second to the Philadelphia Athletics in the first professional race, 1871, the Red Stockings won the next four championships, all with rather ridiculous ease, as they rolled up such percentages as .830, .729, .717, and .899. The 1875 Boston Red Stockings were especially formidable, winning seventy-one games and losing only eight for that phenomenal .899 performance. The second place Athletics won fifty-three games and lost only twenty for a percentage of .726 and couldn't even make it close.

As early as 1874 the Red Stockings of Boston crossed the ocean and showed the sports followers of Britain and Erin their sturdy shanks wrapped up in flaming red. The Boston club and the Athletics of Philadelphia were baseball's first missionaries. Al G. Spalding, the Boston Red Stocking pitcher, was the prime mover of the expedition, while Al Reach, the Athletic second baseman, was his right bower.

The names of Spalding, Reach, and Wright all became famous among the nation's sporting-goods manufacturers.

The Red Stockings and Athletics played fourteen games in England and Ireland, Boston winning eight of them. At the time, baseball still was quite new in the United States, and the Britishers were neither curious nor interested to know more of the American game. They stayed away from the silly Yankee game in great numbers. So the Americans put aside their baseball cudgels and took on the British cousins at cricket. A third Wright, Sam, accompanied the party, and with a cricket team built around the three Wrights, Cap Anson, and Al Reach, the brash Americans blew down the wickets with their lethal clouts and cleaned up the Britishers at their own sport.

2

After the 1875 season, William A. Hulbert of Chicago got tired of seeing Boston win all the pennants with their almost unbeatable Red Stockings. Appealing to Al Spalding's midwestern pride, he induced Al and three of his fellow stars, Ross Barnes, Cal McVey, and Deacon Jim White to sign secret Chicago contracts for 1876. Adrian Anson of the Philadelphia Athletics, a member of Spalding's British tour, also was persuaded by Spalding to sign with the Chicago White Stockings.

There was a National Association rule that any player signing with a rival club while under contract would be barred permanently from the loop. As a result everyone involved was pledged to strictest secrecy. However, it always has been difficult to sit on a baseball secret, and a Chicago newspaper scooped the nation on the story late in 1875.

The story created quite a sensation and raised the roof in Boston. Spalding knew the jig was up and decided to make a clean breast of it. The jumpers were caricatured, ridiculed, and even accused of treason. Boys along the streets yelled after Spalding, Deacon White, and the others: "You dirty seceders, your white stockings will be soiled." It was only ten years after Appomattox, and "seceders" still was a reprehensible word in Boston.

During the following winter, Hulbert conferred with Spalding on what was best to do, and remarked to Al: "I've got a new scheme. Let us anticipate those eastern cusses and organize an association of our own, and we'll see who does the expelling."

Out of that inspiration came an early get-together in Louisville, and at a meeting in New York's Broadway Central Hotel, February

2, 1876, the venerable National League was born. "Let's get away from the old worn-out name of National Association of Base Ball Players," said Hulbert, "and call ourselves the National League of Professional Base Ball clubs."

Hulbert got his new league with its new name, and with his Boston jumpers won the league's first title with his recolored Chicago White Stockings in 1876. But Harry Wright, the Boston manager, was resourceful. By 1877 he had Jim White back again, and with such players as Orator Jim O'Rourke, Tim Murnane, later a famous Boston baseball writer, Ezra Sutton, John Morrell, Harry Schafer, George Wright, and himself, he had his Boston Red Stockings fluttering again from the top of the National League pennant pole in 1877 and 1878. Boston National clubs also won dramatic pennants with spectacular teams in 1883, 1891, 1892, 1893, and 1897 and 1898. With the passing of time, the nickname of Red Stockings seemed to become passé, and at the turn of the century the club became known by the more prosaic and less dignified name of Beaneaters.

Early in the present century the club became run down and was known as the Doves and Rustlers, but as late as 1907 the Boston Nationals retained some red in their uniforms, especially in the stockings. But that year manager Fred Tenney, the famous old-time first baseman, told Peter F. Kelley, baseball writer of the old Boston *Journal*, that he would abandon the old red-stocking tradition in the Boston National uniform in favor of white hose. He feared the red dye in the stockings might cause leg cuts and other spike wounds to become infected.

On reading the story, John Irving Taylor, the president of the Boston Americans, which heretofore had been known as the Somersets, Puritans, Plymouth Rocks, and Speed Boys, called Peter Kelley to his office and said: "Pete, I've got a scoop for you. I'm going to grab that name Red Sox, and from now on we'll wear the red stockings."

It was a happy hunch, and John I. had good precedent for his action. When Comiskey put an American League club into Chicago, he brought back the old nickname of Chicago's early pennant winners, the White Stockings, and condensed it to White Sox. The American League team in St. Louis also resurrected the nickname of von der Ahe's famous four-time champions of the original American Association of the eighties—the St. Louis Browns. And the name Red Sox, a modernized version of Red Stockings, was in the best Boston tradition. While the modern Red Sox frequently have stumbled deep in the cellar dust, many fine Red Sox clubs have

brought new fame and distinction to the old Red Stockings of
Boston. And if the Wright brothers, Deacon Jim White, Tim
Murnane, and Orator Jim O'Rourke follow present-day major league
baseball from the sport's Valhalla, they can't help but put their
stamp of approval on the sturdy athletes that wear Boston's historic
red socks today.

2

BAN DECIDES TO TAKE IN BOSTON

I

WHEN Ban Johnson, youthful, vigorous, aggressive president of the American League, decided to spread east in the fall of 1900, his original plan did not include the placing of a team in Boston. As a result of the National League reduction from twelve clubs to eight in 1900, Cleveland and Louisville were left vacant in the west and Washington and Baltimore in the east. Ban took over Cleveland in 1900, and his expansionist plans for 1901 called for taking up the vacated territory in Washington and Baltimore and placing a second club in Philadelphia, which in the days of the old major American Association had supported the old Athletics and Phillies. Johnson hoped he could win his expansion program peaceably, and with the consent of the National League, and deliberately stayed out of Boston, then a National League stronghold, so as not to antagonize unduly the club owners of the older loop.

However, the National League early let Ban know that if he hoped to expand his American League into a full-fledged major he would have to fight for it. In his conversations with the National League, he said his move was necessary in order to checkmate a move to revive the old major American Association. In fact, such a move was pretty well past the talking stage, and John McGraw, who later became headman of the American League in Baltimore, was offered an

8

Association franchise in that city. Other Association clubs were planned for Philadelphia, Detroit, and Washington.

Two weeks after the National League at its winter meeting in New York decided to ignore a communication from the upstart Johnson, delegates gathered in Chicago to form a new American Association, and they appointed a committee to form an alliance with the National League and work under the National agreement. Ban already had advised the National that he no longer could work under the agreement unless it was substantially changed.

Early in the winter, Arthur Irwin, formerly a crack National League shortstop and manager, was a strong booster for an American League club in Boston. At the time, he ran the Charles River bicycle track; it was located at Charles River Park on a piece of property owned by the Massachusetts Athletic Association and the Charles River Land Company. Though born in Toronto, Arthur grew up in Boston, played with Boston's famous Aetnas Club in the seventies, was a member of the early Red Stockings, managed Boston to a pennant in the Players' League in 1890, and then directed the Boston American Association club to another championship in 1891. After that he led the Phillies and Giants. Arthur always kept his ears close to the ground, and word now came to him over the grapevine that the newly organized American Association intended to put a club into Boston. In fact, he was approached on his Charles River property.

However, Ban Johnson also got around and knew what was going on. He acted quickly, and in early January 1901, he advised a special meeting of his league that he would drop Buffalo and go into Boston. Johnson, Charles W. Somers, new vice-president of the league, Charley Comiskey, John McGraw, Tom Manning, and Henry J. Killilea attended the meeting, which officially voted to drop Kansas City, Indianapolis, Minneapolis, and Buffalo and to go into the eastern cities of Boston, Philadelphia, Baltimore, and Washington. It was agreed that the new league would not molest the players of James Franklin in Buffalo.

Somers, who with Killilea had financed the Cleveland club in 1900, was Connie Mack's original backer in the Athletics when the league first decided to go major at an earlier meeting, October 14, 1900. Somers also had advanced Comiskey ten thousand dollars to help him finance his new major White Sox. A coal and lumber man and lake shipper, Charley was Ban's original "angel" and he sent his bank roll where it did the most good. Though he had no riches to compare with the wealth of such present-day baseball owners as

Tom Yawkey, Phil Wrigley, Walter O. Briggs, and Powel Crosley, Somers' money made the American League possible.

Johnson and Connie Mack induced old Ben Shibe, a Philadelphia manufacturer of baseballs, to take over controlling interest in the Athletics. That left Charley Somers free to put his capital and efforts in the Boston club, but at that early American League period, Somers had a big chunk of four clubs, Boston, Cleveland, Philadelphia, and Chicago, something that wouldn't be permitted in present-day baseball.

The name of Hughie Duffy, captain and center fielder of the Boston Nationals, who had hit an amazing .438 for Frank Selee's Red Stockings in 1894, began to appear in the Boston press in connection with the new American League and as a Johnson representative and spokesman in Boston. Duffy and Tom McCarthy, who were known as the "Heavenly Twins" when both played in Boston, looked up Irwin to sound him on the Cambridge lease, but found him strangely disinterested; they attempted to contact the owners and were met with another rebuff.

However, there is another version that Arthur Irwin was given the old run-around. It appears in a rather amusing news letter from Peter Kelley, the Boston correspondent of the *Sporting News*, in the issue of January 12, 1901. Pete then worked on the old *Record* and and Sunday *Advertiser* under Steve Mahoney, and he signed the interesting nom-de-plume "Hi Hi" to his letters in the St. Louis weekly.

The derivation of Hi Hi is a little story in itself. There was a rather noisy but kindly Boston fan of the period named Arthur Dixwell. He was a bit balmy, but everyone liked him, and baseball was his outlet. He would cup his hands and yell, "Hi Hi," to start rallies, and won the nickname of "Hi Hi" Dixwell. He had a rival, Al Bjorkland, whose slogan was, "Hurry! Hurry!" Both were known at Boston ball games almost as well as the players.

Anyway, Pete Hi Hi Kelley's column read as follows:

There is no question but that Ban Johnson, Somers and Comiskey gave Arthur Irwin and "Juley" Hart (his associate in the lease) the dinky dink. I think I can read between the lines and see it all. I figure that Hugh Duffy went over to Philadelphia with his smooth, clever brother-in-law, who is a legal light, and convinced Johnson and his conferees that he could make the Boston end of the American League a big go.

I rather suspect that Ban Johnson saw a chance to deliver a blow to the solar plexus of the Boston National League club and tipped the wink to Somers and "Commy" [Comiskey, the Chicago owner], that it would be a good plan to give Arthur the go-by. You see they could keep up the people's interest, and I am sure it will all come out in the wash.

A week later, January 19, Hi Hi brings that beloved New Englander, Connie Mack, into the picture, and Connie was to have quite a hand in launching the Boston American League club. This week he wrote:

There was quite a breeze in Boston baseball circles Saturday. Connie Mack—you know we all hate to call him by his complete name of McGillicuddy, was in town. He was going to his home at East Brookfield, Mass. But I rather guess that the Brookfield part of the report was manufactured. Mack was here on business, and for business only. He was closetted with Hugh Duffy, and they had several long talks. They went to the theatre together and discussed baseball's troubles. It is now given out that Mack is to have Philadelphia in the new league, but still own Milwaukee, where Hugh Duffy is to be manager.

And the gossipy Hi Hi seemed to think the new league was sitting in a game of bluff, as he added farther down in his letter: "It will be red-hot stuff if the American League organization declares war. The American League is doing a great deal to bluff the National, and how far they will go cannot yet be determined."

Hi Hi was right on one count and wrong on another. Connie Mack was in Boston on business, but the American League wasn't bluffing. By January 26 he had to report that Connie Mack signed a lease on a big area of land "out towards Brookline and on the road to Roxbury." It had been used for the "chutes" and for various carnivals, and was opposite from where Buffalo Bill's Wild West show and Barnum and Bailey's circus used to play in Boston. "There is no doubt that the Huntington Avenue grounds are a splendid site for a ball park," Hi Hi admitted.

The field was located after a diligent search by Duffy, Mack, and McCarthy, who had to consider transportation and proximity to downtown Boston. Duffy strongly recommended the site. It extended 425 feet on the main thoroughfare, and had an area of 287,000 square feet, about 100,000 more than the little National League ball yard on Columbus Avenue on the other side of the New Haven tracks. The plot's biggest drawback was a deep pond, or pool, at the base of the chutes, which required immediate filling. So while Chris von der Ahe of the Browns once put in a chute-the-chutes at Sportsman's

Park, St. Louis, to stimulate business, the first problem of the new Boston Americans was to remove all traces of their chutes.

The ground was owned by the New York, New Haven and Hartford Railroad, and the Boston Elevated Railway had a lease on it. When Connie Mack handed the agent for the railway company a check signed by Somers, the agent asked his Boston bank to ascertain from its Cleveland contact what kind of a man Somers was and something about his financial standing. The answer came back from the Cleveland bank: "Draw on us to the extent of $100,000."

Boston was impressed; this fellow Somers could talk with real money.

In the meantime, President Arthur Soden of the Boston Nationals gave Arthur Irwin permission to put a new American Association club in Boston, and Soden announced it would have the support of the National League. Arthur said he would play his games at Charles River Park, and that his team would be called the Boston Reds, a reminder of the Boston Players League and old American Association clubs that played on Congress Street. But the revised American Association dillydallied too long; Ban's vigorous young league had too big a jump, and the American Association never got past the paper franchise stage.

2

At the time Mack signed the first lease on the Huntington Avenue grounds, it was freely hinted that the new manager would be Hughie Jennings, the former crack Oriole shortstop, who in 1900 played first base for the Brooklyn National League champions, as it had been determined that Boston's own Hughie—Duffy—would manage the American League team in Milwaukee.

However, when it came time for naming the new Boston American League manager, Ban Johnson and Charley Somers had a ten-strike for the Hub fans. The pilot was the great third baseman of the Boston Nationals, Jimmy Collins, still considered today as the number one third sacker of all time. Collins was only five feet seven and a half inches tall, weighing 160 pounds, but was fast as a cat on his feet and introduced a new style of third-base play. Up to his time, no other third baseman had his faculty for coming in on bunts, and when a batsman tried to cross him by whistling a line drive past his ears, Jimmy always seemed to anticipate the play and was ready for it. He enjoyed matching his wits with such smart hitters and bunters as John McGraw, Willie Keeler, Jesse Burkett, Jack Doyle, and Jennings, who always were trying to outguess him.

The game's greatest third baseman didn't start at the hot corner, having played shortstop and the outfield for his home-town team in Buffalo. He went to Boston in 1895 and played his early games in right field. The Red Stockings then loaned him to the Louisville National League club. Jimmy started in center field for the Colonels, but in a game with Baltimore, the old Orioles made a monkey out of Walter Preston, the young Louisville third baseman. They bunted on the kid until he didn't know whether he was coming or going, and Preston was guilty of four errors.

In desperation, manager McCloskey pulled Collins out of center field, put him on third, and sent Preston to the outfield. With mock solemnity Hughie Jennings patted Collins on the back and said, "We aren't going to bunt any more."

"That's all right, Hughie," replied Collins. "You bunt 'em, and I'll field 'em." He did, and threw them out so regularly that when Collins returned to Boston in 1896, he was Selee's regular third baseman. And from then on, his third-base reputation grew with the years.

Jimmy also could hit and got surprising power behind his drives. He usually was well over .300, and though he fell under that mark in his later years, worrying about his team in Boston, he had a fourteen-year major league batting average of .296.

Collins was the last of the 1901 American League managers to be engaged, and Hi Hi said on March 16, "Manager James Joseph Collins came to town with the staidness and quiet of Sunday and registered at a hotel 25 yards from Newspaper Row." His salary as manager, captain, and third baseman of the new Boston Americans was $4,000, and that apparently was a lot more than he had received from the triumvirate guarding the pursestrings of the National Beaneaters, Arthur H. Soden, J. B. Billings, and William H. Conant. Collins' "big salary" was guaranteed by Somers, and there was a provision that in the event Jimmy was enjoined from playing with the Americans, he still would receive his $4,000 under a civil managerial contract.

Facing a group of Boston sports writers of nearly half a century ago—some of them strongly attached to the National League, Jimmy told his interrogators: "I like to play baseball, but this is business with me, and I can't be governed by sentiment. Repeatedly in the past, I've asked the Triumvirate for a salary increase, but always was put aside with some flimsy excuse. Only this winter, with the American League in the field, have they shown any sign of granting it."

Jimmy bristled at a suggestion he had deserted the Boston Nationals, and when asked whether Hughie Duffy, former captain of the Beaneaters, had been instrumental in his jumping, Collins replied in the negative. "I wasn't influenced by Duffy," he said. "Hughie is looking out for his welfare and sees a good opportunity in managing the American League club in Milwaukee, and I am looking out for James J. Collins."

3

The war between the National and American Leagues, which had been smoldering since Ban Johnson announced his intention to spread east in the fall of 1900, broke in full intensity when the new league invaded Boston. In a baseball sense, that was the "shot heard round the world."

Johnson and his leading raiders, Comiskey, Connie Mack, John McGraw, Jimmy McAleer, Clark Griffith, and Hugh Duffy, already had put tempting bait before the National League stars, and many were nibbling. The early raids were directed at the Philadelphia Nationals, where Mack had signed the second-base king, Napoleon "Larry" Lajoie, and pitchers Bill Bernhard and Chick Fraser. Now with Boston in the new loop, Johnson and his lieutenants turned their attention to the Boston Nationals, who under Frank Selee had won pennants in 1897 and 1898, finished a good second in 1899 and a satisfactory fourth in 1900.

The capture of Jimmy Collins, the Beaneater third baseman, as playing manager was only the first step. Practically all of Selee's players were approached, with the New Englanders Mack and Duffy doing the early spade work. Collins succeeded in winning center fielder Chick Stahl, right fielder John "Buck" Freeman, and pitcher Ed "Parson" Lewis. Lewis later coached Harvard, became president of Massachusetts State College, and was president of the University of New Hampshire at the time of his death in Durham, New Hampshire, May 24, 1936.

Freeman, never much of a fielder, had been a pitcher, first baseman, and outfielder and was one of the outstanding sluggers at the turn of the century; he attracted nation-wide attention by hitting twenty-five home runs for the Washington National League club in 1899, a believe-it-or-not feat in that day.

Collins also made strong efforts to entice Fred Tenney and Herman Long, fellow infielders with Jim on the great Selee infield of Collins, Long, Lowe, and Tenney; Long later jumped to the New York Americans, but Tenney persistently resisted American League greenbacks all through the scrap.

In his first press interview as manager, Collins said his pitching staff would consist of Bill Bernhard, the former Philly, Bill Dinneen, and Vic Willis of the Beaneaters, and that he was hopeful of getting Cy Young from the St. Louis Cardinals. As events turned out, Jimmy had only Young, as Connie Mack decided to keep Bernhard for himself in Philadelphia, and Dinneen and Willis, after flirting with the American League, decided to stick with Selee. Dinneen then jumped to the Boston Americans a year later.

However, next to the engagement of Jimmy Collins as third baseman–manager, the big prize won by the club was pitcher Cy Young, one of the game's real immortals. He had much to do with the early success of the Red Sox and still remains one of Boston's great all-time sports heroes. With Jimmy McAleer, who had played with Young on the old Cleveland Spiders, doing most of the negotiating, the Boston club landed not only Young but also his famous St. Louis batterymate, catcher Lou Criger, and another fair Cardinal-country pitcher, George Cuppy.

Young was a manager's dream, a two-hundred-pound, rubber-armed pitcher, who was always in condition to pitch, was willing to work in or out of turn, never knew what it was to have a sore arm until his forty-fifth year, and who turned in the amazing total of 511 major league victories, fairly well divided between the two big leagues. The closest any other pitcher came to Cy in total victories was Walter Johnson's 413, nearly 100 away. Those two National League pitching wizards, Christy Mathewson and Grover Cleveland Alexander, both closed their careers with the same figure—373 victories.

A farm boy from Gilmore, Ohio, Young was known throughout his active career as Denton Tecumseh Young. It wasn't until after he retired from baseball that he set the world right and said his middle name was True. And how that name True fitted him! "Some smart reporter took my middle initial, T, and made Tecumseh out of it, and I never bothered to have the sports writers change it," he said. He got his nickname, "Cy," from the fact that in the middle nineties it was a common practice to call boys from the farms Cy or Cyrus.

And Cy was a real rube when he first joined the Cleveland Spiders of the National League in midseason of 1890. A no-hit game that included eighteen strike-outs for Canton, Ohio, against McKeesport, Pennsylvania, in the old Tri-State League was his steppingstone to the majors. When he reported, he wore a low-crowned derby hat, about half a size too small, while his clothes were so outgrown that his trousers reached just above his ankles and his coat sleeves stopped before they came to his wrists. Davis Hawley, secretary-treasurer of the Cleveland club, fearful that the other players might laugh Cy off the team, rushed him to a Euclid Avenue haberdasher and got him an entire new outfit before he showed up at the Cleveland clubhouse.

In his first National League game Young defeated Cap Anson's famous Chicago White Stockings with three hits. The night after the game Anson dropped in to see Hawley at Cleveland's old Hawley House, and after talking of almost everything but baseball, gradually veered the subject around to Young. "That big rube had a lot of luck beating us today," he observed. "He is too green to do your club much good, but I believe I might make a pitcher out of him in a couple of years. Anyway, I am willing to give you a thousand dollars for him."

Hawley puffed at his cigar for a moment and replied between rings of blue smoke: "If I remember correctly, Cap, that big rube struck you out twice. And what's more he can do it again. I'm sure he can do us as much good as he would Chicago, so I guess you better keep your thousand, and we'll keep the rube."

In his first complete season with Cleveland, 1891 Young participated in fifty games and won twenty-seven; he jacked up that fine mark to thirty-six and thirty-four victories in 1892 and 1893 respectively. Yes, even without Anson to polish off his rough edges, he developed into quite a pitcher. When Frank DeHaas Robison, the Cleveland owner, acquired the St. Louis club in 1899, he shifted most of his Cleveland stars to the new club, and Cy accompanied the Spider delegation to the banks of the Mississippi. His two years in St. Louis were not overly happy, and they were not up to the Young standards; he won twenty-six games in 1899 and twenty in 1900. He didn't care too much about pitching in the heat of St. Louis, but he was loyal by nature, and it took a lot of persuasion and a $3,500 contract to induce him to make the big hop to Boston in March 1901. And if anything, Cy became even more of a headliner in the young American League than he had been in the National. He was within a fortnight of his thirty-fourth birthday when he signed his first Boston contract, but still in his very prime, with many of his historic games in the years ahead. He became to that early edition of the Red Sox what Mathewson soon became to the Giants, Rube Waddell to the Athletics, and Walter Johnson to the Washington Senators.

4

While Collins failed to win any such names as Nap Lajoie or Herman Long for the middle of his infield, he put together a nimble second-base pair that was destined to write a lot of interesting early Boston American history. His shortstop was Freddy Parent, an agile stubby chap from Biddeford, Maine, who later lived in Sanford, Maine, and his second baseman was another native New Englander, Albert S. "Hobe" Ferris, who came from Providence.

Parent was built close to the ground—he was only five feet five inches tall, and weighed 152 pounds, but he had surprising dexterity in getting over the ground, took the spikes of the toughest base runners, was a fast runner himself and a dangerous hitter in the clutch. He had played for a spell with the Cardinals in 1899 on a loan, but Collins snatched him from the Providence Eastern League club.

Ferris played with Norwich in 1900 and was drafted for the 1901 season by the Cincinnati Reds. But the American Leaguers saw him first, and Hobe never wore the red hosiery of Garry Herrmann. Hobe played the second-base bag, having been converted from catcher, at the Huntington Avenue grounds until his sale to the Browns in 1907. Ferris, five feet eight inches tall, weighing 180 pounds, was a little bigger than Freddy Parent. He was one of the leading battlers on the early Red Sox, a rough and tough old-time player that could take it and dish it out.

In the last twenty-two years of his life Ferris lived in Detroit, where he died of an unusual heart attack, March 18, 1938. Hobe, by this time sixty-one, had become heavier and rounder. He became much disturbed when he read in a Detroit newspaper that Bob Fothergill, the fat former Tiger and Red Sox outfielder, had died suddenly of a stroke, March 16, at the early age of thirty-nine. Ferris fretted so over this early death of "Fat" that he joined Fothergill two days later.

To help Lou Criger, a top-ranking catcher in 1901, on the receiving staff, Jimmy Collins had two frolicsome fellows that later became well-known big league names, Ossie Schreckengost and Larry McLean. Schreck had caught for the Cleveland Spiders and St. Louis Cardinals of the National League, and after one season in Boston Ossie took his talents and shenanigans to Philadelphia, where he won his greatest fame as Rube Waddell's battery partner and the man that had Connie Mack and his Athletics tossed out of a swank New Orleans hostelry for nailing his steak to a dining-room wall. Shreck and Waddell were inveterate cronies and even slept in the same double bed; Ossie wanted Mack to put a clause in Rube's contract that he couldn't eat crackers in bed, and Rube filed a countercharge that Schreck ate his famed "Pizzazza sandwiches," heavily spread with Limburger and sprinkled with onions, between the bed linens.

McLean had little more than a tryout with the 1901 Boston Americans, though for years he was a well-known character around Boston. Everyone knew him as Larry, but his name was really John Bannerman McLean, and he originally came to Cambridge from Frederickton, New Brunswick. He was a handsome giant, six feet five inches tall, weighing 220 pounds, and was something of a baseball John L. Sullivan; Larry had most of the "Boston Strong Boy's" good looks, also most of his weaknesses. He played his best ball for the Cincinnati Reds and New York Giants and hit .500 for McGraw in the 1913 World Series. Larry once dove into a two-foot pool on a hotel lawn in St. Louis, was a playboy all of his life, and eventually came to a tragic end. He was shot and killed in a Boston saloon brawl in 1921.

Collins expected to get Pat Dougherty for his 1901 outfield, but something went wrong, and the slugging Patrick didn't report until a year later. The American League then sent a pair of outfielders to Boston—Tommy Dowd, a former Cardinal, who was with Comiskey's 1900 Chicago club, and Charley Hemphill, who had been with Ban Johnson's American League team in Kansas City.

Connie Mack also did Jimmy Collins a good turn shortly after the season got under way. Frank Foreman, a brother of one of Connie's old Pittsburgh pitchers, was the baseball coach at Gettysburg College. He told Connie, "I've got two pitchers in Gettysburg, and they both can win in the American League, a left-hander named Eddie Plank, and a right-hander, George Winters."

Mack took Plank, and still wishing to do Somers a good turn, recommended Winters to the Boston club. Foreman's judgment on both of his boys was correct; both sons of Gettysburg scored immediate successes in the new major league, and while the left-hander became more famous, Winters proved an early find for Boston and was right behind Cy Young in winning games in that first Red Sox year.

3

⊖

COLLINS' TEAM AN EARLY CONTENDER

I

WHEN we think of the time, money, and labor it requires to build a major league ball park today, it is almost startling to recall that ground for the new American League park on Huntington Avenue wasn't broken until March 12, giving the contractor a little less than two months to get ready for Boston's first game in the new circuit. Hi Hi Kelley was at his best in telling of the little party, with popping champagne corks, which got the modern Red Sox under way in his *Sporting News* letter of March 16.

The Huntington Avenue grounds, where the American League will play, were dedicated last week. Big Mike Sullivan, who would have made a great pitcher only for weakness in his cardiac region, was the high muck-a-muck. He presided at all toasts, and didn't forget to imbibe himself. It was champagne, you know! And it flowed freely. General Dixwell [no doubt "Hi Hi," the oaf] turned the first spadeful of mother earth, and mumbled something about success. Yes, it was a great day for digging and oratory.

It turned into a success far beyond the expectations of Hi Hi and the General in 1901. Nothing was said of the presence of Ban Johnson, the new league promoter, or Charley Somers, backer of the Boston club, at either the digging or champagne-imbibing activities. Melville E. "Mel" Webb, veteran sports writer of the Boston

19

Globe and member of the permanent Cooperstown Hall of Fame committee, recalls the spading on the Huntington Avenue lot. "I grabbed a spade and did a little digging myself," Mel admits. "But I guess they kept that fast-flowing champagne hidden away from me. I know I didn't get any. I suppose they figured I was too young and didn't need any to pep up my youthful enthusiasm." Mel wasn't overlooked some years later when the Boston Americans celebrated the winning of league pennants and world championships in fitting fashion.

Jimmy Collins' Bostons did a few weeks of training at Charlottesville, Virginia, and played their first game with McGraw's scrappy Orioles in Baltimore, April 26, 1901. It wasn't an overly happy occasion for Jimmy Collins and his new Hub organization, as Boston lost by a score of 10 to 6, with Winford Kellum and Lou Criger serving as the Boston battery against "Iron Man" Joe McGinnity and Wilbert Robinson. Turkey Mike Donlin was especially tough on the Bostonians, thumping Kellum for a pair of triples.

Collins' team lined up that day as follows: Tommy Dowd, left field; Charley Hemphill, right field; Chick Stahl, center field; Jimmy Collins, third base; John "Buck" Freeman, first base; Freddy Parent, shortstop; Hobe Ferris, second base; Lou Criger, catcher; Winford Kellum, pitcher. Big Larry McLean, who batted for Kellum in the ninth inning, had the distinction of making the first pinch hit in the American League.

If the story of Boston's first American League game made poor reading on Beacon Hill, the tale of the second reverse in Baltimore brought even sadder tidings from the Maryland front. This time the Orioles really climbed all over Cy Young and Fred Mitchell, later a Boston Brave manager, and crushed the new Boston club by a score of 17 to 6. After yielding three runs in the first inning, Cy Young was blown out two innings later when McGraw's toughies exploded an eight-run bomb under him.

"Who said this Young is so good?" said some of the doubting Thomases back on Commonwealth Avenue and old Newspaper Row. "The farmer is thirty-four, and he probably left his fast pitch in Cleveland." They then used to speak of a "fast pitch" instead of a "fast ball."

The news continued to be poor, as Collins took his battered band to Philadelphia, April 29, when George Cuppy lost to the Athletics to the tune of 8 to 5. The first Red Sox victory came next day, when Young downed Mack's Philadelphia club by almost the same score, 8 to 6, as the Bostonians broke out with a blistering sixteen-hit attack against Bill Milligan. Everybody but Freddy Parent took a hand; Dowd and Ferris both smacked out three, and even Cy Young blew himself to a pair of safeties.

In the second week, the club lost four out of five to Washington and Baltimore, and Collins remarked: "We are too anxious. Everybody is trying too hard, and we are beating ourselves. But I know I have a better ball team than we have shown so far, and once we really get thawed out, we are going to win plenty of games. Dinneen and Willis disappointed me, when they decided to stay with the South Side team [the Boston Nationals], but we are going to show better pitching in the near future."

2

The event that rooters for the new league had been awaiting eagerly finally rolled around. May 8, when the new American League team made its first bow on its Huntington Avenue grounds, was no such unforgettable date as the Fourth of July or February 22, but nevertheless it was a historic date for New England. Since then, fans from the northeast corner of the nation—as well as many Red Sox converts in other sections of the country, have followed this famous team through ups and downs with unswerving loyalty.

Within the two months allowed, the contractors had the field graded, a sodded diamond laid out, while a little grandstand, seating 2,600, with bleachers for another 6,500, mushroomed on the former Huntington Avenue carnival lot. There was also plenty of space for standees in both right and left field, as outfield ropes for overflow crowds were standard equipment at all ball parks. The "Standing Room Only" sign went up early, as the opening day crowd was given as eleven thousand.

With war on between the two majors, no attempt was made by the two leagues to draw up a nonconflicting schedule, and the two Boston clubs clashed on twenty-five of their 1901 playing days. Whether by design or otherwise, the Boston Nationals clashed with Jimmy Collins' May 8 opening and came out a poor second best. The Beaneaters played Brooklyn, the 1900 pennant winner, and according to Boston newspapers, they drew only two thousand to their Walpole Street grounds. They had a good interesting game, too, as the Beaneaters defeated the champions in twelve innings by a score of 7 to 6.

However, for most of Boston and the surrounding country, the new ball club, the new league, and the new ball field on Huntington

Avenue were the center of attraction. And Collins' team behaved itself admirably, as the Bostons easily defeated Connie Mack's Philadelphia Athletics by a score of 12 to 4. Cy Young, the victor, by this time was getting his stout arm into shape, and while he yielded eleven hits, most of them came after Boston had the game well in hand. Managers didn't pamper pitchers in those days, and Mack kept in Bill Bernhard despite the fact that he was bumped for nineteen hits. Collins' early team was a worthy predecessor of the slugging Red Sox of today. Starting in with four runs in the first inning, the Bostons scored in each of the first five innings, and then probably feeling sorry for Bernhard, layed off, as they simmered down to one run in the last three frames.

All hands enjoyed a fine batting picnic, with Buck Freeman, the hefty first baseman, having the biggest helping with a home run, triple, and single. Even Cy Young hit a triple and single and stole a base. There was only one fly in the ointment; center fielder Chick Stahl suffered an injury that proved to be a broken rib, and Charley Jones had to fill in for him.

And Boston liked what it saw. "Jimmy's team is all to the mustard!" "That new league is all right." "The Bostons'll be right up there!" "They'll give Soden and his triumvirate plenty of trouble," fans observed on the trolley ride back on Huntington Avenue.

Boston started to pick up from the time of its first home opening-day victory. Collins' club followed up with a 9-to-2 victory over the Athletics, as George Cuppy defeated Chick Fraser, suffered a poor series with Washington, only to have a humdinger with McGraw's fighting Orioles. Despite a five-run Boston rally in the ninth, the Orioles won an 8-to-7 Friday game as Joe McGinnity outlasted Parson Lewis. During that ninth-inning rally, McGraw had been pretty rough with umpire Haskell, and by the next day Ban Johnson wired the scrappy Oriole chief to sit out the next five games. In the Saturday engagement, Cy Young then pitched Boston to a 7-to-2 victory over the leaderless Orioles.

It gave whimsical Hi Hi a chance for a little fun, as he related:

Boston drew 8,000 for its first Saturday game with Baltimore. This was a pretty good game, too, and the people talked about it because McGraw did not play, and they read in their newspapers that John J. Muggsy had been told to sit on the bench for five days.

This added to the interest and while it was felt that the Orioles wouldn't battle as stubbornly as if their manager and captain were playing, yet there was so much talk that everybody felt inclined to go see the menagerie even though the "great animal" [Muggsy] was not exhibited.

And talking of the business end, Hi Hi tells of how those early Boston American fans went for two-bit baseball. "There is a strong sentiment here for the 25 cent article of ball," he relates, "but it is surprising how poorly the grandstand at the Huntington Avenue grounds has been patronized."

3

Collins' Bostons soon fought their way into the thick of the race, and for the greater part of the 1901 season, Jimmy's energetic club was the only serious threat to Clark Griffith's White Sox. There was an early warfare of the two Soxes, though the words Red Sox were not yet used, and in Boston the club generally was referred to simply as "the Bostons." On the road, some of the more imaginative sports writers coined the term the "Somersets," as Charley Somers was the president-owner, and Boston had its Somerset Street, Somerset Club, and Somerset Hotel. But the name found little favor in Boston, though occasionally the nicknames "Puritans," "Pilgrims," and "Plymouth Rocks" found their way into Boston print.

Through the months of July and August, Boston was treated to its first red-hot American League race as the clans of Griffith and Collins ran nip and tuck through the hot summer months, and as late as August 27, Chicago had a lead on Boston of only .604 to .600. But in a September finish, the White Sox gradually drew away and won by a four-game margin. The second place Bostons finished with seventy-nine victories and fifty-seven defeats for a percentage of .581. Griffith, the winner, came home with eighty-three wins and fifty-three defeats for a .610 rating. The league then played a 140-game schedule, and both contenders had four unplayed games.

Fans of the new Boston Americans got a lot of satisfaction from the fact that its club won the year's series from Comiskey's new champions, twelve to eight. "If we could only play Griffith every day, it would be easy," chortled the fans. McGraw's truculent Orioles really were tough for Collins' team. The best they could do with the scrappy Marylanders was an even break in eighteen games, whereas Muggsy's Roughnecks became Little Lord Fauntleroys when they played Griffith, and won only four games from Chicago out of eighteen.

Ban Johnson was fighting his warfare for clean baseball, but it still was a rowdy era in baseball, and Griffith, the Chicago manager, was almost as much of an umpire fighter as McGraw and George Stallings of Detroit. Collins' team was made up of no shrinking violets, but in the August 31 issue of *Sporting News,* at the hottest spot of the race, Hi Hi reports on how two Boston players, Chick Stahl and Parson Lewis, rescued Pongo Joe Cantillon from the wrath of some overzealous Boston fans.

Umpire Cantillon was treated a bit rough here on Saturday. His work was not as good as he has done, and the Bostons got the worst of two important decisions. Some of the irresponsibles called out "Robber," "Thief" and other choice remarks, and after the game started to make a demonstration. Stahl and Lewis went to Cantillon's rescue, fought their way into the crowd and shoved the brawlers away. Cantillon was very cool, and acted like a gentleman throughout the trying ordeal. I think Ban Johnson is weak in having an umpire at one place too long. The people of Boston got very tired of Monossan early in the season.

There were inferences, especially in Boston, that as a result of the close personal friendship and association between Johnson and Comiskey, the young president's umpires favored Comiskey and the Chicago club. During the hot Boston-Chicago battles, there were cries at the umpires from the Huntington Avenue stands of "Comiskey's pet," and, "Do you have to favor Comiskey to hold your job?"
But your investigator, Hi Hi, quoted umpire Frank Dwyer, later a Detroit manager, to refute these charges:

Frank Dwyer said that Ban Johnson told him to go ahead and umpire his games and not to be bulldozed by Comiskey or any one else, and that even if Comiskey bothered him to put him off the grounds, and in a very severe case to forfeit the game. This was to show that he never received instructions to favor the Chicagos, as claimed by some persons. He said he had no instructions of that kind at all, and said Johnson always had backed him up on everything he did.

And Griffith came in for a scolding in a later Boston letter:

Did you see that interview with Ban Johnson in which he gives Mr. Clark Griffith all that was coming to him and said if he paid more attention to leading his team and less to thinking of ways to harass the umpires that the White Sox would have won the pennant from the Bostons ere this? Pretty warm, eh? And then Mr. Johnson kind of gave

Griffith a hint that if he didn't lay off his umpires, he could sneak out of the American League and back to the National.

4

The Boston American League club broke in with a lot of power and led the young loop at bat in its first year as a major with a hefty team average of .293, pretty good socking for a club in the days of the dead ball and freak pitching deliveries. The figure has been matched by few Boston clubs since. High man on the club was Buck Freeman, whose .346 was second only to the magic mark of .405, with which Lajoie of the Athletics won the 1901 American League batting crown. Buck had a robust collection of extra base hits, too—twenty-two doubles, fifteen triples, and twelve home runs. Other Bostonians high up were manager Jimmy Collins with .329, Ossie Schreck, .320, Freddy Parent, .318, and Chick Stahl, .310. Collins did little monkeying with his material, and Boston fans didn't need a score card to tell who his players were. At the end of the campaign, Hi Hi observed, "Captain Collins took the players turned over to him, and with few exceptions never changed the batting order throughout the season."

Despite those early shellackings in the spring, Cy Young wound up the season with thirty-one victories against only ten defeats for a percentage of .756. His mark was excelled only by Clark Griffith, who won twenty-four games and lost seven for his Chicago champions. The one that came nearest Cy's total of thirty-one victories was McGraw's iron man, Joe McGinnity, who won twenty-six games for the Orioles.

The pitchers that were of greatest help, next to Young, were George Winters, Mack's early-season recommendation from Gettysburg, with sixteen victories and twelve losses, and Parson Lewis, who won sixteen and lost seventeen. Cuppy, Mitchell, Kellum, Beville, and Braggins filled in at various times.

Boston also made a strong start at the turnstiles, and despite the club's humble early stands and the fact that the very thought of Sunday ball in Boston would have been considered sacrilegious in 1901, the club drew 527,548 at its Huntington Avenue grounds, only 18,000 less than the attendance of the Chicago champions, who topped the league with 545,859. And of particular interest to Johnson and Somers was the fact that the Boston Americans outdrew the Boston Nationals by nearly 200,000. Crippled by American League raids, the Nationals with a .500 percentage and fifth-place club, attracted only 340,606.

With the background and great record of the Boston Nationals in the nineteenth century, the enthusiasm that greeted the new league and Collins' team still must occasion surprise. There were a number of contributing factors, not the least of which was the fact that Jimmy's entry participated in a grueling race in its very first year. Nothing like a torrid nip-and-tuck race to make the turnstiles sing!

The old Boston Nationals also had lost popularity by their tight-fisted policy. There was an old National League rule in force at the time that no club could pay a player more than $2,400. There were subterfuges to get around it, but they never were employed by the conscientious members of the triumvirate—Arthur H. Soden, J. B. Billings, and William H. Conant, the owners since the seventies. Not only the players of Selee's old champions but also the Boston fans felt that the team was underpaid.

Soden, who was in the roofing business, was really a fine chap, but he had a real old-time New England sense of thrift. In 1890, when the Players League war almost wrecked the National League, he went to the rescue of the Giants, and his heirs had stock in the New York club until well in this century. But Arthur and his associates could pinch pennies in many ways. Apart from the few passes made out to newspapers, each of the two owners had only two cardboard passes. And it took a good man to pry one loose from any one of the triumvirate. Fred Tenney, the first baseman who succeeded Duffy as captain, didn't help the club's popularity when he jumped over the right-field bleacher rail and wrestled with a fan for a foul ball that had been hit into the open seats.

The American Leaguers also were lucky in their raids, for in Collins, Stahl, Freeman, and Lewis, they had four of the National League club's most popular players. All had their individual followings that now rooted for the players in their new American League uniforms. Hughie Duffy and Connie Mack, managers of the new Milwaukee and Athletic clubs, also had legions of friends in Boston and the surrounding area, and if the Boston crowds didn't like McGraw and Griffith, they enjoyed coming out to badger them and root against them.

And in one season Cy Young became the particular darling of the Boston fans. Everybody liked the big farmer, and he quickly became the town's number one baseball idol. Cy was likable and friendly and far from a prude. While he never was a troublemaker on a ball club,

Cy liked his drink, and he could stand up at the bar and knock 'em off with the best of them.

The late Jimmy Isaminger, former Philadelphia sports writer, used to enjoy telling a story of how he and Stony McLinn, now a Quaker City sportscaster, met Cy Young at Hot Springs, Arkansas, where old Cy was doing some early training. After a little conversation Cy suggested they adjourn to the Majestic Hotel bar for a little libation.

Both Jimmy and Stony were young at the time, and they had been told that it was dangerous to imbibe alcoholic beverages while drinking the resort's medicinal waters. As Young was in training, they also thought it advisable not to set any bad example. So when Cy asked, "What will you boys have?" they ordered mineral water.

"Make mine Kentucky bourbon," said Young, and when he got the bottle he filled his glass to the brim. When they came to a second round, Jimmy said boldly, "Make mine the same as Mr. Young's."

Cy laughed. "I guess they kidded you about drinking beer and likker here being fatal," he said with a wink. "Well, it never seemed to be fatal for me."

Somers was too busy in Cleveland with his coal, lumber, and lake shipping interests to pay much attention to his ball team in Boston, though he made several trips to the Hub with the idea of interesting local capital in the club, but got nary a nibble. However, Charley put in a capable business manager in Joe Gavin, and made quite a hit when he appointed a popular Boston newspaperman, Joe Callahan, as Gavin's assistant. The club leased a fine suite of offices at 8 Beacon Street, which early became a popular rendezvous for New England baseball men and sports writers.

On the whole, the new club was greeted with a friendly press. At first, a few writers referred to them as "the Invaders," but as Collins' club won the fancy of the town, they soon changed their tune. The outstanding Boston baseball writers in 1901 were Tim Murnane of the Boston *Globe*, Walter Barnes of the *Journal*, and Jake Morse of the *Herald*. They were a great and able trio; their output was read avidly all through New England, and they were as worthy pioneers of the game as any of the early players and managers.

In fact, Murnane had been one of the famous early players. A native of Naugatuck, Connecticut, he had played with the Philadelphia Athletics in the original National Association, made that early baseball pilgrimage to Britain, and was a member of the Boston Red Stockings in 1876, when they were charter members of the National League. He was fifty when the American League first invaded Boston, and the shock of white hair that later made him such a distinguished figure in the Boston press box had just started to turn.

Having played in the early National League, Tim naturally was partial to the old league and the Beaneaters, though later when his employer on the *Globe* acquired the Red Sox, he became one of the American League team's most enthusiastic boosters. It was reported in 1901 that Somers had offered him the presidency of the new Boston club, which Tim refused, though later he served for years as president of the New England League.

But even in 1901, when Tim's heart still was with the National League, he was fair, and at the end of the season, he spoke well of the new league in his Boston *Globe* column, and then quoted Arthur Irwin as saying: "The National League has made a poor fight with the American League; in fact it has laid down as far as I can learn. Their game always has been to make the opposition lose money and quit. In this case, the American League came in under full sail and has won out on every end, and is going after the old fellows in better shape than ever."

5

The American League stepped up the ferocity of its raids in 1902; most of the remaining big stars of the Phillies, Ed Delahanty, Elmer Flick, Al Orth, Frank Donohue, Bill Duggleby, jumped to the new league, and a new club that Ban Johnson put into St. Louis, the modern Browns, wrecked Frank Robison's St. Louis Nationals, taking the cream of the Cardinals, pitchers Jack Powell, Charley Harper, and Willie Sudhoff, infielders Rhody Wallace and Dick Padden, and outfielders Jesse Burkett, the heavy hitter from Worcester, and Emmet Heidrick.

The Boston club also did more raiding, and its prizes were pitcher Bill Dinneen of the Boston Nationals and a battery from the New York Giants, pitcher Frank Sparks and catcher Jack Warner. Dinneen, who had been on the brink the winter before, finally took the leap into the richer Huntington Avenue pasture. However, all winter treasurer Billings of the Beaneaters claimed that he had Dinneen safely in his fold, and wasn't convinced that Bill had jumped until the burly pitcher reported to Jimmy Collins in Washington as the Boston Americans passed through the capital city on their way to the Augusta, Georgia camp. Dinneen, a native of Syracuse, New York, quickly joined Cy Young as one of the great pitchers of the early Red Sox staff and served the American League loyally for years as a top-ranking pitcher and first-class umpire.

It is interesting to note that Cy Young, the Boston pitching ace, spent the better part of the 1902 training season coaching the Harvard baseball team, and as late as April 5, Hi Hi reported Cy doing a fine job with the Crimson college boys and that he soon would join Collins' team in Georgia.

Other worth-while acquisitions on the 1902 Boston Americans were first baseman George "Candy" LaChance, outfielder Pat Dougherty, and pitcher Tom Hughes. LaChance was a big French Canadian from Putnam, Connecticut, who had played the previous season for Cleveland. As Somers then still owned Cleveland and was heavily interested in the Athletics, he brought LaChance to Boston and sent Ossie Schreck to Philadelphia. With Candy's acquisition, Buck Freeman, who was no gazelle around first base, shifted to right field. LaChance was no Fred Tenney at the first corner, either, but a big playful, likable guy. Dougherty, the new left fielder, was the slugging pitcher-outfielder from Bridgeport who almost joined the club in 1901 but was sidetracked. Hughes came from Baltimore; he had jumped from the Cubs the year before.

Collins' team was in the race practically all of the 1902 season, yet had to be satisfied with a good third, six and a half games behind the leading Athletics. The new Browns, who had replaced Milwaukee in the league, slipped by Boston into second place by a margin of a game and a half. It was a disappointing season for Collins; during most of the first half of the season he ran second to Griffith's White Sox, and in most of the second half he trailed Mack's Athletics.

The Athletics were an absolute dark horse and could not have won without the help of the Boston club. On the eve of the season it looked as though Mack's club had been absolutely wrecked when the Pennsylvania Supreme court upheld the legality of the reserve clause in the Philadelphia National contracts, and ordered Lajoie, Flick, and pitchers Bernhard, Duggleby, and Fraser, all of whom had jumped to the A's, to return to the Phillies. Only the latter two obeyed, as Lajoie, Flick, and Bernhard moved on to Cleveland, out of the jurisdiction of the court.

Mack was so badly off for pitchers that at a special meeting of the league called by Ban Johnson, Somers let Connie have three of his secondary pitchers—Bert Hustings, who had come from Duffy's old Milwaukee club, Fred Mitchell, and Howard Wilson. The June capture of Rube Waddell, whom Mack snared from the Los Angeles club, and the midseason acquisition of Danny Murphy made

Connie's first pennant winner possible. Waddell won twenty-three games for the Athletics after June 26, and games between Connie Mack's big left-hander and Cy Young became the season's biggest treats at the Huntington grounds. Hustings and Mitchell were Mack's third and fourth pitchers, and there would have been no 1902 flag for Connie without these Boston "gifts."

Danny Murphy, a favorite with New England fans all during his career, joined the Athletics in Boston on July 2 of that year, and he hit the Huntington Avenue ball field like an atom bomb. Old Boston fans still shudder as they recollect Danny's pre-Fourth pyrotechnic display in his American League debut, and it was a good thing Murphy didn't start at game time. He might have blown the Sacred Cod right out of the State House. Mack had just acquired Murphy from Norwich, and the recruit didn't show up at the park until the second inning. But there still was time for terrific damage; the rookie from Connecticut collected six hits, including a grand slam homer, from his victims, George Prentiss, Cy Young, and Merle Adams. It wasn't at all a happy afternoon for Boston fans. When it was over, Collins' team was on the wrong end of a 22-to-9 score.

One thing that vexed Boston fans in 1902 was the club's inability to beat the second-division teams. They blew the 1901 pennant because they couldn't lick the fifth-place Orioles. In 1902, the Bostons had a percentage of .600 against the other first-division teams, the Athletics, Browns, and White Sox, and only .532 against the four second-division clubs, Cleveland, Detroit, Washington, and Baltimore. The champion Athletics, on the other hand, played only .508 ball against the first division but blistered the teams of the lower half for .688.

"The Bostons have guts, or they wouldn't go so well against the top teams," the fans remarked ruefully. "But what the thunder ails them when they play soft clubs like Washington and Baltimore?"

Collins, himself, didn't know the answer. Today it would be termed "screwy baseball" that just didn't make sense. "What's wrong with us?" Jimmy asked Cy Young. "We play our hearts out when we play Mack, Griffith, and McAleer, but the bottom teams kick hell out of us."

Wholesale disabilities also held back the club, or it would have won that year. After getting off to a strong start, pitcher George Winters, the find of 1901, became ill and was out for weeks. His illness threw Jimmy's entire staff out of kilter, and Pat Dougherty, manager Collins, and Chick Stahl all were out for long periods with injuries. Pat played in only 106 games, and Jimmy in 105, and the three "Cripples" were the team's leading hitters; Dougherty was Boston's top man with .335, Collins followed with .324, and Stahl with .318. Buck Freeman remained the American League's leading slugger with 110 extra bases, 11 more than the collection of the great Ed Delahanty. Buck's productive "wagon tongue" yielded 37 doubles, 20 triples, and 11 homers.

Old Cy Young again was prince of pitchers, and despite that mid-season shellacking from Danny Murphy, the Ohio farmer won thirty-two games and lost twelve. The only pitcher to have a higher winning percentage, Bernhard of Cleveland, was in only about half as many games, winning eighteen and losing five. Cy still was the toast of all Boston.

Collins also worked the tail feathers off his latest Boston National prize, Bill Dinneen. If Somers paid him good money to entice him away from Conant and Billings, he made Dinneen earn it. Bill had little chance to twiddle his thumbs as he won twenty-one games, and lost as many, in a 140-game season. The semi-invalid Winters won eleven games and lost nine; Hughes had ten victories against nine defeats, and Sparks won seven while losing nine. Late in the season the Boston club brought up that jovial Cincinnati Dutchman, south-paw Nick Altrock, on the recommendation of Hughie Duffy. After Johnson moved the Milwaukee Americans to St. Louis, Hughie stayed in Brewtown to handle Milwaukee in the newly organized minor American Association, and Altrock became the pitching gem of Duffy's staff, winning twenty-eight games and losing fourteen. Collins used the whimsical Altrock in three games; Nick won one and lost two.

The management had made some improvements in its Huntington Avenue grounds, and before the 1902 season Joe Gavin put in a new main entrance on Rogers Avenue and a bleacher entrance behind third base. The club also had learned it couldn't make ends meet and pay high salaries with mostly quarters coming in at the gate. It hiked the price of the third-base bleachers to fifty cents, which got quite a rise out of the public-spirited Hi Hi, who was apprehensive that the "gambling element" among the two-bit fans would take over in the right-field sun seats, which still sold for a quarter.

The baseball people here are madder than hatters over the action of the American League in raising the price of the third base bleachers. This act of the American Leaguers will hurt them here, and cost them many friends. . . . All the cheap gamblers who claim that they run base-ball in this town will flock over to the first base bleachers. And may the

"Lord have mercy," when they bet a man is to reach first base and fails by a few feet.

If Hi Hi carried the banner for two-bit baseball, he also was a crusader for clean baseball. Ban Johnson set down Hobe Ferris for five days for shoving around an umpire, and the Boston correspondent's sympathy was all with the arbiter. "Ferris deserves his suspension, and while it will hurt Collins' club, I am glad of it," he proclaimed. "We do not want any of the John McGraw biz in Boston, and the sooner that certain players become reconciled to that fact the better it will be for Boston baseball lovers. I hope this will be a lesson for Hobe, for if he behaves himself, he will make a big name for himself."

4

⊖

PILGRIMS SINK PIRATE CRAFT

I

AFTER being in the thick of the fight in 1901 and 1902, Collins' team went over the top in 1903 and won Boston's first American League flag. And though the club had a lot of stubborn competition from the Athletics in the first half of the season, the Bostons eventually won with such ridiculous ease that they cantered home sixteen and a half lengths ahead of Mack's second-place White Elephants. It was the only runaway race in the first ten years of the American League's existence as a major.

Peace came to baseball in January 1903, when the National League gave up its costly fight and admitted Johnson's hustling American League as a full-fledged major and equal partner. Under the peace treaty, the National League consented to Ban Johnson's last circuit change, the shift of the Baltimore franchise to New York, provided the American League agreed to stay out of Pittsburgh. The two leagues accepted the National commission form of government, headed by Garry Herrmann—then president of the Cincinnati Reds, while a joint committee awarded fifteen disputed stars amid much acrimony and dissatisfaction.

The Boston Americans hadn't any of the disputed men, though Vic Willis of the Beaneaters, who finally had followed Young, Collins, and Dinneen to the new league, was returned to the Boston Nationals. Ban Johnson, however, got all the better of the barter, as he saw to it that his league was awarded Ed Delahanty, Nap Lajoie, Willie Keeler, Sam Crawford, Bill Donovan, George Davis,

33

Kid Elberfeld, Dave Fultz, and Wid Conroy, while the National
League was awarded three big fish, Christy Mathewson, Willis, and
Tommy Leach, and such lesser fry as Harry Smith, Rudy Hulswitt,
Sam Mertes, and Frank Bowerman.

With baseball peace established, there also was a change in the
Boston club's financial setup. Somers, who had got nowhere trying
to interest Boston capital, sold the better part of his interest in the
club to Henry J. Killilea, an able Milwaukee lawyer. There had been
two Milwaukee Killileas in Ban Johnson's young organization, as
Matthew Killilea was Hugh Duffy's boss as president-owner of the
Milwaukee club in 1901. Matt suffered from tuberculosis and died
suddenly on July 27, 1902, at Winneconn, Wisconsin. He also had
been an attorney and had been with Johnson as Milwaukee owner
since Ban's early Western League days. However, Henry was one
of the early intellects of the American League and played a big part
in the negotiations which ended the National-American war. Charley
Comiskey used to say that Henry knew more baseball law than any
other man in the game and that he repeatedly had outsmarted John
T. Brush, the shrewd owner of the Giants.

With the coming of Killilea to Boston, Joe Gavin moved out of the
business office, and he was succeeded by another Joe—Joseph H.
Smart. And the name of the newcomer gave Boston writers opportunities for plenty of puns. "Our new business manager arrived
today," comments Hi Hi in the April 13 issue of *Sporting News.*
"He is Joseph H. Smart of Milwaukee, and he takes the place of
Baird, the western college man, originally selected to succeed Joe
Gavin. He is said to be a very clever business man, but at any rate,
we know he's smart."

The first job of Killilea and Smart was to fill in and grade their
ball field. As the Huntington Avenue park was built largely on
filled-in ground, the ball field almost sank out of sight after the
winter snows and the March thaw, and it was quite a feat to have
it in readiness for the Patriots' Day opening. Gradually the club
began to be known as the Pilgrims and Puritans, as Boston sports
editors and headline writers had to find some way to differentiate
it from its Boston National League rival, but these stiff-necked
nicknames never found much favor with the fans, especially those
of Irish extraction.

The club trained at Macon, Georgia, with Criger and a few of the
pitchers going to Hot Springs, where their conduct was hardly up
to the best puritan standards. At least, there was criticism of Collins
for letting some of the players get from under his watchful wing.

Criger started the season in poor condition, and while Collins expressed a lot of confidence in his team before the opening gong, he had great fears for Criger and remarked, "Lou is not in good health, and he may not be able to do much catching for us this season."

The catching seemed to come in for a lot of attention and comment. Before the baseball peace, Jack Warner, a New Yorker, had jumped back to the Giants, by this time managed by the scrappy McGraw, who had returned to the National League in midseason of 1902. Yet feuding between conflicting cliques, which hurt several later Red Sox clubs, seemed to have had something to do with Warner's going, and in certain quarters he wasn't missed.

The loss of Jack Warner will be severely felt this year [wrote our old friend Hi Hi, who shows himself as an early crusader for tolerance]. Warner was partly the cause of a religious feud in the ranks of the Boston Nationals a few years ago, when the men of Hibernian extraction and one religion were hounded by the others, who hate Celts as the devil hates holy water.

That is why Warner's return to a Boston club in 1902 did not make some of the cranks enthusiastic. If there is one place where bigotry and disputes on religion should be tabooed, it is in connection with baseball and any other sport.

Warner later returned to the American League with Washington and then became a taxicab driver in his native New York, where he died in 1944.

To fill Warner's shoes the Boston club acquired a real New England Celt, Charles "Duke" Farrell, of Oakdale, Massachusetts, and Lowell, who jumped from the Brooklyn club before the peace. The Duke was a jovial, good-natured chap and a great kidder. At the time, he still wore a big fat black mustache à la John L. Sullivan and had the start of a potbelly. Charley had been in the National League since 1888, and though thirty-seven, still was regarded as a dangerous hitter and good catcher.

Unfortunately Duke broke a leg in an early spring game, after the old fellow had started like a whirlwind; eventually he got into seventeen games and hit .404. It left the sick man of the early spring, Lou Criger, the club's only available backstop until Collins signed Jake Garland Stahl, the catcher of the University of Illinois, who a decade later was the Red Sox manager. At that time Stahl was known as Garland. He helped out by catching thirty-eight games, but despite Collins' dire April predictions, Criger caught ninety-six games for him.

2

Nothing shows better how the Pilgrims captured Boston than the opening day crowds for Patriots' Day, April 20 (the holiday fell on a Sunday, and was celebrated on Monday), when the Nationals put on a rival show at their South Side grounds. With the dove of peace hovering over the two leagues, schedules that generally were nonconflicting were drawn up in two-team towns. But both Boston clubs decided to scramble for the Patriots' Day plums with scheduled morning and afternoon games. Each club played its rival from Philadelphia, which naturally gave the Americans all the better of it, as the Athletics were the champions. But even Ban Johnson in his fondest dreams did not anticipate the extent of the Americans' turnstile victory. In the morning the Pilgrims played to 8,376, and in the afternoon 27,658 were jammed into the park, half of them lined along the foul lines or herded behind ropes on Joe Smart's newly sodded outfield. At Columbus Avenue, the Beaneaters drew 1,800 in the morning and 3,867 in the afternoon.

Those two Patriots' Day games at the Huntington grounds really were historic. In the morning game Mack started Rube Waddell, his strike-out star, against Winters. Now Rube never was one to get up early, and present-day night ball, which permits a player to stay in the hay until noon, would have been his meat. Collins knew the Rube had been making whoopee with Boston companions the night before and directed his strategy accordingly.

From the first inning on, he directed a bunting attack at the Rube, and the Pilgrims had him running around the infield until his tongue hung out. Repeatedly Waddell looked over to Connie Mack on the bench for sympathy and succor, but Connie had his eyes on the outfield fence, while Harry Davis, the Athletics' first baseman, repeatedly yelled, "Get in there and pitch, you yellow so-and-so." Boston morning fans enjoyed the frolic; it was a bit sadistic but funnier than a circus. When it was over, they almost had to carry Rube out of the park, as Boston won the bunting game by a score of 9 to 4.

The afternoon tilt before that great crowd also was a noteworthy one, as it was the contest in which Chief Albert Bender, the great Indian pitcher, then a sinewy youth of nineteen, made his American League debut and won his first major league game. Boston fans whetted their lips in anticipation of a double victory when Collins' men jumped early on Eddie Plank and gave Cy Young a substantial lead to work on. Mack called in the young Indian after six runs had been scored on Plank, and Bender held the Bostons to one additional run, a homer by Buck Freeman, while the White Elephants trampled down Cy Young and his successor, Tom Hughes, by a score of 10 to 7. "Who was that fellow Bender that pitched for Mack after Plank was knocked out?" fans asked on the Huntington Avenue cars on their way back from the ball park. "Don't know; never heard of him," was the reply. They were to hear plenty about the crafty Chief in subsequent years.

The Bostons didn't start that 1903 season as if they would make a runaway of it. They divided their first eight games, and on May 26 the Pilgrims still stood at the .500 mark with fifteen victories and fifteen defeats. The loss of Duke Farrell in Washington on April 27 was a heavy blow. Then one good week over the Memorial Day holiday enabled the Bostons to leap into the lead, June 2, but by the crazy margin of only a half game over the fourth-place Athletics. It then looked like a real horse race, as the four leaders were so closely bunched one could have covered them with a towel. Boston had a 21-to-15 showing, St. Louis 19-to-14, Chicago 20-to-15, and the Athletics 21-to-16.

On June 16, the Athletics led for the last time, but in the following six weeks they gave the Bostons a relentless chase. As late as August 4, Collins' lead was only two games, but around that time Jimmy opened the throttle, and soon the Pilgrims were so far in front that the rest of the league couldn't even see their dust. At the finish the second-place Athletics trailed by 103 points.

It was a clean-cut victory for the new American League champions, as they led in team hitting with .292 and in fielding with .960. Pat Dougherty was the club's leading hitter with .332, and among the league's regulars he was topped only by Lajoie, the champion batsman, and Sam Crawford of the Tigers. Young showed he could hit as well as pitch; he was right up there with Pat with .330 for forty-one games, while others well up were Parent, .304; Collins, .296; and Freeman, .285. Buck was the league's home-run king with thirteen; he also had thirty-nine doubles and twenty-one triples. Even present-day Ted Williams will admit that is fair socking.

Though Jack O'Brien, an outfielder from Troy, New York, hit only .212 in ninety-six games, he was a warm favorite with the Boston fans that season and got a lot of credit for keeping the team in the running after Chick Stahl was disabled for half of the season.

Chick played in only seventy-eight games, and while O'Brien's hitting and fielding didn't approach the Stahl standard, for that one season O'Brien proved a most useful player.

However, it really was the pitching which made the Boston team stand out so formidably in that early American League season. "When a team has pitching such as I have, it is bound to win a lot of games," said Collins modestly, taking little credit for himself.

Though the staff was lopsided with right-handers, the Pilgrims had the second-, third-, and fifth-ranking pitchers of the league in Cy Young, Tom Hughes, and Bill Dinneen. Cy, by this time thirty-six, still was magnificent; while he fell under thirty victories for the first time in his Boston career, his twenty-eight victories easily were tops for the league. The Ohio farmer lost only nine for a percentage of .757. As in 1901 and 1902, Young was preceded in the averages by a pitcher that saw considerably less service, this time Earl Moore of Cleveland, who won twenty-two games and lost seven.

Hughes and Dinneen both chalked up twenty-one victories, but Long Tom lost only seven to eleven for Bill. Collins had picked up another capable twirler, Norwood Gibson, a former Notre Dame collegian, from the Kansas City club late in 1902, and in 1903 "Gibby" won twelve games and lost nine. Winters, the Gettysburg find of 1901, rounded out the quintet with a ten-and-eight showing. For some reason, Nick Altrock didn't make much of an impression on Collins. The Cincinnatian liked his brew, but most players of that day were pretty good two-fisted drinkers, and managers weren't squeamish about the personal habits of their players so long as they delivered on the ball field. Anyway, Nick was sold to the White Sox in June, and in Chicago he quickly developed into one of Comiskey's aces.

3

With baseball peace having been restored only the previous January, there still was much bitterness during the season of 1903. John T. Brush, the Giant owner, was one of the National League diehards and almost started the war all over again when in midseason he tried to play shortstop George Davis, who was awarded to Comiskey in the peace settlement. The Giants had become incensed when the Detroit club traded Norman Elberfeld, the famed Tabasco Kid, to the New York Highlanders. The Kid had jumped to the Giants the previous winter but had been ordered back to Detroit by the peace commissioners. Brush and McGraw thought it was rubbing it in for the effervescent kid to sport himself in a New York American uniform. And Ban Johnson hated John McGraw with an unmitigated hatred for leaving the American League in July 1902 and taking a sextet of his Baltimore American players with him to the Giants. McGraw, on his part, had no greater love for Ban. The enmity between the pair lasted until Johnson went to his grave in 1931.

Barney Dreyfuss, owner and president of the Pittsburgh Pirates, was one of the first of the National League club owners to realize that the war was over and that baseball would flourish and pay richer dividends if the two leagues learned to live harmoniously together as spirited rivals. While Dreyfuss eventually lost his great spitball pitcher, Jack Chesbro, catcher Jack O'Connor, and infielder Wid Conroy in the last days of the war, he had been hurt less than any other National owner; he had held onto such stars as Hans Wagner, Fred Clarke, Tommy Leach, Deacon Phillippe, and Sam Leever, had won the National League pennants of 1901 and 1902, and under the peace settlement the American League had agreed to stay out of Pittsburgh. So Barney held no grudge as a war hang-over.

When it became apparent that Boston would win an easy pennant in the American League in 1903, while the Pirates were having a third straight romp in the National, the fans and many of the nation's top sports writers began talking of a World Series between the two major champions, along the lines of the early world championship series of the eighties between the pennant winners of the National League and the old major American Association. Both presidents Killilea and Dreyfuss of the two leaders fell in with the idea, and in early September they met in Pittsburgh and signed an agreement for the playing of the first modern World Series.

The two clubs agreed to play a five-out-of-nine series, three games in Boston, four in Pittsburgh, and two more in Boston if such games were necessary. The two clubs agreed to divide the gate receipts evenly, use no player that was not under contract on September 1, and to make their own pecuniary arrangements with their players. This was all to Barney's advantage, as his players were signed to October 15 in their regular seasonal contracts, whereas the Boston contracts ran out September 30.

Killilea had to pay his players two weeks' additional pay to have them play the series. Present-day club owners who think some of their players are tough hombres to deal with should hark back to 1903 when the Pilgrims threatened to strike and not play the series unless they got the entire Boston club's share of the gate. Killilea held out for a club owner's share and got it by paying the players extra for their series chores. The threat of the strike didn't go so well with the Boston fans, who had set up their new American League champions as little tin gods.

The two clubs battled through eight games, and the total attendance of 100,429 was considered something quite remarkable at the time, but major league club owners and players must smile at a total gate of $55,500. Joe Smart announced there would be no two-bit admissions for the World Series, though the bleachers and standing room sold for fifty cents. Grandstand seats sold for one buck, but even at these prices there was a Boston World Series ticket scandal which blew Joe Smart out of the picture and had many repercussions, including the sale of the club.

In the van of the Boston fan contingent were the famous Royal Rooters, 150 of whom accompanied the Pilgrims to their games in Pittsburgh. Their victory song was "Tessie," which they sang at each and every occasion. They "Tessied" until fans of other towns were ready to commit mayhem if they sang it again.

The leading spirits in the Royal Rooters were Mike Regan and a famous Boston fan of that period, "Nuff Ced" McGreevey. McGreevey had a liquor business near the ball park; his walls were covered with baseball pictures, and many players frequented his establishment. He had a stock phrase, "Enough said," and the roguish Boston *Post* baseball writer, Paul Shannon, condensed it to "Nuff Ced." McGreevey liked the nickname, put Shannon's simplified spelling on his personal card and on his saloon, and there were some Bostonians so crass in their thinking that they believed "Nuff Ced" used his association with the Royal Rooters to ballyhoo his grog shop.

The Royal Rooters' history actually went back to Selee's National League champions of the nineties, and they made their first pilgrimage out of Boston to Baltimore in 1897, when Selee's great team won a vital series from Ned Hanlon's rowdy Orioles to give Boston the National League flag that year. As the Boston Pilgrims of the Johnson loop came forward and the Columbus Avenue gang dropped back, the Royal Rooters climbed on the American League band wagon.

4

Fred Clarke brought a powerful club to Boston for the first game, October 1, one of the best ever to represent the National League. If they weren't quite as tough as the Orioles, they did their best to live up to their name of Pirates. Clarke, himself, was the dynamic left fielder of the club, Clarence "Ginger" Beaumont was the center fielder, and Jimmy Sebring played right. The club had a crackerjack infield with Tommy Leach on third, the immortal Honus Wagner at shortstop, Claude Richey on second, and William "Kitty" Bransfield of Worcester on first. Wagner was the National League's batting champion and Clark the runner-up, while Beaumont had led the league the year before.

Harry Smith and Eddie Phelps were the Pirate catchers, and while Clarke came up in the series with only one dependable pitcher, Charles "Deacon" Phillippe, during the league season he had a formidable staff with Sam Leever, Ed Doheny, Bill Kennedy, Irvin "Kaiser" Wilhelm, and Fred Vail backing up the Deacon. In fact, that 1903 Pirate pitching staff still holds the major league record by pitching six successive shutouts (fifty-six innings) from June 2 to 8 inclusive; Phillippe and Leever each pitched two, and Wilhelm and Doheny each one. Leever led the National pitchers with twenty-five victories and seven defeats, and Phillippe was second with twenty-five wins and nine setbacks. Ed Doheny, a tall left-hander from Andover, Massachusetts, went berserk right after the series and had to be put in a madhouse. He won sixteen and lost nine during the season, and Clarke's inability to use this undependable character was a sore blow to his team and National League hopes.

The Pirates stopped at the Vendome Hotel in Boston, and before the first game, played on a Thursday, hundreds of fans milled around the lobby hoping to get a glimpse of the National champions. "Hey, Dutchman, we're going to give you and the Pirates a good licking," one Boston fan yelled at Hans Wagner. "Who with—that old man, Cy Young?" grinned Honus good-naturedly. But other Pirates, sputtering tobacco juice, replied more belligerently. It was reported that $10,000 was wagered in the Vendome lobby on the series and the first game. Imagine that happening in the lobby of the hotel housing World Series players in the reign of Judge Landis! Ban Johnson picked Tommy Connolly of Natick, Massachusetts, as his umpire, and Hank O'Day called 'em for the National League. The official scorers were the venerable Tim Murnane for Boston and the bewhiskered John Gruber for Pittsburgh.

The Pilgrims didn't give the Pirates much of a licking in the first game, played before a rather unruly crowd of 16,242. Smart packed them along the foul lines and behind outfield ropes. Young took a good going over, the Pittsburghers jumping on him for four runs in the first inning and going on to win by a score of 7 to 3. Deacon Phillippe held the Pilgrims to six hits, while the Pirates shelled old Cy for twelve, little Tommy Leach prodding Young for two triples and two singles, and Sebring firing the first modern World Series home run and two singles. Buck Freeman was the only Bostonian who lived up to his reputation; he hit a three-bagger and a single and scored two of the Pilgrim runs. Boston also played poorly in the field, with Ferris and Criger each tossing in a pair of errors.

"Well, that's only one game," Collins told his men. "We've rid ourselves of a lot of bad baseball, and Cy won't give us another game like that one again."

Jimmy called the turn. Before a considerably decreased Friday crowd of 9,415, Bill Dinneen pitched the Pilgrims back to even terms with the Pirates, October 2, winning a 3-to-0 shutout as he limited the National League champions to three hits and struck out eleven. This time the Bostons got all the butter off their fingers, as they gave Bill perfect and brilliant support. Pat Dougherty shared honors in the Boston headlines with the chunky pitcher from Syracuse, as the popular outfielder, leading off for Collins, was the Pilgrim spark plug, with two home runs and a single. Except when he was pitching against the gusty Patrick, Sam Leever, the Pirate hurler known as the Hoosier schoolmaster, put dunce caps on most of the other Pilgrims.

The third game was played on a Saturday, October 3, before a crowd of 18,801, the greatest of the series. The crowd was so big that it became unwieldy, got out of hand, and interfered with the fielding. There also was a mix-up over reserved-seat tickets in the grandstand, and late comers found their seats already occupied. Railroads with terminals in Boston ran special excursions for the Saturday afternoon game, and a real carnival spirit prevailed. Men broke through the outfield ropes, encroached more and more on the playing field, and made it difficult for the outfielders. Though the Boston fans tried to open avenues for Collins' outfielders, the Pilgrims suffered more from the mob on the field than the Pirates, and the National League champions prevailed by a score of 4 to 2. The Pirates had a flock of ground-rule doubles.

Phillippe came back after only one day's rest to hold the Bostons to four hits, two by manager Collins, who scored both Hub runs. The Deacon was a smooth worker, and discussing his pitching, the capable Pittsburgh writer Ralph S. Davis wrote: "Phillippe, who officiated in both of Pittsburgh's victories in Boston, unquestionably is the pick of the Pirate staff. He does not get as much credit, perhaps, as is due him, because he goes about his work so unostentatiously and so consistently, but nevertheless, his record shows him the most dependable man of the bunch."

Collins started his third ace, Hughes, but Long Tom was knocked out in the third inning, yielding four hits and three runs before Jimmy yanked him. Collins didn't think the game was gone, and sent in Cy Young to quell the Pirate bats in the third; Young gave up only three additional hits, but with the Bostons almost helpless before Phillippe, the game already was in Davy Jones's locker.

That finished the early fighting in Boston, and with the next four games scheduled for Exposition Park in Allegheny, the hangout of the Pirates, Boston fans didn't feel too happy about the situation. Many believed the series would be over before the Pilgrims ever had a chance to return to Boston. Remaining Boston National League sympathizers were gleeful as they taunted Pilgrim fans: "Collins' team may be champions in that Ban Johnson league, but the National still is the real major league."

The National League partisans had even more occasion to gloat, when the series was resumed in Pittsburgh, October 6, after a two-day interruption. The fourth was a Sunday, then an idle day in both contending cities, and rain washed out the game scheduled for Monday, the fifth. That break worked to order for Fred Clarke, as his pitching headliner, Phillippe, again was rested and ready to resume work. Collins came back with Dinneen, his second-game winner, but Bill had an off day, the Pirates winning by a score of 5 to 4. That gave the Pennsylvanians a lead of three games to one, and Pirate fans were so sure the series was over that they dashed on the field after the fourth contest, lifted Phillippe, the three-game winner, on their shoulders, rode him majestically around the park and to the clubhouse, where for a half hour the Deacon was compelled to shake hands with his admirers.

The Bostons were in no mood for handshaking and backslapping when it was over; they were sputtering and cursing. It was a difficult game to lose, even though Dinneen was blasted for twelve hits, Beaumont and Wagner each getting three. At times big Bill had his stuff, and he struck out seven. The score was 2 to 1 in Pittsburgh's favor after six innings, when it seemed anybody's game until the Pirates slugged Dinneen for three runs in the seventh, with Beaumont and Leach hitting triples.

Boston's gladiators didn't quit; they had a lot of fight left and put on a spirited three-run rally of their own in the ninth, but it fell just one run short of tying the score. What made the Boston players so sore was that that last rally had come too late.

5

Deciding it was curtains for the Bostons, and wishing to give the Royal Rooters something to cover themselves with when they finally were deluged by Pittsburgh base hits, a group of Pirate fans presented "Nuff Ced's" Boston delegation with a large many-hued umbrella. Perhaps that "rainbow bumbershoot" changed the luck, or it was the three-run ninth-inning rally in the fourth game which lit the fuse, for from then on, the Collins gang was a changed team.

The Pilgrims became terrific fighting galoots as they tore the Pirates limb from limb in Pittsburgh, October 7, winning by a score of 11 to 2. Even though the crowd was 12,322, ground rules were necessary. With Phillippe having fetched in three victories, Clarke now took a chance with "Roaring Bill" Kennedy, a pitcher with a ten-and-five record, and the final score makes Bill look much worse than was really the case.

For five innings Kennedy held Cy Young to a scoreless tie. In fact, Roaring Bill tried to start something himself in the third inning when he lit on Young for a clean double with none out, and then had to stand around and watch Cy set down Beaumont, Clarke, and Leach.

The big break came in the sixth inning, when for about ten minutes three of the Pirate immortals played as though they were members of the Rinky Dinks rather than stars on the famous three-time Pirate champions. Wagner, the Flying Dutchman, booted two, Clarke and Leach each one. Kennedy couldn't hold up against that kind of support; ten Bostons went to bat, and six scored. The Royal Rooters were pretty well exhausted when that inning was over, but their larynxes were completely used up when four more Boston tallies were scored at the expense of Jack Thompson in the seventh.

Everybody but Lou Criger took part in a fourteen-bingle Boston Tee Party, with Pat Dougherty again having a most profitable afternoon with two triples and a single. Oddly enough, he didn't score a run. Even Young lived up to his .330 American League average by hitting a single and puffing around to third on a three-bagger.

That was just the start of the fun for the Royal Rooters, and they had many opportunities to stage their umbrella dance after that. The sixth game on the eighth wasn't as lopsided as was the fifth game victory, but Boston won by a comfortable 6-to-3 margin while tying up the series at three victories each. Dinneen was back on the hill for the Pilgrims, and Schoolmaster Leever tried it again for the Pirates. Each pitcher gave up ten hits, with Ginger Beaumont being a ball of fire at the top of the smoky city batting order with four safeties and two stolen bases.

Dinneen won largely on his superior support, as Leach again was guilty of two errors, one of them, a wild throw, helping the Bostons to three runs in the third, and Wagner giving them another with a strong-armed peg in the fifth. However, had the game been tighter, Dinneen probably would have borne down harder. Propped up by an early 5-to-o lead, Bill eased up and gave the Royal Rooters an uncomfortable session in the seventh. But Dinneen got the fire out, after the Buccaneers rushed over three runs on hits by Sebring, Phelps, Beaumont, and Clarke. Bill was tougher in the eighth and blotted out the Pirates without difficulty in the last two innings.

The seventh game was to have been played in Pittsburgh on the ninth, but Barney Dreyfuss decreed it was too cold for baseball and postponed it until the tenth, a Saturday. Barney didn't exactly have cold feet, and there was a purpose in his action. Where he had averaged 10,200 for his first three games in Exposition Park, he packed in 17,038 for the Saturday battle, almost as many as Killilea and Smart had sold tickets to in Boston a week before. And it gave the hard-worked Phillippe another valuable day of rest before being called on to face Young again.

Oddly enough, with the two teams again starting off even, the Pilgrims reversed the score of the first game, when the Deacon beat Cy, 7 to 3. This time it was Young who prevailed by that margin. Yet, in appreciation of his efforts to carry the Pirates almost single-handed through the series, Pittsburgh fans presented the Deacon with a diamond stickpin before the game.

It still was cold, but Young, the farmer, fared better in the frigid atmosphere than Phillippe, the Deacon. Hits into the big overflow crowd were ground-rule triples, and Boston profited by this arrangement; five of their eleven hits landed in the crowd, and most of them would have been easy outs on a clear field. The five triples were hit by as many different players, Collins, Stahl, Freeman, Parent, and Ferris. The Royal Rooters howled with glee and derided the Pirate rooters during the extra-base shower.

Young also gave up ten hits, but he limited bingles into the crowd to blows by Clarke and Bransfield and pitched brilliant ball with runners on base, striking out six. The fielding was erratic, no doubt due to the numbed fingers of the athletes, as the Pilgrims committed four errors and the Pirates three. Even so, there was some spectacular play around second base. On the Boston side, Freddy Parent handled nine out of ten chances, and Ferris eight, while Richey of the Pirates accepted thirteen chances at second, and Wagner eight out of nine at shortstop.

Collins' players were a happy crew when they boarded their special train back to Boston. "That was the game we had to win, Cy," Jimmy said to Young gratefully. "They'll never catch us now."

"Didn't Cy and Bill make the Dutchman look good?" laughed Hobe Ferris. "National League batting champion, my eye!" In the fifth, sixth, and seventh games, Young and Dinneen had held the famous Honus Wagner hitless in eleven official times at bat.

Newspaper cartoonists in Boston, and elsewhere around the country, were drawing an infuriated Pilgrim staving in the skull and cross-boned hat of a rapidly retreating Pirate with his descending musket shaped like a bat. Or if the Boston Pilgrim wasn't doing that, he was shooting the Freebooter full of holes. It reflected the spirit of the occasion. Sir Barney, Pirate skipper Clarke, and his Buccaneers distinctly were on the run.

Another two days elapsed before the Pilgrims had a chance to nail down their fifth win and clinch the series, after a gallant uphill fight that yielded them four straight victories. October 11 was the second idle Sunday of the series; October 12 was a rainy Monday, and the baseball marathon finally came to an end, on a Tuesday, October 13. By that time, the series had dragged through nearly two weeks, and the poorest crowd of the eight games, 7,455, saw the Boston Americans win their first world championship, five games to three.

If the seventh game saw the first contest reversed, the eighth was a duplicate of the second game. Bill Dinneen won his third victory of the series by the same score as his first, 3 to 0, giving up four hits, against three on October 3. Everybody was pretty well fed up with the series, officials, players, fans, writers, and Bill took no chance of it dragging to a ninth game. "I want to get back to Syracuse; I got a lot of things I want to do," he said. "This thing has gone far enough." He pitched like a man that wanted to go home.

Clarke played out his string to the end and pitched Phillippe for the fifth time. The two idle days again rested his arm; the Deacon was rarin' to go, and would have beaten a lesser opponent. He gave up only eight hits but again was handicapped by three errors. The Pilgrims, on the other hand, backed Bill with perfect support. Six of the Boston hits were made by the bottom of the batting order, including a run-producing triple by Candy LaChance, who had been a drag at bat in the earlier games. Two Boston runs crossed the plate in the fourth and a third two innings later.

One of Pittsburgh's few chances to score was broken up by a great play by the brainy Criger. Leach was on third and Wagner on second when Lou bluffed a throw to second to catch the Dutchman. But he didn't go through with it, and half wheeling around, completed the throw to Collins and nipped Leach off third.

The game and series ended appropriately enough with Dinneen striking out the great Honus Wagner. What the final crowd lacked in numbers, it made up in enthusiasm. Reach's 1904 *Baseball Guide* says: "The demonstration which followed Dinneen's strike-out of Wagner equalled that seen at any big football game in this country." The fans had no goal posts to pull up, but they all tumbled on the field, shrieked, sang, and danced, while the new world champions were carried to their dressing room on the backs of the crowd. The rainbow-hued umbrella was in the center of the parade.

Heroes of the series were Bill Dinneen, who won three games, two of them shutouts, and lost only one; Cy Young, who broke even in four games; Pat Dougherty, who hit two homers in Dinneen's first victory; and Pittsburgh's lionhearted pitcher, Phillippe, who won three games and lost two. The series produced only two .300 hitters, Stahl for Boston with .309 and Sebring, who batted .366 for the Pirates. The "goat" unquestionably was Wagner, the National League batting champion, who hit a modest .214.

The players of the two clubs fared well, considering 1903 salaries and that the total gate for the eight games was only $55,500. Thanks to Dreyfuss' generosity, the losers divided bigger shares than the winning Bostonians. Barney threw his share of the receipts into the Pittsburgh players' pool, and each Pirate drew a share of $1,316. Killilea kept his club owner's share of $6,699.65, and each Boston player pulled down $1,182, plus full salary up to October 15.

However, the fact that the Pirate players fared better than the new Pilgrim world champions didn't sit well in Boston, and the series left a smell that didn't fade from the nation's sport pages until the winter snows. Everyone was taking a crack at Killilea and his business representative, Joe Smart. J. Ed Grillo, a fair and fearless writer, then the Cincinnati correspondent to the *Sporting News,* a publication which then had American League leanings, denounced what he termed the "skinflint" methods of the Boston management. He claimed that Barney Dreyfuss, president of the rival World Series contender; the Boston National owners, Messrs. Soden, Billings, and Conant, as well as the visiting sports writers, had to pay their way into the Huntington Avenue grounds. Of course, today, it is a practice for all persons, except working press and radio men, to pay their way into the World Series.

Grillo also said the sale of the seats was handled wretchedly, intimated collusion with speculators, who he said sold the choice dollar grandstand seats for five dollars, and "even score cards sold for 15 cents." That really was profiteering! Hi Hi admitted that a lot of things could have been handled better, but reported a lot of "specs" got stuck, especially in the last game.

5

⊖

JOHN I. TAYLOR ENTERS THE
SCENE

I

DISSATISFACTION with alien ownership, and a carry-over of the
1903 World Series scandal, found expression in a number of changes
the following winter. Joe Smart, who had gone back to Milwaukee
after the series, was especially in the Boston doghouse, and both
Ban Johnson and Killilea decided a change in his department was
in order. When there was a news leak of a contemplated shift, Ban
and Killilea were deluged with applications, especially from Boston.
It put Ban in a spot; he didn't want to hurt the feelings of any of
his Hub friends, so he recommended Carl M. Green, the Chicago
Record-Herald baseball writer. Green kept Hughie McBreen, who
had worked with Smart, as his assistant.

Even though the post went to a Chicagoan, the change was well
received. "We got tired of having our news disseminated from
Milwaukee," wrote Hi Hi, and added, "Heretofore nobody had any
authority to speak a word for the club." About the same time that
Green came in, the club procured a new seven-year lease on its
Huntington Avenue grounds, the original lease signed by Connie
Mack for the American League in 1901 having run out.

However, a much more important announcement than the shift
in business managers and the signing of a new lease soon was to be
sprung by Ban Johnson on Boston fans. Shortly after the opening
of the 1904 season, the city was pleased to hear that henceforth its

popular new club could operate under home ownership. Killilea, spurred by Johnson, sold the Pilgrims to General Charles Henry Taylor, owner, publisher, and editor of the Boston *Globe*. The General purchased the club for his rather wild son, John I. Taylor, with the idea that it would give him something to do and occupy his mind.

General Taylor, a Civil War veteran who was wounded at Port Hudson, Louisiana, in 1863, was a lifelong student of military affairs and served on the military staffs of Massachusetts governors Claflin and Russell. At one time he was private secretary to Governor Claflin, and he served in the Massachusetts House of Representatives and as clerk of that body. He was an able, hard-hitting journalist, a public-spirited Bostonian, and one of New England's foremost publicists.

It is unlikely that the General would have gone into the baseball business if it hadn't been that he wanted to find an interest for his son, John I. The son was something of a playboy; he didn't have the General's drive or ability, but he was interested in all sports— polo, golf, and tennis, with baseball his especial hobby. He knew quite a bit about the game, had a pleasant side to his many-sided nature, and many friends in Boston and the suburbs. General Taylor also had assured himself that the Boston Americans, world champions of 1903, were a promising business venture. John F. "Honey" Fitzgerald, later Boston mayor and father-in-law of Joseph B. Kennedy, former ambassador to the Court of St. James's, "Big Mike" Sullivan, and other Boston politicians also had bids in for the property, but Ban was happy to see the club go to the publisher of the *Globe* and his son.

"John I.," as he was invariably referred to, had worked a little on his father's newspaper in both the advertising and editorial departments, but he wasn't cut out to be a newspaperman, and in his first statement on acquiring the Boston club, announced he had withdrawn entirely from journalism to become a full-time baseball club owner.

"I intend to give up newspaper work, which has been my business, and devote myself entirely to the advancement of the interests of my team," he said. "I have the utmost confidence in Jim Collins and consider him as good a manager as there is in the country, and shall co-operate with him so far as it lies in my power to give Boston as good ball as it has had in the past, and will spare neither money nor effort in that direction.

"Boston is a great baseball city and deserves the best there is in the market. I want another pennant to fling from the top of that pole at the close of the season, and I see no reason why there shouldn't be another world's pennant as well." He added that he had been hopeful of swinging a deal for the club for two years, and that he would retain Carl Green as his business manager.

The Taylor regime was to prove an eventful one in Red Sox baseball. By nature, John I. was better fitted to ride with a champion than take the bumps with a loser. With later inefficient teams, he developed a hot temper, was impatient and sarcastic with erring and inefficient ballplayers, became a turbulent character in baseball, and in the years to come was a severe taskmaster for many of his athletes and managers.

Even though the Boston Americans now were *Globe*-owned, young Taylor was careful never to give his father's newspaper any break in giving out news, while other Boston newspapers treated the club as kindly as before the sale to the General. However, *Globe* ownership of the team converted Tim Murnane, the newspaper's famous baseball writer, to a 100-per-cent American Leaguer. While Tim was the Boston club's official scorer in the 1903 World Series, many of Murnane's fellows believed his heart still belonged to the old league; but Murnane worshiped Charles Taylor, and when the General acquired the property, Tim, one of the National's 1876 charter-year players, became heart and soul a Boston American partisan. And what Tim thought and felt, his baseball assistant, Mel Webb, also thought and felt.

John I. Taylor took over on April 18, and the following day, April 19, Patriots' Day, 28,000 passed through the portals of his Huntington Avenue grounds to see morning and afternoon games between the Pilgrims and Senators. With George Winters opposing Dunkle, the Bostons won the after-breakfast game, 1 to 0, and Cy Young nosed out Case Patten, 3 to 2, before a great overflow crowd in the afternoon.

John I. gleefully clapped his hands. "So far, so good," he laughed.

The double victory over Washington was a good augury of what was in store for Taylor in his first year as president. The Pilgrim world champions of 1903 remained a formidable compact club; they won many tight, well-pitched games and hoisted their second successive pennant after one of the American League's greatest races. It was another season which gave Boston fans many interesting and thrilling afternoons.

2

Collins' team already had undergone some changes before John I. Taylor took charge. Ban Johnson still pulled a lot of strings behind the scenes, and Jesse Tannehill, strong-armed left-handed pitcher, came to Boston from the New York Highlanders, and the Boston battery of Tom Hughes and Garland Stahl was sent to Washington. Jimmy picked up a new third-string catcher, Tom Doran, to help out the aging Lou Criger and Duke Farrell.

The new Boston management made a deal with the New York Highlanders on June 19 which had Boston fans seeing red. The popular and hard-hitting left fielder, Pat Dougherty, was traded to New York for Bob Unglaub, a utility infielder. If the Pilgrims hadn't repeated that season, it would have been difficult for them to live down that deal; as it was, the alleged "trade" stuck in the craws of Boston fans for many years. Until Frazee ruined the Red Sox in the post–World War I period, it unquestionably was the worst deal made by the Boston club.

In his weekly letter to the *Sporting News*, Johnny Hallahan, who succeeded Pete Hi Hi Kelley as the Boston correspondent, wrote:

The fans are greatly disturbed over the change made by President John I. Taylor, by which we lose that peerless wielder of the stick, Pat Dougherty, and get in return an untried player in fast company, and if the reports we hear are true, a sick man in one of New York's hospitals.

There is not the least doubt in my mind, and the vast majority of people who are interested in the World's Champions are of the same thought, that we got all the worst of the exchange, and all deplore the deal.

And Hallahan was mild compared to some of the other things which were printed and said in Boston about the deal. "They must have got John I. plastered to pull anything like that on him," said many a fan. The trade really was Ban Johnson's handiwork, but how he hornswoggled John I. Taylor, a new owner anxious to make good and please his fans, into being a party to the deal remains a mystery today. Johnson was anxious to build up a strong club in New York to buck McGraw and Brush. The 1903 New York Americans, led by Clark Griffith, the former Chicago manager, were dubbed the "All-Stars" by friendly writers, but the stars didn't click and only finished fourth. McGraw was winning his first pennant in New

York in 1904, and Johnson no doubt wanted a powerful American League club to give the rejuvenated Giants the stiffest kind of opposition. So Dougherty was added to the New York Stars.

Jack O'Neill, the 1903 outfield substitute, tried to fill the departed Patrick's big brogans in left field, but it was too much of an assignment, and on July 2, Taylor purchased Albert "Kip" Selbach, from the Washington Senators. Kip, only five feet seven inches, was one of the leading lead-off men in the game; before the baseball war, he had played for Washington, Cincinnati, and New York in the National League, jumping the Giants in 1902 to cast his luck with McGraw's early Baltimore Americans.

Collins and Taylor owed their 1904 pennant to the fact that the club was almost immune to injury. No other championship club of modern times ever compiled such a record for daily attendance. Talk about Ned Hanlon's tough old National League Orioles shaking off bruised shins, mashed fingers, and twisted ankles—they didn't hold a candle to Collins' doughty Puritans of 1904. The American League played a 154-game schedule for the first time in 1904, and the Pilgrims played three tie games—157 contests in all. Chick Stahl, Buck Freeman, and Candy LaChance played in all 157; manager Jimmy Collins and Hobe Ferris each missed one, and Freddy Parent two. Between Washington and Boston, Al Selbach played in 146 games, while Lou Criger, the first-string catcher, caught 95 contests.

The pitchers also worked with clocklike consistency, and it was only on rare occasions that Collins yanked a pitcher because of ineffectiveness. Young produced twenty-six victories against sixteen defeats and was second in wins only to the majestic peak of Jack Chesbro of New York, who won forty-one games and lost twelve. Right behind old Cy were Dinneen, with twenty-three victories and fourteen setbacks, and the new left-hander, Jesse Tannehill, with a twenty-one-and-eleven record. Norwood Gibson followed with seventeen and fourteen and George Winters with eight and four.

The season of 1904 was famous for the many brilliant pitching duels involving Boston pitchers. On May 1, that impish child of nature, Rube Waddell, pitched a one-hit game against the Pilgrims at the Huntington Avenue grounds and won by a score of 3 to 0. Only two Boston batters reached base, as Jesse Tannehill, the left-hander, was the defeated Pilgrim boxman.

Waddell had a lot of fun crowing about his feat the next few days, and he unquestionably inspired Cy Young to pitching the classic of his brilliant career. He taunted Cy to face him, and shouted, "I'll give you the same what I give Tannehill."

The two met in the last game of the series in Boston, May 5, and it really showed what Young could do when he had his dander up. He retired the twenty-seven Athletics who faced him in order, one of the six perfect games of major league history. He reversed the former score, defeating Waddell, 3 to 0. "How did you like that one, you hayseed?" farmer Young yelled happily at the disgruntled Rube when it was over. It was Young's second no-hit game, as he had pitched his first with the old Cleveland Spiders of the National League in 1897.

Connie Mack was as much impressed with Young's victory as Collins was, and made no effort to hide it. "I never saw such a game pitched," said the tall man from Brookfield with unfeigned admiration. "He knew what he was doing with every pitch. Cy was perfect! Just perfect!"

Then, on August 15, Jesse Tannehill hurled Boston's second no-hit game of the season in Comiskey's park in Chicago, defeating Altrock, the former Boston southpaw, and Ed Walsh by a score of 6 to 0, in a game in which only two runners reached base. But there was one game Jesse pitched that season that brought him and his Boston teammates a lot of woe. Many players of that period were tough and hard-boiled; they slid with their spikes high, and pitchers loosened batters at the plate, but no one really wanted to do a fellow player any harm. Tannehill hit Danny Hoffman, popular fleet-footed Athletic outfielder from Manchester, Connecticut, with a fast inside pitch; the ball struck Hoffman under the right eye, and he went down like a felled steer, the eye dangling out of the socket. Hoffman narrowly escaped death, and for weeks Jesse's pitching was affected; he couldn't, or wouldn't, let go a fast inside pitch at a left-handed batsman.

Young lost a thirteen-inning heartbreaker to Eddie Plank, of the Athletics, 1 to 0, in the Philadelphia park on September 10. The author saw this game as a boy fan from Connie Mack's old Columbia Park two-bit bleachers. In one of the later innings, Danny Murphy opened the frame for Mack with a three-base hit. Young then struck out the next three men, Monte Cross, Mike Powers, and Eddie Plank, on nine pitched balls. There wasn't a called strike, nor a foul strike, among the nine pitches; all three men took their three cuts, hit nothing but the Philadelphia air, and returned to their bench. The writer has attended some five thousand big league games as a baseball writer, but never again did he see a pitcher retire the side in exactly that manner.

There was one game with the Athletics, however, before a capacity crowd at the Huntington park, in which the Boston pitchers had rough sailing. It was a hot midsummer day, and the A's were hammering Young, Dinneen, and everybody else. Chick Stahl, the Boston center fielder, doing his stuff in front of the center-field ropes, ran first to his right and then to his left, trying to stop the slashing drives from the Philadelphia bats.

Finally, a fan, stealing a page from Willie Keeler's book, yelled, "They sure are hittin' 'em where you ain't, Chick."

"Yeah," replied Stahl, as he started after another line drive. "Why the hell don't they hit 'em where I am for a change."

3

The 1904 American League race was a humdinger from start to finish, and during the better part of the campaign, baseball was at a fever heat in Boston, New York, and Chicago. From the getaway to May 19, the early fighting was between the Pilgrims and their early rivals, Mack's Athletics. Then in late May and early June, Cleveland was "the club to beat," but Lajoie's Naps fell back, and New York and Chicago alternated in second place, as the Pilgrims led continuously from April 19 to August 4, when the White Sox led for a day, only to be dislodged by Griffith's Highlanders on the fifth. Chicago led again for several days, only to have Boston shoot out in front at Comiskey's South Side park, August 18, before a then record White Sox crowd of 30,178, when Jesse Tannehill hurled that 6-to-0 no-hitter.

As late as August 23, only five games separated the first five contenders. New York led with sixty-two wins and forty losses, for a .608 percentage, followed by Boston, sixty-three and forty-two, .600; Chicago, sixty-three and forty-four, .589; Athletics, fifty-eight and forty-two, .580; Cleveland, fifty-seven and forty-five, .559.

The three lower contenders eventually fell slightly back in the spirited hand-to-hand early autumn fighting, and the Pilgrims and Highlanders played leapfrog with each other all through September and early October. Collins led from August 29 to September 3, when Griffith shoved his nose in front for two days. On September 5, Boston again dislodged New York, but the next day Griffith's men seesawed in front and held the lead three days. Then Boston set the pace from September 9 to 14, when the Highlanders captured first place for a day. The Pilgrims were in the van September 15 and 16, when New York stepped out again and led the procession until September 29, after which Boston had three days in the front seat.

They seesawed in and out of first place in the first week in October, and it was New York by half a game after the game of Friday, October 7, when the Highlanders, playing on their old Hilltop Park at 165th Street and Broadway, now the site of New York's Medical Center, won over Boston by a score of 3 to 2. Happy Jack Chesbro, winning his forty-first victory of the season, won the close decision from Norwood Gibson. It was an amazing season for Happy Jack, a native of North Adams, Massachusetts, who later lived and died at Conway, Massachusetts. A big-chested spitball pitcher, he had jumped the Pirates to join Griffith's New York Stars shortly before the baseball war ended, and his individual efforts made New York's great 1904 fight possible.

Boston fans and the Puritans then got a good break, partly the result of the greed of Frank Farrell, the New York owner, for a few extra dollars of football revenue. The two clubs were scheduled for a Saturday double-header at Highlander Park, October 8, but at a time when the New York club's chances hadn't looked so good, Farrell had rented his park to Columbia University for a Saturday afternoon football game.

The double-header was transferred to the Huntington Avenue grounds in Boston, as the National League Beaneaters were playing that day in Philadelphia. Believing that he would need Chesbro for another double-header in New York on the following Monday, the tenth, the final day of the season, Clark Griffith instructed his big spitball pitcher to remain back in New York. But when the players entrained at Grand Central, there was Happy Jack at the depot, and "Griff" didn't have the heart to chase him back. So a last minute ticket was purchased for Chesbro, and he accompanied the New York mission to Boston.

So long as Jack went to Boston, he wasn't the kind of a pitcher to sit on his haunches when a pennant was at stake. "Who're you going to pitch?" he asked Griffith on the Saturday morning.

"Well, I figure Al Orth for the first game, and Jack Powell for the second game," Clark replied.

"What the hell's the matter with me?" Chesbro asked. "Don't I work for this club any more?"

"But you worked yesterday," said Griffith. "You don't want to pitch them all."

"You want to win the pennant, don't you?" persisted Chesbro.

Griffith gave in to him and let him start the first game against Bill Dinneen before a crowd of over twenty thousand which sprawled all over the Huntington grounds.

"That fellow again," said Freddy Parent when he saw Chesbro go out to warm up. "Don't he ever have enough?"

But it was one day the Pilgrims had no need to be fearful of "that fellow." The Highlanders got Jack a run in the first inning, and for three frames it looked as though it might stand up for the stout-hearted veteran. However, the Boston bats sent hits whistling around his ears in the fourth inning, when he was belted for four runs, after which Griffith called in Walter Clarkson, the former Harvard great. The pesky Pilgrims poked the pair for fourteen hits, with the infielders doing especially heavy damage, as Jimmy Collins, Hobe Ferris, and Freddy Parent each cracked out three hits. The resultant shellacking was to the tune of 13 to 2.

Johnny Hallahan tells about the mortification of Griff's pitchers in his October 15 *Sporting News* letter.

Chesbro had nothing that could puzzle the Champs, for they took kindly to all of his curves once they got started in the fourth inning. Then Walter Clarkson, who had pitched such great ball for Harvard, was given a chance to display his ability as a professional to Boston fans, but like his predecessor, he had nothing that could fool the Champions, as eight additional hits and seven runs were made off him in the remaining innings of the game.

By winning that romp, the Bostons again found themselves in front by half a game. It made the second game of vital importance. If Boston won, the Pilgrims would have a lead of a game and a half; if New York won, the Highlanders could return to New York with the same half-game lead they had brought to Boston. Collins had Young primed for the game, and Griffith pinned his hopes on big Jack Powell, his second-best pitcher, who had a twenty-three and nineteen record. It was a bitter duel, halted by darkness after seven innings, but the Puritans tallied a precious run in the fifth, giving them the game by a score of 1 to 0. Powell gave up only four hits to seven off Cy, and all of the Boston writers admitted that the Ohioan won on his superior support. "If there ever was a game decided on fielding, this was it," wrote Tim Murnane.

"We were lucky to get away with the second game, but such is the fortune of baseball," wrote Hallahan. "We profited by the Highlanders' mistakes, one of which proved fatal, allowing Boston to score the only run, which also was the winning run. It was a pitchers' battle in which Powell had slightly the better of old Cyrus Young, but the support given the latter was far ahead of that tendered to big Jack."

The next day was a Sunday, but the two clubs made use of it to backtrack to New York for that second double-header on the tenth. By this time, Jimmy Collins was more or less in the driver's seat. He was leading by a game and a half, and if he split even, he was sure of the flag. Griffith, on the other hand, was in the unhappy position where he had to win both games; if he could do it, the Highlanders would win by two points. The fact that Boston was completing its full schedule of 154 games, whereas New York had three unplayed games, complicated the mathematics of the standings.

4

The first game of that historic double-header of October 10, 1904, always has remained a bitter memory for old New York fans, but it was a gala occasion for the delegation of several hundred Royal Rooters that came down from Boston to sink or swim with Collins. The pitchers were Bill Dinneen, who had won the easy Saturday game, and Happy Jack Chesbro, who was starting his third game in as many playing days. Jack again was gunning for number forty-two, and for quite a while it looked as though the big man from North Adams would get away with it.

The little Highlander Park stands seated only about twelve thousand, but the rooters stood twelve to fifteen deep in the big outfield, and New York newspapers gave the attendance as 28,540. The Highlanders were the first to score, getting to Dinneen for two runs in the fifth, Syracuse Bill's only poor inning. It all started with the bottom of the line-up after two were out, but the New York battery was tough at bat, Kleinow and Chesbro getting four of the six hits off Dinneen. Kleinow lashed out a single, and Happy Jack bounced another off Dinneen's brawny chest. Then came a blow that was like a darting pain for the Royal Rooters; Pat Dougherty, the old Boston favorite, hit a torrid single to center, scoring Kleinow. Dinneen then walked the dangerous Willie Keeler, filling the bases, and when Kid Elberfeld worked Bill for another pass, Chesbro was forced home. With the bags still laden with New Yorkers, Dinneen pulled himself together, retiring Williams on a roller to Parent.

Erratic Highlander fielding enabled the Puritans to tie up the game at 2 all in the seventh. Candy LaChance opened with a scratch single, and Hobe Ferris sent a drive through Williams which was hot enough to go for another single. Lou Criger sacrificed the pair along, and Dinneen hit a hopper down to second baseman Williams. In his haste to make a play on LaChance at the plate, Jimmy threw wildly, with the result that not only LaChance but also Ferris scored.

In the historic ninth, Chesbro's luck still ran bad. Criger, not a particularly fast man, opened with a slow roller to Elberfeld, so slow in fact that the catcher outfooted it for an infield poke. Lou advanced to second on Dinneen's sacrifice and to third on Selbach's out.

Then came the play about which as many words have been written as any ever executed on the big league chessboard. While he was pitching to Parent, one of Chesbro's spitters took wing after sliding out of his hand, climbed over catcher Jack Kleinow's head for a wild pitch, and Criger streaked in with the winning run from third. It was the pennant, won on a wild pitch.

Ever since then there has been a controversy between two schools of thought as to whether that really was a wild pitch for Chesbro or should have been scored as a passed ball for the other Jack— Kleinow. In 1941, a New York newspaper reopened the story, said Chesbro had been maligned all these years, and that the pitch on which Criger scored actually was a passed ball which got away from Kleinow. The following winter, the author ran into Kid Elberfeld, the 1904 New York shortstop, in Florida. I asked the Tabasco Kid whether it was a passed ball.

"Hell no, Fred," he ejaculated between squirts of tobacco juice. "That ball rode so far over Kleinow's head that he couldn't have caught it standing on a stepladder."

Dinneen took care of the dejected Highlanders in the bottom half of the ninth, and another pennant was ready to be nailed to the top of John I.'s mast.

The second game that day must seem an oddity for present-day fans and players. One naturally would assume that after the race was decided, and the tension of the first game was removed, everyone would let down and that the second game would be a farcical contest between second-string players. But these two teams had been fighting each other so long and so hard that they couldn't ease up and get out of the habit. They battled in the nightcap as hard as they had in the curtain raiser.

With both Collins and Griffith sticking to their regular line-ups, George Winters pitching for Boston and Ambrose Putnam for New York, the Highlanders eventually won the second game in ten innings by a score of 1 to 0, in a contest in which each team made only four hits. It gave New Yorkers a chance to say, "If it hadn't been for Chesbro's wild pitch, we would have won the championship."

But there were no ifs for the Boston fans; they knew they had it, as their club's final lead was one and a half games and eight points.

Most of the players returned to Boston with the happy John I. Taylor and the Royal Rooters, and a lot of wine flowed at Putnam's Hotel, on Huntington Avenue—near the ball park, where a good part of the team was housed. Even as late as 1904, many ballplayers did not bring their families to the town for which they played. Jimmy Collins kept his family back in Buffalo, and Mrs. Dinneen remained in Syracuse. So, "Put's," as the players called it, was the rendezvous for the ball club. It had a large downstairs drugstore, but among the baseball fraternity, its bar was better patronized than its soda counter. In later years, after his baseball career was over, Cy Young served at "Put's" as an official greeter.

Charley Lavis, accompanied by some of his pals on the Royal Rooters, brought a trophy for the new champions. Collins accepted it for the team in his usual modest manner. "The players did it all," said Jimmy. "I had a great team of ballplayers to manage; they did everything I asked of them."

5

With the winning of the American League pennant for the second successive year, the Boston players naturally looked for another crack at the world championship, especially as McGraw's Giants won in the National League, and a series in which half the games would be played at the Polo Grounds promised to provide rich purses for the athletes.

However, to the dismay not only of the Red Sox but of the Giants, John T. Brush, the Giants' owner, refused to accept John I. Taylor's challenge, issued after the double-header of October 10, to play a World Series. Brush replied his club "was content to rest on its laurels." As early as August 5, when the Highlanders first went into the lead, John McGraw said his club would not meet the American League champions in a postseason series.

Had Collins won as easily in 1904 as he did in 1903, there is no doubt that a World Series would have been played. At one time, when the Highlanders were leading in September, some of the New York newspapers already were clamoring for an all–New York World Series and speculating what Mathewson could do against Chesbro and McGinnity against Jack Powell. That merely infuriated Brush. He hated Ban Johnson and the entire New York American League crowd, Frank Farrell, Chief Bill Devery, Joe Gordon, the figurehead president, and Clark Griffith, and still thought of the Highlanders as the "Invaders," a term for the newcomers still used by New York writers friendly to Brush.

Brush resented the stipulation in the 1903 peace treaty which permitted the American League to come into New York, and even took legal steps to restrain the enforcement of the peace compact. He felt that if he permitted his Giants to play the Highlanders, he would be extending the hand of friendship to Farrell and Devery, the backers of the New York Americans, and accepting the Highlanders as an equal of his Giants. He announced in September that there would be no series with Griffith's team.

So when Boston won and Brush received Taylor's challenge, he was more or less behind the eight ball. He had said he wouldn't play the American League champions, having New York in mind, and now had to go through with it, even though he had nothing against Taylor and the challenging Puritans other than his natural antipathy toward all American Leaguers.

Ban Johnson strove to bring pressure to have the series played, but the National League president, Harry Pulliam, tried to find an out for Brush and McGraw when he said, "Playing of games outside the regular schedule is left to the discretion of individual clubs."

However, Barney Dreyfuss, the Pirate owner, who had been in a succession of bitter feuds with McGraw that season, more or less sided with the American League. After giving permission to his fourth-place Pirates to play Cleveland, the fourth-place club of the American League, Dreyfuss, who was chairman of the National League's schedule committee, issued a statement which rather accused Brush of running out on an agreement made by the two schedule committees.

"It was the National League schedule committee, or a majority of it, which meant the whole, which passed its word to the American League that postseason games would be played," said Barney. "I never agreed to play Cleveland until now. I agreed to play the team which finished in the same American League notch that my team did. The American League managers understood this, all along the line, I think, and I will keep my word with them as far as the Pittsburgh club is concerned."

McGraw tried to square things for Brush with some remarks belittling the American League and the Boston champions, which was in poor taste inasmuch as the Pilgrims were world champions in 1903. And it didn't go very well with his players. At a time of low salaries, the Giants didn't take kindly to passing up a chance to make from $1,000 to $1,500 a man. They held a meeting, requested permission to play the Bostons a series, but Brush remained adamant.

The failure of the Giants to play the Pilgrims was sharply criticized by the nation's fans and press. Only the most partisan National Leaguers sided with Brush and McGraw. The *Sporting News* termed the 1904 Boston Americans "World's Champions by default."

Even in New York, the sports writers generally were critical. Bob Edgren, then the nation's foremost sports cartoonist, made no attempt to hide from Brush and McGraw how he felt about it. In a famous sports cartoon appearing in the New York *World* and St. Louis *Post-Dispatch*, and reprinted in the *Sporting News*, he had Jimmy Collins leaning over the Polo Grounds fence, saying, "Trot out your champs, Mr. Brush." But Brush is crawling into a hole near the home plate. Alongside of the hole is a note, "Challenge to play for the World's Championship. The American League."

Over the cartoon appeared Brush's lame remarks for not playing the series: "We are content to rest on our laurels—John T. Brush," and underneath, Edgren had his own caption: "To a man down a hole, the American League champions look like the REAL Giants."

AN AWFUL LETDOWN

I

OPTIMISM bubbled at the Pilgrims' 1905 camp at Macon, Georgia. The full squad was there with the exception of Cy Young, Criger, Freeman, and Selbach, who were sent to Hot Springs, Arkansas, for the baths.

John I. Taylor, son of the G. A. R. veteran, headed the Boston delegation to the heart of Georgia. In his retinue were Fred Doe, owner of the New Bedford club, and Mike Regan, described as "the best rooter of them all." And for that period the two-time champions had quite a press delegation, Tim Murnane and photographer Chapman of the *Globe*, Jake Morse and artist Wallace Goldsmith of the *Herald*, Walter Barnes and artist Bartholomew of the *Journal*, Frederic P. O'Connell of the *Post*, and A. B. C. Mitchell of the *American*.

It was an enthusiastic, wishful-thinking aggregation, and nobody could see anything but a third pennant. And with the adoption of the Brush World Series rules by the major leagues and the National Commission, there would be no such mix-up as followed Boston's pennant victory of 1904. If the Pilgrims made it three straight (and who doubted it?), there was real dough in the offing.

Taylor was especially enthusiastic about Chick Stahl, who had shown signs of putting on weight in 1904. "I'm well pleased with 'heavyweight' Chick Stahl," laughed the owner. "He looks like a new man." Chick explained that through winter baths and exercise, he had brought down his waistline and generally streamlined himself.

Apparently no one realized that a championship club had aged

63

from one season to another; most of those old National League jumpers were getting into their thirties—and all at the same time. Almost overnight the spark went out of their play.

The team got off to a wretched start, losing its first six games and seven of its first nine. They made a bad beginning when Chief Bender defeated Cy Young in the opener in Philadelphia, 8 to 2, and they were nosed out the next day, 6 to 5. Then followed three straight defeats to Washington, 1 to 0, 3 to 2, and 3 to 1. The first loss in the capital was an especial heartbreaker. Winters pitched a one-hit game, but that lone hit by second baseman Jim Mullin beat him. Opening at the Huntington Avenue park, Collins' club lost to the Athletics, 5 to 4, as Coakley and Waddell won over Gibson. It wasn't until their second game at home and the seventh of the season, April 22, that the Pilgrims scored their first victory, Winters winning a 3-to-0 shutout from Henley of the Athletics.

There was a pickup in early May, when the club won a long series from their 1904 foemen, Griffith's Highlanders, and Freddie O'Connell was able to chortle a little as he recorded: "Collins is looking like himself once more, and so is the army of loyal rooters, for four out of five from the Highlanders has restored all of the confidence that some of the timid fans lost a week ago. It no longer is a joke to call Collins' team 'world-beaters.' "

Yet there was little world beating for the 1905 team. By July 4 the Pilgrims had worked themselves into fifth place, when they dropped both holiday games to the Athletics, who were on their way to Mack's second pennant. In the morning game, by using his entire first-string pitching staff, Plank, Coakley, and Waddell on the mound and Bender as a pinch hitter, Connie Mack had eked out a 5-to-2 decision over Jesse Tannehill.

The afternoon tilt was another memorable pitching duel between Young, by this time thirty-eight, and Rube Waddell, and the battle made conversation for Boston fans for weeks. The two pitching knights—the grand old right-hander and the king of southpaws, fought it out for twenty innings before Rube triumphed by a score of 4 to 2. An error, a hit batsman, two hits, and a force play finally gave the Athletics their winning runs. It was the longest major league game played up to that time in the east, passing a Boston-Providence eighteen-inning game of 1878, and tying the then major league record, a Chicago-Cincinnati National League 7-to-7 tie game of July 30, 1902.

Perhaps the most remarkable thing about the game was that Young went through the entire twenty innings without giving up a single base on balls, though in the twentieth inning an inside pitch hit Jack Knight, the young Philadelphia shortstop, on the head, knocking him unconscious. Losing the game after that near-perfect control really vexed the old fellow.

"I don't walk anybody in twenty innings, and I still lose," said Cy. "Well, I'll be damned!"

Young gave up eighteen hits to fifteen for Waddell, and after Boston scored twice in the first inning, the Rube turned back the Pilgrims scoreless for the next nineteen frames. Harry Davis tied it for the Athletics when he smacked Young for a sixth-inning home run.

"Talk about box work—Young and Waddell never did better work," enthused Frederic O'Connell. "And some folks say that Young is all in. If they had only seen him on July 4, they would change their opinion quickly and say he still is the G. O. M. [Grand Old Man]."

There were fielding gems aplenty, but a news dispatch gave special mention to Hobe Ferris' second-base play, saying, "Ferris gave the finest exhibition of infielding seen in Boston in years, accepting 13 out of 14 chances, and most of them difficult."

Boston remained in the second division until middle September, when Cleveland's collapse helped the Pilgrims to wind up fourth. As it was, Collins' veterans came strong at the end and lost third place to Detroit by only a half game. Boston won seventy-eight games and lost seventy-four for a percentage of .513; Bill Armour's early Tigers won seventy-nine and lost seventy-four for .516. And the Boston attendance held up nicely for John I. Taylor, the club ranking third to Chicago and Philadelphia with 468,828.

The big cause for the slide from first to fourth was a terrific letdown in the team's hitting. The Pilgrims slumped to .233 at bat, ranking sixth, while the leading regular was manager Jimmy Collins, with .276 for 131 games. In the face of this kind of hitting, lefthander Tannehill had a really remarkable record, twenty-two victories and nine defeats. But he was the only one over .500. Winters broke even in thirty-two games; Young had eighteen wins and nineteen defeats; Dinneen slipped back to twelve and fifteen, and Gibson to four and eight.

Several changes were made in the club, and Taylor pulled a spring deal with the St. Louis Browns which proved a blunder. The Boston club had owned a young, hitting outfielder, George Stone, since 1902 and had optioned him to Milwaukee in 1903 and 1904. Maybe Hughie Duffy, Stone's 1903 manager, had given Collins an adverse report on him, as the Boston club swapped Stone to St. Louis for Jesse Burkett, one of the three major league hitters who compiled three .400 averages. But by this time Jesse was thirty-five and long past his .400 days. He came from Worcester, had many friends in Boston, and his baseball nickname was "the Crab." Jesse had plenty to crab about that season, hitting only .257. A year later he was out of the league, and Stone was the American League batting champion with the Browns.

LaChance was the first of the regulars of the 1903–04 champions to go. Candy was released after the club's poor April getaway, and Buck Freeman and Myron "Moose" Grimshaw, a newcomer from Buffalo, divided his old first-base position. Lou Criger, now thirty-three, still caught 109 games, but Duke Farrell was dropped, and Collins introduced two young catchers, Armbruster and McGovern.

And after the season was over, Ban Johnson's front-office appointee, Carl Green, stepped out as business manager and was replaced by his assistant, Hughie McBreen, a native Bostonian. The shift was most popular, especially with the sports-writing fraternity.

2

If the descent from first place to fourth seemed quite a drop in 1905, the great debacle came in 1906, when the Pilgrims plunged through the cellar door into the bottomless pit. It was a season-long nightmare for Boston fans, when even a soothsayer wouldn't have dared to predict what would be their later fate under Harry Frazee. In all the history of major league baseball, no championship ball club ever faded as fast as did the pennant winners of 1903 and 1904.

From the Macon training camp came no word of warning that a once great team was about to sing its swan song. Maybe it was a touch of the Georgia March sunshine—or moonshine—as Freddie O'Connell chirped contentedly:

Collins can't see where his team won't fit. This can be said in the Boston team's favor for the coming season: Collins is at the helm again and he won't be bothered. Collins always has been a king with his players and all will work their hardest for him. Every one has started practicing willingly and is anxious to work into condition as rapidly as possible.

There is no doubt in the world but that the Boston team will start the race in vastly better form than a year ago. It is no secret that last

Cy Young

Jimmy Collins

Reproduction of painting by Abbot H. Thayer, in
National Baseball Museum, Cooperstown

Bill Dinneen   John I. Taylor

summer the men were overweight, and their poor start in the spring
kept them down for a long time. That won't happen again.

Mr. O'Connell soon had to sing a different tune. After losing their
first three games to New York, the Pilgrims seemingly found themselves and finished the month of April with six victories and seven
defeats. On April 30, the Puritans really shot up the Highlander
park; they rattled twenty-three hits off Frank Farrell's fences and
defeated Chesbro and Newton by a score of 13 to 4. That was
pleasant music, coming over the ticker, for Boston fans. "Collins'
boys are hitting again; we'll soon be on top again," laughed many a
Pilgrim partisan.

But that twenty-three-hit game stood out in Boston's 1906 attack
like one thin sunbeam in a dungeon of darkness. The next day in
New York, May 1, Bradley Hogg of the New Yorkers won an
8-to-0 shutout from Norwood Gibson. That was the game which put
wax on the chutes. The next day the club returned home for a long
string of games at the Huntington grounds, in which Boston played
every team in the league. And how they fattened in that visit to the
Hub! By the time the losing streak was checked by Jesse Tannehill
winning a 3-to-0 shutout from the White Sox, May 25, the Bostons
had lost twenty straight. That still stands as an American League
record for ineptitude, though it twice was tied by the Athletics—in
1916 and 1943.

Much of the trouble was due to the illness of Criger and the
inability of two catching novices, Graham and Peterson, to handle
the veteran pitchers. Collins also missed the latter games of the
streak with a bad knee; he played only thirty-seven games that
season. When the streak was halfway over, Jimmy no longer was
king. Freddie O'Connell wrote he was a fine chap but "cold and
independent" and wasn't up to the job of "correcting the situation."
He called Boston the "citadel of the American League," and he
didn't intend to stand idly by while it was being battered down.

Attendances fell off sharply as the Pilgrims dropped game after
game. And then a curious thing happened; after about twelve defeats it perked up again. Everybody wanted to be on hand when the
streak was broken, and when Tannehill finally pitched that May 25
shutout, a goodly midweek attendance of eight thousand was on
hand. As further testimony of Boston's loyalty, twenty-five thousand
saw the two Memorial Day games with the Athletics and were
rewarded with two unexpected victories.

Where the 1904 club was almost free of injuries, the 1906 club made up for it. The casualty list of the Pilgrims on July 14 was like a bulletin from Bunker Hill. Collins, injured knee. Winters, ill at home. Criger, ill all season (when he did get back, he promptly split a finger). Peterson, bad injury. Graham, broken wrist and called home by wife's illness. Tannehill, twisted ankle.

Friction naturally developed between Collins and his boss, John I. Taylor. A drop from the champion's seat to the cellar in two years would have disturbed a more sweet-tempered boss than John I. Taylor. Collins discouraged the boss from going into the clubhouse, but the players had to go through a passageway between the grandstand and bleachers, and Taylor frequently sat by the passage and lectured his athletes on their shortcomings. Those inclined to be chubby were the especial target of his displeasure.

There was an open break between Jimmy and John I. in late June. Collins no longer was putting on his uniform. Some of the Boston sports writers said he was seeking the seclusion of the bench to get away from the barbs of the fans, who had been riding him hard. Then a statement came from the club physician that Collins' knee was well enough for him to play. Jimmy didn't think so; he said his nerves were on edge; he put the team in Chick Stahl's charge and went to a near-by beach for a rest. It developed that Jimmy took his salt-air holiday without the permission of the club, and John I. placed him under suspension.

Ban Johnson rushed to Boston and tried to pour oil on the troubled waters. "After Collins' great work in his first five seasons as manager, I do not hold him accountable for the slump of the Boston team," pontificated Ban. "He has had to contend with many injuries and conditions beyond his control. However, I think Collins should put on his uniform because of the advice he can give younger players." Ban didn't explain why Jimmy couldn't give this advice in mufti.

Several weeks later there apparently was another crisis, as Johnson again rushed to Boston, this time to deny that through the intervention of the league some of the young Detroit players would be sent to Boston to strengthen the harassed Pilgrims. One of those young Detroiters was a fiery Georgian named Cobb, then playing his first full season in the league.

The final blowup came on August 29, when busy Ban again was on the scene. Charley "Chick" Stahl, the center fielder, was named acting manager, and Collins again was placed under suspension. Chick, a native of Fort Wayne, Indiana, was one of the original jumpers from the Boston Nationals, an affable, good-natured fellow now thirty-three, and the only Boston player to take part in all of the team's 155 games. With Stahl holding the tiller in September, the club limped in a bad last with 49 victories, 105 defeats, and a percentage of .318. The unhappy Pilgrims had ten more defeats than the seventh-place Washington team.

If those old men of the champions of 1903 and 1904 aged fast in 1905, they grew whiskers to their knees in 1906. "The poor tailenders of 1906 presented the most melancholy spectacle ever witnessed in major league ball," is recorded in Reach's 1907 *Guide*. "The cause of this awful slump was the decadence of the team's veterans, which had set in the year before."

Efforts were made to enlist new blood. Ban Johnson used pressure to bring about the reinstatement of Mike Hayden, an outfielder who had jumped to York in the old outlaw Tri-State League. Mike played in eighty-five games, and got into a memorable row with Hobe Ferris. Hayden was a high-class fellow, a graduate of Villanova College and a dental student at the University of Pennsylvania. He became involved in an argument in the field with Hobe Ferris, and it grew hotter when the pair returned to the bench. Swinging from the top of the dugout, Ferris, with all the instincts of an old Oriole, dented his spikes into the young dentist's face.

And two stars of a crack 1906 Holy Cross team, outfielder Jack Hoey and catcher Bill Carrigan, were signed by Taylor. Carrigan had the nickname of "Rough"; he came from Lewiston, Maine, and played his baseball hard. He was a collegian but no "panty-waist." With Criger out, and both of the other young catchers, Peterson and Graham, incapacitated, young Carrigan got into thirty-seven games and hit a rather meek .211. But from the start, Rough was a character, and Boston was to hear plenty of Holy Cross Bill before he put away his uniform for the last time.

The club had a young pitching rookie, Joe Harris, a Melrose, Massachusetts, right-hander, who was procured the preceding fall from Fall River. Joe had one of the sorriest pitching records ever compiled; he was credited with two victories in that hapless season and charged with twenty-one defeats for an almost incredibly low percentage of .087. But for one day, September 1, 1906, Joe reached baseball immortality. On that day, Harris pitched a twenty-four-inning game against Jack Coombs, then a young Colby College recruit with the Athletics, which still is the American League's long-distance record and was the major league mark until the Braves and Brooklyn excelled it by two innings fourteen years later.

Harris eventually lost the game, 4 to 1, when a flock of extra-base hits, Ossie Schreck's double and triples by Socks Seybold and Danny Murphy, broke up the contest with the Athletics scoring three runs in the twenty-fourth inning. But young Harris obtained almost as much glory out of it as Coombs, the winner.

Stahl, who had taken over only a few days before, slapped the tired youngster on the back, saying: "That game made you, Joe. Keep on pitching like that, and you'll stay in the league for a long time."

But it was Harris' last good game in the majors. He became ill the following winter and was released to Providence in midseason of 1907. As for Coombs, he went to the very top with the Athletics, becoming one of the great pitchers of baseball.

3

Boston American League baseball was rocked with one sensational story after another in 1907, the year that John I. Taylor told Peter Kelley he would put red stockings on his players and call them the Red Sox. But long before that—in the very early spring, things began to happen, as Boston had four managers and one acting manager in that hectic season.

There is reason to believe that Chick Stahl never wanted the management. He had always been a loyal Collins man, and in the fall of 1906, he went to the front to have Jimmy's suspension lifted. John I. Taylor returned from a trip around the world in November and requested Hugh McBreen to get in touch with Stahl and advise him to attend the league meeting in Chicago in December. Hughie didn't have to look far for Chick, as he was in Boston at that very time, making arrangements for his wedding, November 14, 1906, to Miss Julia Harmon, who lived in the same neighborhood as the ball park.

A hitch developed in negotiations for Chick to manage the club, as Stahl insisted that certain things be done for Collins. Eventually Taylor stopped off at Fort Wayne on his trip to Chicago, and announced he had signed Stahl to a new contract as captain-manager.

After several training seasons in Macon, with some of the overweight boys boiling out at Hot Springs, John I. Taylor decided on a new training base at Little Rock, Arkansas. The club started working out on March 4, and the first few weeks in Arkansas were fairly harmonious. After Collins' difficulties had been straightened out, Jimmy returned to the team as a private, and said he would be glad to serve his old friend Chick to the best of his ability.

Moving eastward, the club stopped off at West Baden Springs,

Indiana, and on the morning of March 29, Boston awoke to hear some terrible news from the Red Sox training jaunt. In a fit of moody depression, player-manager Stahl had committed suicide the previous night by swallowing three ounces of carbolic acid. A minute after Chick put the stuff to his lips he was dead.

In his early training, Stahl suffered a stone bruise, which was slow in healing. A doctor at the resort gave him a prescription for carbolic acid and told him to wash the bruise with a solution of water and the acid. Instead, Chick drank it.

There seemed little explanation for the outfielder's rash act, unless he brooded over the material he was taking over, and the magnitude of his job frightened him. He had been married less than a year before, apparently quite happily. He was the offspring of German Roman Catholic parents, and all through his career, no matter what demands baseball made upon him, he never forgot his religious duties. John I. Taylor was not at the training camp, and as far as is known Stahl had no arguments with the chief in Boston, though it developed later that Chick had tried to resign in Louisville three days before.

All baseball grieved at Stahl's untimely exit. Fred O'Connell, who was at the Indiana camp, reported Collins looked ten years older and had black rings under his eyes such as he never had seen on a man in so short a time. Tears welled in Cy Young's eyes as he addressed a group of players and said: "It is mighty tough, boys. I never dreamed such a thing could happen. In fact, none of us could imagine Stahl doing away with himself. Players may come and go, but there are few Chick Stahls."

"My God, it is awful," said Lou Criger. "I can't realize it yet, but thank goodness he did not suffer long. Stahl was a king among men. He was the squarest man I ever knew. He had only one fault— he was too generous. I never saw him go back on a friend or a deserving acquaintance. In fact, he was often bunkoed because he believed in the goodness of all mankind."

It was a tragic training season for Boston fans. Harry "Cozy" Dolan, Boston National outfielder, died in a Louisville hospital of typhoid fever while his team was homeward bound.

And Frederic O'Connell, the Boston *Post* writer who recorded Stahl's suicide, was destined to join Chick in the great beyond within a month. Freddie was stricken with pneumonia at West Baden Springs, rushed to a hospital there, and died April 21, at the early age of 25. A graduate of Boston College and Harvard, he seemed to have a great sports-writing career ahead of him. He had a brother,

Joe, a congressman from Massachusetts, and another, Dan, now a judge in a Massachusetts Superior Court.

A third brother, James, later an attorney, succeeded him as the Boston correspondent to the *Sporting News,* while Freddie's untimely death gave that imp of the press box, Paul Shannon, a chance to break in as a full-time baseball writer. Before that Paul had been on the city side of the *Post,* but he liked sports and his clever breezy style quickly won favor with Boston fans.

4

After Stahl's suicide, Taylor, in Boston, wired Cy Young to take charge of the team, but the Ohio farmer had no more managerial ambitions than did Stahl. Cy took over reluctantly, because it was "orders," but let it be known that he had no wish to hold the job permanently. He also felt that after his mediocre thirteen-and-twenty-one season with the 1906 tailender he had a chance to put on a strong comeback and wanted nothing to interfere.

On April 6, he issued a statement: "Judging from the way I have been going this spring, I believe I will have one of my best seasons this year, and I would not have anything worry me. I also believe I do not have the ability to manage the team. I feel highly honored by Mr. Taylor's offer, but I could not do justice to both positions."

However, Young agreed to carry on until Taylor could name a permanent successor to Stahl. Lou Criger's name was mentioned, as was that of Hughie Duffy, but the report was that Hugh wanted $10,000. He had just completed a three-year managerial term with the Phillies. But when Taylor named his manager, it created almost as much of a stir as Stahl's lamented suicide. The new man was George Huff, a Dartmouth graduate, who was Athletic Director at the University of Illinois and a Cub scout on the side. Huff was a huge 225-pounder who had a short minor league catching career with Fort Wayne, Rockford, and Burlington, Illinois, and as head of the Illini's athletic department had developed Jake Garland Stahl, pitchers Carl Lundgren and Fred Beebe, outfielder Wildfred Osborne, and others.

One report had it that it was Jake Stahl who recommended him to Taylor. On April 17, he severed relations with Illinois. When a thousand students at Urbana gave him a banquet, the college band played, "He's a Jolly Good Fellow," and Dean Clark made the good-by address. Huff responded by saying he'd do his best to make good in Boston.

A lot of nice things were said about the newcomer, and *Sporting News* commented editorially:

Expert Huff will have a grand opportunity to develop a winning team in Boston. President John I. Taylor will turn over to his new manager a club which, if properly handled, should make a good showing this season, and with the infusion of young blood of the quality that Huff has secured for the Chicago National League team for several seasons, should be a contender in 1908. If, as has been charged, there is a clique in the Boston ranks, Manager Huff's first move should be to break it by exchanging its members for players who possess loyalty as well as skill.

Huff didn't wait around long enough to break up any cliques, and he bounced back to Urbana so quickly some of the students didn't know he'd been away. George and John I. promptly got into each other's hair, and some of the old-timers on the Boston squad didn't take kindly to the "Professor," as they called him. Maybe they resented him releasing Buck Freeman, who caught on with Washington. The Professor's managerial tenure was exactly thirteen days, and under the heading "Huff Hikes Home," James E. O'Connell reports the end of the brief Huff reign, May 1:

With a real rude bump, full of stars [did he mean scars?] and other funny things, George Huff got his dose of medicine, when he threw up his new job as manager of the Boston American League club. It was not one of those nice pleasant awakenings, but a severe jolt, which comes to all men, sooner or later. With George, it came sooner. And it was a case of back, back to the wild and wooly west for the giant manager, that is a giant in physique, as his managerial abilities were not in evidence and the players were not in the least cowed by his bigness in avoirdupois.

The new manager was the infielder Bob Unglaub, who came to Boston from New York in the unpopular Pat Dougherty deal of 1904. By this time, Unglaub had become the team's regular first baseman and under Huff had been named captain. Bob began with a bang, for in his first day in charge he won a game from the Highlanders by cleaning the bases with a triple.

Soon after Bob took over, Bill Dinneen was traded to St. Louis for Albert Jacobson, also a pitcher, which was another poor deal for Boston. Bill still did a lot of steady pitching for the Browns. And Jimmy Collins finally severed his Boston connections. Connie Mack was in the hunt for another pennant in Philly, and he traded

Jack Knight, his young shortstop–third baseman, and a check for
$7,500 to Taylor for the veteran Jimmy, by this time thirty-four
years old. Mack also sugared Collins with $3,000 as compensation
for moving to Philadelphia.

However, it wasn't long after this deal that Ban Johnson again
bobbed up in Boston. He had gone to New York to see off some
friends who were sailing for Europe, and his next stop was Beacon
Hill. And when Ban appeared, fireworks usually exploded on Bunker
Hill. This time, the pyrotechnics blew Bob Unglaub out of the
managerial seat. Ban spent a Sunday with John I. at Buzzard's Bay,
and the week-end party was followed with an announcement that
the new manager would be Jim McGuire, a veteran catcher who was
being procured from the Highlanders. Jim had a long career with
Philadelphia, Cleveland, Washington, and Brooklyn in the National
League and Detroit and New York in the American. He now was
forty-two years old, and Clark Griffith made no effort to block his
transfer to Boston. Unlike Professor Huff and the novice Unglaub,
McGuire, a cagey veteran, could command the respect of his players.

Jim took over June 17, and his first move was to restore Heinie
Wagner to short, play Knight, the recently acquired Athletic, at
Collins' old third-base spot, and shift Freddy Parent to left field.
New acquisitions were outfielder Bill "Bunk" Congalton, pitcher Cy
Morgan, the crossroads cutup who later developed into a winning
pitcher for Connie Mack. Bill Carrigan kicked up a bit of a fuss
when sent to Toronto to gain experience, wanted his release, but soon
realized the move was for his own good. Under their many 1907
managers, the Red Sox boosted their position to seventh place, exchanging places with Pongo Joe Cantillon's black-garbed Washington
tailenders. The 1907 club won ten more games than the 1906 tailender, so John I. could grin and say, "We again are headed in the
right direction."

A pleasant feature of the season was the continued amazing pitching of old Cy Young. He was beginning to show his forty years, had
developed quite a bay window in front, but after dropping under
.500 in 1906, he had the noteworthy record of twenty-two victories
and fifteen defeats. He still could pitch—and win. Only twice all
season was the Grand Old Man taken out of the box. He wasn't
blowing off steam in the spring, when, called on to take Stahl's place,
he said he felt he was in for another great season.

He had only one complaint. "Those young fellows keep bunting on
me," he would say. "They know I've got this in front [pointing to
his pouch], and I don't stoop the way I used to."

By this time young Cobb was in his third year in the league and winning his first hit parade as the Tigers, under Hugh Jennings, were salting away their first American League pennant. Perhaps it was because of the ragging which Lou Criger gave Cobb, but there was an early feud, with the potbellied pitching veteran and his chattery catcher on one side and the tempestuous young Georgian on the other. They would fight the Civil War all over again. Cy would call Ty a "fresh rebel," and say, "My Pappy used to chase yours all over Georgia." Ty would come back with: "So that's your best pitch, you old mossback; down where I come from, the kids throw 'em faster than that. Throw another one like that, and I'll ram it down your throat, and when you choke they can cart you away to the G. A. R. home where you belong." Yet Cy still fooled Ty more often than the speed boy made hits off him.

For a time, Criger was one of the toughest catchers in the league for Ty to steal bases on. Lou seemed to sense when the fleet-footed cracker intended to go down, and usually had the ball at the base ahead of him. That was a challenge to the audacious Georgian, so one day he told Criger that when he reached base, he would go down to second on the first pitch and then steal his way around. He stole second as advertised, sliding into the bag ahead of Lou's peg in a cloud of dust.

Then he yelled to Criger, "And now, you old ice wagon, I'm on my way to third." And despite Criger's quick throw to Knight, Ty slid safely into third base.

"And now I'm coming home, you old baboon," Cobb announced. By this time Lou was fit to be tied, but Ty came in with the pitch and slid safely under Criger.

"Well, I'll be damned!" said Lou. "He did it!" And from then on, Criger never gave Ty much trouble.

7

☻

RED SOX ROPE A TEXAS COWBOY

IN early September 1907, a fine-looking, keen-eyed young Texan reported at the Huntington grounds and told McGuire, "I'm Tris Speaker, the new outfielder from Houston."

"Well, get yourself a uniform; you *look* as though you might be a ballplayer," said Jim.

He *might* be a ballplayer. And *what* a player! Boston later had Babe Ruth, and in recent years Ted Williams, but to many Boston fans Tris Speaker still is the number one player who ever wore the crimson socks of the Red Sox. He was the game's matchless center fielder, and though we've had our Earl Combses, Max Careys, Joe DiMaggios, Terry Moores, and Dom DiMaggios, Speaker was the greatest of them all. He was the player without a weakness; he could hit, run, and field and had the daring, aggressive winning spirit of a real champion. But for the fact that his career was contemporaneous with Cobb's, he would have stood out even more strongly. He managed to squeeze in one batting championship in the thirteen years that Ty ruled the roost, but Tris had a remarkable lifetime batting average of .345.

On the defense, Speaker had it all over the Georgia Peach. Tris played a short center field, as he could come in or go out with equal speed and ability; he was an uncanny judge of fly balls and caught the sphere in front of him with an easy grace. Players of his day often spoke of him as a "fifth infielder"; he could dart in and trap unwary runners off second base, and his rifle arm is attested by 461 outfield assists.

His full name was Tristram Speaker, though ballplayers called him "Spoke," and he was only a youth of nineteen when he first presented himself to Jim McGuire. Tris came from Hubbard City, Texas, and as a prep-school athlete, was a crack left-handed pitcher with Fort Worth Poly Institute. In his youth he served as a telegraph linesman and cowpuncher. "Spoke" still can rope a steer today when occasion demands.

Speaker started his professional career with the Cleburne, Texas, team of the North Texas League in 1906. He pitched seven games and never won one. In his last game as a pitcher, he was being belted, 24 to 6, when his manager, Benny Shelton, yelled from the bench: "Stay in there, Tris. They haven't got a *single* hit off you yet." They were all for extra bases.

One of Cleburne's outfielders became incapacitated, and Shelton, being short of hands, put Tris in the outfield. There the young cowboy fared better, but he was only eighteen and hadn't developed his full power. He hit .268 but was a greyhound from the start, stealing thirty-three bases in eighty-four games. He showed enough to land with Houston in the Texas League in 1907, where he won the batting crown with .315, and title to his services was purchased by the Red Sox for the bargain price of $750. Tris was scouted by George Huff, the thirteen-day manager, who also recommended another Houston outfielder, George Whiteman, who eventually was turned back after a brief trial and landed with the Red Sox eleven years later.

Tris was no immediate success in his first fall with the Red Sox, and there was little commotion in the Boston newspapers when Speaker played his first of 2,789 big league games for the Boston team in Philadelphia, September 12, 1907. Relieving Congalton in right field in the latter innings, "Spoke" had two hitless times at bat and no fielding chance. He was just another of the many rookies being brought in for trial by Taylor. McGuire worked Speaker into seven games, and the Texas kid got only two hits in nineteen times at bat for an average of .158.

In fact, as Tris tells it, the Red Sox thought so little of him that they forgot to send him a contract the following spring. And then John McGraw, the old Giant leader, booted an opportunity of a lifetime. Speaking of the incident, Speaker recalled: "I went to Marlin, Texas, where the Giants were training, on two occasions, told McGraw I was a free agent, and begged him for a chance, but he said he already had more players at his camp than he knew what to do with."

After wiring to several other clubs for a job, young Speaker eventually landed in Little Rock, where the Red Sox trained in 1908. Tris was left there by the Boston club, apparently for ground rent. The only stipulation was that if he developed, Boston would have first call on his services. Tris came fast that season, leading the Southern League at bat with .350, its highest winning average up to that time. By the fall of 1908, the Giants, Pirates, and Senators all became interested in the Mercury-footed fly chaser, but Mickey Finn, the Little Rock owner, making good his gentleman's promise to Taylor, permitted John I. to buy Tris back for five hundred dollars.

With the Red Sox in September 1908, Tris, now twenty, again had only indifferent success, hitting .220 for thirty-one games. But baseball men liked his style, recognized his potential greatness, and predicted once he got used to big league ways, he would develop into a star.

2

There were many other important changes in the 1908 club, as Taylor disposed of most of the remaining holdovers of the 1903–04 champions. Hobe Ferris followed Bill Dinneen to the Browns; Freddy Parent was sold to the White Sox; and during the season Bob Unglaub was disposed of to Washington. Filling their places were a new third baseman, Harry Lord, a Bates collegian from Porter, Maine, and second baseman Amby McConnell, a North Pownall, Vermont, boy who had played for Beloit College in Dalton, Massachusetts. Both Harry and Amby had played with Providence in 1907, and Lord soon was looked upon as a second Jimmy Collins.

In midseason the Red Sox regained Jake Garland Stahl, the 1903 University of Illinois catcher. By this time, everybody called him Jake. He was more or less a protégé of Ban Johnson and had had a busy career since Boston let him go to Washington in 1904. Jake went to first base and at Ban's suggestion was made playing manager of the Senators in 1904 and 1905, the youngest pilot then in the loop. Released to Chicago, he refused to report to Comiskey but joined Jim Callahan's Logan Squares, a strong Chicago semipro club of 1907. Johnson helped him get his reinstatement in 1908, when he started the season with New York, but he didn't click with tough Kid Elberfeld, Griffith's midseason managerial successor, and Farrell, the New York owner, sold Jake back to Boston. Stahl immediately took over at first base, and almost before Boston fans realized it, they had another fine infield in Lord, Wagner, McConnell, and Stahl.

Taylor was spending money right and left, and new outfield acquisitions in 1908 were Jack Thoney, a famous speed boy who had played with Cleveland, the Senators, and the Yankees; Harry Gessler, a former Dodger and Cub; and Clifford Cravath, later a National League home-run champion. Thoney could run like a deer but spoke with no real authority at the plate.

Bill Carrigan had learned a lot in his season in Toronto, and along with Pat Donohue, took much of the catching burden off the aging shoulders of Lou Criger. A raft of new pitchers were brought in; Eddie Cicotte, Fred Burchell, Elmer Steele, and Jack Thielman, a former St. Louis Cardinal. And Joe Wood, later the famous Smoky Joe, came up as an eighteen-year-old in the late summer. When he first was in the league, they added a final *s* to his name and called him Joe Woods.

John I. Taylor's scouts practically snatched the youngster from the cradle. His price tag was only $3,200 when the Red Sox purchased him from Kansas City, his home-town team, August 12, and Taylor immediately issued orders for the boy to report at the Huntington grounds. Even so the kid had had some experience, pitching in 1907 for Hutchinson, Kansas, and before that for a team of Bloomer Girls. One story had it that Joe dressed up as one of the gals, and in his early career, fans would yell, "How about those bloomer girls, Joe?"

He had a record of only seven won and twelve lost when he left Kansas City, but already he had established a reputation as a Bob Feller of his day; he pitched a fast ball that literally smoked. Though he later grew to be five feet eleven and a quarter inches tall and brought his weight up to 185 pounds, at the time, he was a tall, skinny, thin-faced but handsome lad, and people marveled where the boy got his speed.

For immediate purposes, Cicotte was the best of the 1908 pitching newcomers; Eddie was a chap who was to make both good and bad marks in baseball. A Detroit semipro of French-Canadian ancestry, Cicotte tried out with the Tigers in 1905 and was left in Augusta that year to pay for ground rent, somewhat as Tris Speaker later was left in Little Rock. When the Tigers purchased Cobb from Augusta that year, one of the stipulations of the deal was to let Eddie stay in the Georgia town. From Augusta, he went to Indianapolis, Des Moines, and Lincoln, and Taylor procured him from the latter club. Somehow John I. always felt Cicotte could do better, and Eddie repeatedly was in his doghouse.

Cicotte pitched a knuckle ball and a so-called "shiner." One of his nicknames among players was "Knuckles." He pitched his shiner by filling the right pocket of his knickers with talcum powder. He would rub one side of the ball on the talcumed trouser leg until it was smooth as finest silk. It then worked like an emery ball that had been roughened, in reverse. When pitched against air currents, the natural side of the shined ball became rough in contrast, and the sphere wobbled on its way to the batsman. Rulings in 1920 outlawed the shiner, emery ball, and other trick deliveries.

In his first season with the Red Sox, Cicotte won eleven games and lost twelve; "Cutup Cy" Morgan did about the same, thirteen and fourteen; Burchell won ten and lost eight, and the Grand Old Man, Cy Young, now forty-one, continued to carry the staff, winning twenty-one games and losing only eleven. And the stouthearted veteran, at that advanced pitching age, hurled the third no-hit game of his career, against the New York Yankees, June 30, Boston winning by a score of 8 to 0. He was only the second major league pitcher to hurl three no-hitters, and the earlier hurler, Larry Corcoran, performed his feats in the ancient days of the sport when pitchers bowled the ball underhand like a cricketer.

Boston missed seeing this feat, as Cy pitched the game in New York. But Young was given a grand demonstration when he returned to the Huntington grounds. Jimmy O'Connell tells something of Boston's affection for the venerable old fellow in his July 9 letter to the *Sporting News*.

In this city there is one great player of world-wide reputation, who will be honored shortly. And how? That hero is none other than the noblest Roman of 'em all, our own Cy Young, who has done more to keep Boston a fixture in pennant competition of the American League than any other player identified with the Boston Americans since the club was established in this city.

Cy has ever been a favorite of the fans and when he leaves Boston some 10 or 20 years from now, there will be true sighs of regret heard on all sides. Ball players may come and ball players may go, but take them all in all, Cy has it on the whole bunch.

Not only Boston but the American League players told the world of their warm regard for the brilliant veteran. His fellow players of the entire league chipped in to buy him a great loving cup, a spontaneous expression of their feelings for old Cy. On the side was the simple inscription: "From the ball players of the American League, to show their appreciation to Cy Young as a man and as a ball player. August 13, 1908." The cup now is one of the prize exhibits at the National Baseball Museum at Cooperstown, New York.

After a terrible tailender in 1906, and a seventh-place club in 1907, the Red Sox moved up to the top of the second division in 1908, but a fifth-place club wasn't making sufficient progress for John I. Taylor. He wanted to get back into the pennant fighting, and on August 28, in a surprise move, he fired Jim McGuire as manager, paid him off in full, and gave the job to Fred Lake, a Bostonian, who had a varied major and minor league career. A catcher-outfielder, Fred had played with the old Boston Nationals, Milwaukee, Kansas City, and Toronto, had directed minor league clubs in Lowell, Lynn, and Nashua, and had scouted the New England territory for Taylor.

3

Despite Boston's pride in Young's third no-hitter, and Jimmy O'Connell's prediction that Cy would stay on in Boston for one or two decades, John I. Taylor shocked Boston by trading away both members of his famous Young-Criger battery in the winter of 1908–09. No doubt the young owner thought it was a good idea to clear out the remaining old-timers of the 1903–04 champions and to depend entirely on young blood.

Criger was the first to go, being traded in December to the St. Louis Browns for a chubby, frolicsome catcher, Ed "Tubby" Spencer. Some cash also went to Taylor in the deal, and Lou said immediately he would refuse to report to St. Louis unless he got a cut of the cash. Jim McAleer, the Brown manager, took care of that detail. Criger was the only player ever to send an open telegram to the rooters of the city he was leaving. He sent a wire to:

Boston Baseball Fans. I want the Boston fans to know it was no wish of mine to leave Boston. I signed a contract with Taylor in October, and he promised faithfully never to sell or trade me. He gave me a raise in salary and a gift of a shotgun, and I thought for sure I would be with Boston in 1909. I assure you I was dumfounded when I learned of the deal Taylor pulled off.

I love Boston and am sorry to leave, but now that I got my divvy of sales money, I shall go to St. Louis and look out for us. The team that beats us will have to win the championship. I am going to make

Taylor sick and sorry of his deal before the year is gone. Am feeling fine at present, and look out for St. Louis when they get to Boston. January 27, 1909.   LOU CRIGER

It wasn't long after Boston fans digested Lou's farewell address that they received a stiffer wallop. At the so-called American League "schedule meeting" in Chicago, February 17, John I. and Frank Somers, the early Boston owner, now interested solely in Cleveland, sat around for hours imbibing high balls and trying to cook up a deal. Shortly before midnight they sprang their big story on the drowsy sports reporters, which soon had them wide awake. Boston had traded Cy Young to Cleveland for pitchers Charley Chech, a former National Leaguer, and Jack Ryan, a youngster, and an unnamed amount of cash, which later turned out to be $12,500.

A Chicago dispatch from the meeting said: "Somers, the Cleveland magnate, is tickled half to death with the deal, and says that with Cy on the job the pennant for 1909 is safe." (Cleveland had lost the 1908 flag by a half game.)

Many Boston fans were heartbroken; some thought John I. had lost his reason. Was he trying to kill the American League in Boston? Others were sure Somers outdrank Taylor, and then put over the deal when he didn't know what he was doing. It was as though John had traded away a kindly, affectionate uncle whom all the kiddies loved. Jimmy O'Connell tried to find an out for the Red Sox president in his Boston letter to *Sporting News* which followed the deal:

President Taylor's trade during the Chicago meeting was the sensation of the off-season. He had repeatedly stated, and so had Manager Lake, that Cy would remain in the employ of the Red Sox until his days as a star were ended.... But Cy Young wasn't a permanent fixture after all, and as he undoubtedly witnessed his best day, President Taylor took the wisest course in replacing him with younger blood. To many it looked like a foolhardy move on Taylor's part, but to those who stop and consider with mature deliberation, the Boston magnate showed exceptional wisdom in the deal made with the Cleveland club.

Unlike Lou Criger, old Cy let out no beef on being traded, and issued a statement at his Peoli, Ohio, farm that he was well satisfied with his treatment in Boston. "It was just another deal," he said philosophically, "and it was proper for President Taylor to make whatever trade he thinks will work out to his advantage. I am grateful he sent me to Cleveland, where I started my big league career."

Harry Hooper

Tris Speaker

George "Duffy" Lewis

"Old Rough" Bill Carrigan

"Smoky Joe" Wood

If there was a lot of winter bellyaching over the trading of Young and Criger, and though the players received in exchange—Ryan, Chech, and Spencer, proved poor replacements, Boston soon forgot all about the deals when the 1909 club showed remarkable improvement and was in the race for the greater part of the season, despite the fact that the human antelope, Jack Thoney, was out most of the time with illness, and Stahl, McConnell, Lord, and Wagner were ill or injured at crucial stages of the race. The 1909 club finished a good third with a percentage of .583, only five points less than Detroit's pennant-winning percentage of 1908 but nine and a half behind the 1909 Tigers and five in back of the second-place Athletics. But considering the hideous 1906 tailender, it was an amazing three-year comeback, with Reach's 1910 *Guide* remarking, "Boston's climb to third place was one of the brilliant feats of the race, and manager Lake deserves high praise for his capable handling of the team in his first full season as a major league manager."

The club was generally known as the Speed Boys, a term Taylor then liked better than the Red Sox. He liked to say, "My Speed Boys surely were running today." They were second in team batting, and they could fly from base to base, much as do the present-day St. Louis Cardinals. Almost everyone could steal; Harry Lord had thirty-six stolen bases, Speaker thirty-five, Harry Niles twenty-seven, McConnell twenty-six, Harry Hooper fifteen, and a batting average of .282 in eighty-one games. Lord and Spoke, hitting .311 and .309 respectively, were the particular pets of the fans.

Like Speaker, Hooper was to write many brilliant chapters into Red Sox history. If Tris was the game's foremost center fielder, many believe Hooper was the king of baseball's right fielders on the defense. Harry, too, had a rare faculty for judging line drives and fly balls, roamed over acres of territory, was fleet as a deer, and had an arm of steel. He later also made an ideal lead-off man, and his batting average never attested to his full value to the club.

Taylor scouted Harry himself, and the Boston boss was no mean judge of ballplayers. John I. was married to a Social Registerite from San Francisco, the former Miss Dorothy Van Ness. Taylor made frequent trips to California, and he found Harry Hooper playing with Sacramento in the old outlaw California State League and in 1908 signed him to a Boston contract. "Hoop" came from Santa Clara, California, and first attracted attention as a star athlete at St. Mary's College.

Another useful player picked up by Taylor on his west coast meanderings was another California State Leaguer, pitcher Frank

Arrelanes, a California Mexican from Santa Cruz, who had pitched for Stockton and San José and proved Fred Lake's biggest 1909 winner with sixteen victories.

Cicotte won thirteen games and lost five that season, and Joe Wood, now all of nineteen, started to come fast and was credited with eleven victories in sixteen decisions. Cy Morgan was traded in midseason to the Athletics for Vic Schlitzer, and another pitcher with Mexican blood, Charley Lou "Sea Lion" Hall, with the voice of a walrus, was procured from St. Paul in a deal for Chech, one of the pitchers obtained in the sour Young deal. Two young Green Mountain boys, both products of the University of Vermont, southpaw pitcher Ray Collins of Colchester and infielder Larry Gardner of Enosburg Falls, both joined the Red Sox colors in the late summer and were immediate successes. Larry was destined to become one of the game's top-ranking third basemen. Had Taylor kept old Cy Young another season, he might have won his second pennant in 1909, as the old farmer still was good enough to win nineteen and lose fifteen for the sixth-place Clevelanders.

A postseason Red Sox series with the Giants, third place club of the National League, wasn't much of a financial success, but it helped Tris Speaker to gain early national recognition. Neither John I. nor John J. McGraw was particularly interested in playing the series, but Taylor said, "If the boys want to play it, and can pick up a few hundred dollars, let them go to it."

After Joe Wood dropped the first game to the great Christy Mathewson, the Speed Boys won the next four, as Speaker tore through the series like a Texas tornado. He sparkled in every game, smashing out twelve hits for twenty bases in twenty times at bat for a batting average of .600. He hit two home runs and stole six bases.

"I never believed a player could be that good," said Taylor with openmouthed admiration.

John McGraw, who declined to sign Speaker when Tris considered himself a free agent in the spring of 1908, was scarcely a tub thumper for the American League, or its players, but he was enough of a ball man to recognize genius. "I've never seen a greater exhibition in my life," he said. "That Speaker is headed for the top. I think he is a better ballplayer right now than the American League's Ty Cobb."

Everybody admitted Fred Lake did a grand job of running the club, but by November 1909, the Boston fans learned they again had a new manager. The new man was Patsy Donovan, of Lawrence,

Massachusetts, an old-time hitting outfielder with an abundance of major league managerial experience. At various times Pat had conducted the Pirates, Cardinals, Senators, and Dodgers, but usually was in the second division because of mediocre material. Donovan was put on the Taylor payroll a year before as scout and enjoyed John I.'s confidence.

The difficulty with Lake apparently was financial. A month before the season was over, John I. called Lake into his office and said, "Fred, give me some idea of what you have in mind as to your salary next season."

Lake named his figure and got no response.

Tim Murnane reported that in view of the club's substantial improvement, and the money it made in 1909, Lake "upped" his figure, but not to any "princely sum." But John I. seemed to think it was too much, and as Fred didn't come down, Donovan was elevated to the post.

A story was printed in Philadelphia by Horace Fogel, then one of the Quaker City's leading baseball writers and later turbulent president of the Phillies, that there was a lot of bad blood on the Red Sox and that Lake and Taylor had clashed frequently during the 1909 season.

Tim Murnane, chief sports writer on General Taylor's newspaper, took up the cudgels in John I.'s defense, when he wrote:

John I. Taylor is running his own ball club in his own way. Mr. Lake is a man of wide experience and needs no guardian. Then, why should outsiders go around with muck rakes looking for trouble? Fred Lake is a capable baseball man, and will no doubt catch on, while John I. Taylor is not so badly off with a man like Pat Donovan in line. No, Horace, there was no inside trouble of any kind, and today John I. Taylor wishes Fred Lake the best of luck that can come to him.

Lake was signed soon after as 1910 manager of the Boston Nationals.

4

John I. Taylor later confessed: "I believe my 1910 season was my biggest disappointment. After our fine race in 1909, I thought our young Speed Boys had arrived and confidentially expected to win the pennant, but we just couldn't get anywhere." Detroit's three-year pennant monopoly was smashed, but it was by the Athletics not by the Red Sox. And those pennant-hungry young Athletics really feasted on the Red Sox, winning eighteen out of twenty-two from Boston. It was a little satisfaction to Boston fans to win the year's series from the fallen Tiger champions, twelve to ten. Boston finished fourth with a percentage of .529 and twenty-two games out of first place.

Maybe Horace Fogel had something about dissension the winter before, as Harry Lord, captain–third baseman of the team and one of the bright lights in 1909, was demoted and benched in early August after admitted friction with Taylor. Heinie Wagner next wore the captain's shoulder straps. Pressed for the reason for the change, Taylor snapped: "I believe Heinie Wagner is a far better, and more inspiring, captain than Lord, and Clyde Engle [an infielder-outfielder picked up from New York] is every bit as good a third baseman."

The views expressed in a news letter to the *Sporting News* in August 1910 no doubt were one-sided, but they showed how the Boston winds were blowing: "The fact is that Lord was in bad for weeks with Taylor, Donovan and a majority of the Boston players. He has been accused of sulking, of remaining out of the game when his injuries did not warrant his resting, and also of being too grasping. 'Money mad' is the term applied to Lord by one connected with the Boston club."

And Tim Murnane wrote about the same time: "No man should expect to make money out of a losing team, and yet no man goes into the baseball business with a guarantee that his ball players will deliver the goods."

But Lord was an outstanding young player, and there were numerous bids when Taylor put him on the trading block. Offers came from Cleveland, Washington, and the Athletics. Taylor tried to close a trade with Cleveland for outfielder Joe Birmingham and pitcher Cy Falkenberg. That would have been a good deal for Boston, but eventually the swap was made with the White Sox—Lord and Amby McConnell for third baseman Bill Purtell and pitcher Frank "Piano Legs" Smith. It was a steal for Comiskey; he procured a star in Lord for a mediocre infielder who lasted only one season in Boston and a washed-up veteran pitcher.

Yet 1910 is a year to be remembered by Boston fans, as it was the year its great outfield combination, Duffy Lewis, Tris Speaker, and Harry Hooper, first functioned together. Many fans and critics rank this outfield as the greatest of all time. The later Yankee outfield of Bob Meusel, Earl Combs, and Babe Ruth had more slugging power, but it was below the famous Boston trio in defensive skill.

The last addition to the threesome was George "Duffy" Lewis, a 1910 freshman and another of John I. Taylor's California finds. In fact, the young Boston millionaire took an early fancy to Lewis, and long after Taylor severed relations with the club, Duffy was known as "John I.'s boy." Lewis, the present road secretary of the Boston Braves, is a San Francisco boy who grew up in Alameda, where he played on the high-school and town teams. He was early famous for his snappy clothes and fancy vests.

Taylor first spotted him when he played for Yuma, Arizona, in the Imperial Valley League, and he had Dan Long of the San Francisco club wire that he wanted to sign Duffy for Boston. In the meantime, Jim McGuire, the 1907–08 Red Sox manager, by this time Somers' chieftain in Cleveland, wrote to Lewis, saying he was interested in him and wanted him to join the Indians.

"Taylor used to josh Charley Somers of Cleveland on how he beat him to Duffy Lewis by using Western Union against the U. S. mails," said Lewis, relating the story of how he came into the Boston fold.

Lewis played with Oakland in the Pacific Coast League in 1909, and Taylor kept in touch with "his boy" all through that season. John I. went west early in 1910 and celebrated signing Lewis to his first Red Sox contract by taking the young ballplayer to the famous Battling Nelson–Ad Wolgast forty-round fight at Port Richmond, California, on Washington's Birthday. "John I. had me in some fine company," added Lewis, "as Jack London, Nat Goodwin, and his talented wife, Edna Goodrich, were all members of our party."

Chunky little Duffy rewarded Taylor by breaking into the outfield immediately as the regular left fielder in 1910 and hitting .288 in 151 games.

"John I. was a good boss," said Lewis. "Maybe he was sharp at times, but he'd always buy the boys suits of clothes whenever they had big days."

Once Taylor told the young Californian, "You don't fight those umpires enough. You take everything they give you without letting out a peep."

So Duffy thought he would become more aggressive. After a count of two strikes and three balls, he was called out on strikes. He tossed his bat down and raised such general hell around the plate that he was chucked out of the game, the only time he was ejected during his major league career.

That night Taylor said to him: "I've got a damn good notion to send you back to the coast. That strike was right over the middle of the plate. What the hell were you kicking about?"

5

The season of 1911 was a continuation of the previous year's disappointment, the Red Sox sliding back into the second division by
the width of a gnat's eyelash. The White Sox nosed them out for
fourth place with .5099 to .5098, by reason of playing two less games.
Boston won seventy-eight and lost seventy-five, while Chicago won
seventy-seven and lost seventy-four. Though never in the running
for the first two spots—held by the Athletics and Detroit, Donovan's
club ran third until September, when the Red Sox finished in low
and were passed by Cleveland and eventually by Callahan's White
Sox in a photo finish.

Weakness at first base unquestionably prevented Donovan's 1911
club from finishing third. Jake Stahl had decided to sit this season
out in a banker's office. He had married well and left baseball to take
an executive post with his in-laws in the Woodlawn Trust and Savings Bank of Chicago. Donovan had Hugh Bradley, a Worcester lad
who had played well with the Worcester club, groomed for the post,
but on the club's training trip, young Hugh proceeded to break a leg
and was out for the season. The rather slow-moving utility man,
Clyde "Hack" Engle, Alva Williams, a catcher, and Ralph Myers,
a youngster loaned to St. Louis for part of the season, all tried their
luck at first base.

The once injury-proof Bostons suffered from many other ailments.
Catcher Bill Carrigan was out for weeks with a broken hand and
took part in only sixty-two games, but it gave a young catcher from
Nebraska, Les Nunamaker, a chance to show his worth. At times,
all three of the new outfielders, Speaker, Hooper, and Lewis, suffered injuries, as did Heinie Wagner and Larry Gardner. Purtell, the
Chicago third baseman, procured in the Lord deal, bogged down
entirely, and Donovan made the smart move of sending Larry Gardner, his 1910 second baseman, to third, where the Vermonter quickly
blossomed into stardom. Wagner played second base, when his woes
permitted, which enabled a promising infielder, Steve Yerkes, a
former Worcester player recalled from Chattanooga, to get into 117
games at shortstop.

Joe Wood was the lone bright spot of the pitching staff. Donovan
used the Kansas City lad, now aged twenty-one, as though he had
the build of a Cy Young; Wood worked in 276 innings, won 23
games and lost 17, while Smoky Joe's 231 strike-outs were second
only to Ed Walsh's 255. Ray Collins won 11 games and lost 12,
and Cicotte had an 11-and-14 record. Larry Pape and "Sea Lion"

Hall helped round out the staff, as Taylor, getting peeved at the entire corps, cut loose Frank Arrelanes, Frank Smith, Charley Smith, Eddie Karger, and a few others.

A young right-hander, Hugh Bedient, came up in September from the Jersey City club and cost Taylor five ballplayers. He came from Falconer, New York, and pitching for Falconer against the Corry, Pennsylvania, semipro team, he compiled the fantastic record of forty-three strike-outs in winning a twenty-three-inning game by a score of 3 to 1. He was soon to make good use of that strong right arm in the Red Sox service.

And despite another year of heartbreaks, American League writers and fans were more and more enthusiastic about that new outfield trio. Many asked: "How can a team with an outfield of Lewis, Speaker, and Hooper finish fifth? Why, with those boys in the outfield, nothing drops safe. They cover it like a carpet."

8

⊖

EVERYTHING HAPPENS IN 1912

I

THE season of 1912 was a historic one for Boston fans. Everything happened! They acquired a new park, one of the finest in the country; they got a new set of owners, a new manager, a new pennant, and, of course, a new world championship. And Tris Speaker won the Chalmers car for the American League's most valuable player, getting fifty-nine votes out of a possible sixty-four.

As early as 1910, it was known that the Taylors—the General and John I.—would not renew the lease on the Huntington Avenue property and were scouting around for a new home for the Red Sox. Several locations were considered, but the Taylors finally decided on the present site of Fenway Park at Lansdowne and Jersey Streets, in a good residential section, a half mile from the Charles River and less than a mile from the original Boston American League grounds. The plot was owned by the Fenway Realty Company, in which the General was one of the large stockholders, so it was a good business deal all around.

Construction of the new baseball palace, Fenway Park, began in 1911, when the Taylors announced they would have the finest ball park in the country. The steel and concrete baseball era had started only a few years before with the erection of Shibe Park in Philadelphia and Forbes Field in Pittsburgh in 1909 and the rebuilding of the old wooden Polo Grounds in New York after the fire of 1911.

The new Fenway Park had a great single-deck grandstand of steel and concrete, wooden bleachers in left, a right field pavilion, and a large wooden bleacher in extreme right and center field. Because of the contour of the plot of ground purchased, the field is shaped something like a piece out of a jigsaw puzzle, with seventeen facets and walls and barriers breaking off at odd angles. There was a ten-foot embankment in left field of the original Fenway Park, and Duffy Lewis would scamper up it like a Rocky Mountain goat to make some of his best catches. For years it was known as Duffy's cliff. It bothered other outfielders, and once Fat Fothergill of the Tigers rolled down the cliff. A car line had to be extended so that fans could get to the new park.

John I. proudly chaperoned Tim Murnane, Herman Nickerson, Paul Shannon, and Peter Kelley over the newly constructed park in the early winter, talked glowingly of the Red Sox future, and there was little intimation he wouldn't head the club when the new park was opened and a new season dawned. But in late December 1911, there came the unexpected announcement that the Taylors had sold 50 per cent of the club to Jim McAleer, manager of the Washington club, and Robert B. "Bob" McRoy, Ban Johnson's right-hand man and secretary of the American League. The new people would take active control. Jake Stahl would give up his Chicago banking job and return to the club as first baseman–manager. It later developed that Jake, too, had a piece of Red Sox stock in the new setup.

At a reorganization meeting, January 4, 1912, McAleer was elected the new president, John I. Taylor, vice-president, McRoy, treasurer, while these three, along with General Charles Taylor and J. H. Turner, the club's attorney, made up the new board of directors. Hugh McBreen, the club's secretary under the Taylors, withdrew to buy a half interest in the Jersey City club, which became closely affiliated with the Red Sox. Eddie Riley, the former office boy and John I.'s protégé, moved up to secretary.

There is no doubt that this deal was engineered by Ban Johnson, and that he was behind the picture at all times during the brief McAleer-McRoy-Stahl ownership. Neither Jim nor Bob were in the chips, but McAleer had been close to Ban since he was one of his top raiders during the National-American League war. Later he managed mostly second-division clubs in St. Louis and Washington, managerial jobs which then paid little better than $7,500. McRoy had been very close to Ban in American League headquarters. It was said at the time that they paid $150,000 for their half interest. Perhaps the newcomers were to be permitted to buy the club with profits.

The new Fenway Park wasn't included in the deal—it still belonged to the Taylors. They also retained the bonds and preferred stock. One version was that Ban got tired running to Boston and "straightening things out for John I. Taylor"; another was that with the new park about ready to open, General Taylor thought it a good time to get out.

McAleer also brought along his trainer, Joe Quirk, who had been with him in St. Louis and Washington. Quirk replaced Charley Green, uncle of the present Red Sox trainer and for years a character around Boston. Charley used to handle boxers at the Criterion Club and once managed a billiard parlor at 541 Tremont Street.

2

An exhibition skirmish with Harvard gave the Boston fans an opportunity to get a preview of the new park, April 9, but McAleer and McRoy had a difficult time ushering in the 1912 American League season. Their big inaugural day party at Fenway Park, April 17, the game of the eighteenth, as well as two games scheduled for Patriots' Day on the nineteenth, were rained out, costing the club sixty thousand admissions, according to Tim Murnane. Tim thought the new owners could ill afford it, and wrote, "I believe that $90,000 will not cover the salary of the new men under contract for the season," and, "It would not be a bad guess to name $150,000 as the total cost for running the Red Sox this year."

However, the Red Sox eventually got going on a Saturday, April 20, when 27,000 were out to see Stahl's charges outslug the Yankees, 7 to 6, in eleven innings, with Bucky O'Brien, a new spitball pitcher, and Sea Lion Hall beating Jim Vaughn, a huge left-hander. It was the augury for many good things to come as the Red Sox quite properly christened their new park with a brilliant and unexpected pennant victory. (The official dedication date, with Ban Johnson orating and champagne corks popping, was not held until May 17, when the White Sox, scoring four runs in the ninth off Pape, ruined the party with a 5-to-2 win.) Stahl's 1912 team won 105 games and finished with a percentage of .691, which endured as an American League record until Miller Huggins' 1927 Yankees passed both marks with 110 victories and a .714 percentage.

After spectacular pennants and world championships in 1910 and 1911, the Athletics were supposed to be a sure thing for 1912. In fact, Connie Mack still calls his 1912 club his best team. But the A's never could get near the fast-running Red Sox. Stahl never was lower than second. Boston took an early lead by winning five games of their first six and ran second to the White Sox in May. The Red Sox moved into first place for keeps June 18, and eventually finished fourteen and a half games ahead of a surprising second-place Washington club, the Senators nosing out the dumfounded Athletics for the runner-up position by a game.

Stahl gave the club a fine ride, but he had good breaks all year. After injuries crippled the Red Sox for three straight seasons, Jake had a return to Collins' luck of 1904, and none of his regulars suffered more than minor mishaps. Stahl restored Heinie Wagner to shortstop and played Steve Yerkes at second, and they immediately clicked as an adroit double-play combination. Stahl alone took time off, and Hugh Bradley filled in for forty games at first. A good, young, aggressive catcher, Forrest Cady, was acquired from Newark.

The stellar outfield of Lewis, Speaker, and Hooper fairly sizzled, with Spoke hitting a glorious .383, topped only by Ty Cobb and Joe Jackson. The other .300 hitters were the new star third baseman, Larry Gardner, .315, and Stahl, .301. The Athletics still outhit the Red Sox, .282 to .277, but Jake that season also had amazingly good pitching.

If Speaker sparked the team's offense, his new pal and roommate, Joe Wood, was the headliner on the defense. Smoky Joe had a season such as comes to few pitchers, even to top-ranking aces. The Kansas City boy with that smoking fast one won thirty-four games and lost only five for a percentage of .872. Wood's 258 strike-outs were second only to Walter Johnson's 303. Hugh Bedient, the kid with forty-three strike-outs in one game, from Falconer, won twenty games in his first full season and lost ten. Collins, the Vermont left-hander, and the blustering Hall had almost identical records, fourteen and eight and fifteen and eight respectively, while Thomas "Buck" O'Brien, a spitballer from Brockton recalled from Denver after a 1911 tryout, won eighteen and lost thirteen. Eddie Cicotte was sold to the White Sox on waivers in July. Larry Pape rounded out the staff.

Almost as big a kick for Boston fans as the winning of the club's third pennant was Joe Wood's late-season winning streak of sixteen straight. The remarkable thing about Smoky Joe's streak is that it ran concurrently with a skein of similar length by Walter Johnson, Washington's famous star. Johnson started his run on July 3, and Wood five days later. Johnson was stopped by Earl Hamilton of the Browns, August 25, but Wood extended his run to September 20, when he lost to Covington and Lake in Detroit by a score of 6 to 4. In Wood's previous game, Hamilton also had a chance to stop Joe, but Wood won his sixteenth from the Brownies, 2 to 1. The St. Louis club contributed four of the sixteen victories, in which Joe gave up only two runs. Wood also won four games from the White Sox, three each from the Tigers and Indians, and one each from the Yankees and Senators.

The most eventful game of the streak was a pitching duel with Walter Johnson, September 6, which Joe won by a score of 1 to 0. The contest had a terrific build-up, like a Bob Feller–Hal Newhouser game of today, and was played to an overflow crowd at Fenway Park. And the game was worthy of the ballyhoo! The only run scored was with two out in the sixth on successive doubles by Speaker and Lewis. Tris's hit sped past third, and Lewis' was a fairly high fly to short right which fell near the foul line. The outfielders played "around" for Duffy, a right-handed hitter, and Dan Moeller had to make a long run for the ball. With a final lunge, he got his finger tips on the ball but couldn't hold it; it fell safe, and Spoke scored. Both pitchers had terrific speed, and both Tris and Duffy hit to opposite fields from where they normally hit, in coining the game's lone run.

Six of the sixteen games in Joe Wood's streak were shutouts, including an eleven-inning 1-to-0 decision over Willett of the Tigers.

9

SNODGRASS MAKES HIS $30,000 MUFF

I

BOSTON'S brilliant pennant victory gave the Red Sox a chance to meet McGraw's truculent Giants in the 1912 World Series. Aided by Rube Marquard's spectacular nineteen-straight winning streak, starting with the opening game of the season, and the addition of Jeff Tesreau, huge 220-pound Missouri spitballer, to the regular pitching staff, the Giants had won 103 National League games and a comparatively easy pennant. A year before, the Giants had lost the World Series to the Athletics on Frank Baker's dramatic homers and the mighty pitching of Bender, Plank, and Coombs, and the bellicose McGraw was intent on getting revenge on the American League and regaining his loop's old laurels. The two major leagues then were tied at four victories each in World Series competition, and everyone knew this one would be for blood. A tough schedule was arranged by the old National Commission, whereby the clubs alternated between New York and Boston on successive days. The 1912 event proved one of the most historic of all series, and a gate of $490,449 gave Jim Gilmore, the Federal League president and promoter, his big argument when he induced moneyed men to back clubs in his quasi-major league a year later.

As in 1911, the Giants won the toss for the first game, and the series opened at the Polo Grounds on a crisp, clear, early fall day, October 8. The National League had abandoned its silly Columbus

Day schedules of 1910 and 1911, enabling the baseball commissioners, Garry Herrmann, Ban Johnson, and Tom Lynch, to get the series under way a week earlier.

An all-night queue formed at the Polo Grounds for the precious first-game ducats, and by 7 A.M. the line stretched down Eighth Avenue for twelve blocks. Hours before game time the unreserved lower grandstand and bleachers were jammed with loquacious partisan New Yorkers. The crowd of 35,730 included such dignitaries as Governor Foss of Massachusetts, Governor John K. Tener of Pennsylvania, later president of the National League, and the rival mayors, John "Honey" Fitzgerald of Boston and Gaynor of New York. "Honey" had his gang with him, as he led the delegation of Boston's famed Royal Rooters. They had a special roped off section in the extreme left-field wing of the grandstand.

McGraw's players wore their regular white home uniforms, as John T. Brush, the Giant president, gave up the special black uniforms worn by his players in the World Series of 1905 and 1911. Spoke laughed as he came on the field and saw the Giants in their home attire. "I see they aren't wearing their mourning clothes this year," he chirped to Joe Wood.

"These Giants are good; they run on everything, and McGraw has some crack pitchers, but we're a great ball club, and I know we can beat them. Just play your game," Jake Stahl told his players in the New York clubhouse before the game. "Of course, it will be Joe in the first."

Doughty McGraw didn't think the Red Sox would be as tough as the Athletics a year before, but after that third-place series of 1909 he had a wholesome respect for Tris Speaker. "Wood is fast, and he'll get his strike-outs, but he isn't as smart as Chief Bender, and we can hit fast-ball pitching," he told his players. "But watch that Speaker all the time. He's the man we've got to stop."

Wood warmed up for Boston as was anticipated. But when it came time for a Giant pitcher to limber up, the crowd was dumfounded to see big Jeff Tesreau, the man mountain from the Ozarks, warm up with Wilbert Robinson, the New York coach. All New York had expected Christy Mathewson, the Giant pitching master, to go after the first game. He had started the New Yorkers off to victory in the World Series of 1905 and 1911 and was the public's choice to face the brilliant Red Sox youngster. "Where's Matty?" "What's the matter with Matty?" yelled disappointed New Yorkers. But playing percentage, McGraw was willing to gamble with Tesreau, the Nationals 1912 earned-run leader, against Stahl's thirty-four-and-five pitcher, and to hold Mathewson for the first game before a partisan Red Sox crowd in Boston.

The game was a fierce struggle which had the crowd shouting itself hoarse and sweating with excitement almost from the time the first ball was pitched. Smoky Joe started and ended with strike-outs; he had eleven all together, but the Giants also got in their licks and outhit the Red Sox, eight to six. However, Jake's athletes got some good breaks, made the most of them, and when it was over the Royal Rooters were able to stage a war dance on the Polo Grounds infield to the tune of a close 4-to-3 victory.

The scrappy Giants were the first to score, putting over a pair of runs on Wood in the third inning. After Tesreau fanned, Wood walked Josh Devore, the pint-sized lead-off man, and Larry Doyle arched a treacherous fly to short left between Gardner and Lewis which fell safe for a Texas League double. That put little Josh on third. Wood burned three quick strikes over on Snodgrass, but the goat of the 1911 series, Red Murray, streaked a line single to center, and Josh and Larry came tearing over the plate. A year before, Murray, the Giant clean-up man, had failed to get a single hit in the six-game Giant-Athletic Series, and enraged New Yorkers had hung Red Jack in effigy from a lamppost outside of the Polo Grounds.

For five innings, Tesreau clearly had outpitched Wood, blowing down the Red Sockers almost as quickly as they came up, but Boston came back with a run in the sixth. McGraw had advised his players to bear down on Speaker, and they took his advice too literally. With one down, Tris sent a line fly to deep left center, and both Devore and Snodgrass were off for it with the crack of the bat. Josh ran in front of Snodgrass just as the Californian was about to make the catch; Fred barely got his finger tips on the ball, and it rolled to the fence for a triple. Spoke scored as Doyle tossed out Duffy Lewis at first base.

The Red Sox got another break in the seventh inning; they took full advantage of it and rode it into three runs and victory. With Stahl down, Wagner and Cady spanked Tesreau for successive singles, but the rally seemed over when Wood grounded an apparent double-play ball down to Doyle at second. Larry stopped it all right, but in baseball parlance, when he tried to pick it up, he couldn't "find the handle." Larry missed the double play and just barely got the ball to Fletcher in time for a force play on Cady. Harry Hooper followed this slip with a double, scoring Wagner, and then Steve Yerkes came through nobly, driving a single over second which fetched in Smoky Joe and Harry. Tesreau then fanned the dangerous Speaker with a spraying spitball, but the Red Sox now had a two-run advantage. Using their hits with the thrift of a Vermont housewife, they had crowded five of their six safeties off Tesreau into their two scoring innings.

Smoky Joe, however, still had to weather a torrid ninth inning, but he showed the heart and courage of a lion in the day's biggest test. After Murray lifted to Hooper, Fred Merkle, Buck Herzog, and Chief Meyers lashed out successive singles, Merkle scoring. It looked as though Wood was tiring; the Giants had the tying and winning runs on base with only one out, and Sea Lion Hall was warming up in the bull pen. Stahl came over to Wood to talk it over. "Can you make it, Joe?" he asked anxiously. "I'm all right, Jake; I'll take care of things," Wood replied.

Art Fletcher, later the aggressive coach of the Yankees, was McGraw's next batter. Joe had fanned him twice, and now putting everything he had left on every pitch, he again whipped a third strike over on McGraw's disgusted shortstop. One more sturdy hitter stood between Wood and his first World Series victory, Otey Crandall, the Giants' relief pitcher and one of the most dangerous pinch hitters then in baseball. Otey also took three furious strikes and was Smoky Joe's eleventh victim. With Crandall's last lunge, the New York crowd gave a gasp of despair, but from the Royal Rooters' section came a spontaneous paean of victory that could be heard almost to the Charles River. The Red Sox took turns in slapping the tired but grinning Wood on the back, while his pal Speaker exultantly exclaimed: "You were great, Joe. Great! I'm proud of you."

2

The scene shifted to Fenway Park the next day, October 9; the weather had turned much colder than in Harlem the preceding afternoon, and the Red Sox were lucky to get out of it with a 6-to-6 eleven-inning tie on a raw cloudy day before 30,148 of the faithful. McGraw's strategy of saving Mathewson to oppose a lesser Boston pitcher than Wood in the second game would have worked out but for the erratic play of his team. The Giants piled up five errors behind Matty, with Fletcher, the chattering shortstop, the main culprit with three. "Shall I get you a net, or do you want a basket?" sympathetically asked his Red Sox rival, Heinie Wagner, while McGraw frothed before it was over.

"Honey" Fitzgerald had the center of the stage at the start; as the Royal Rooters paraded into the park a red-bedecked automobile also was driven to the home plate. "Honey" presented it to Boston's first pennant-winning manager in eight years, Jake Stahl, and then fetched out a silver bat with a red ribbon for Heinie Wagner. Both were gifts from admiring Boston donors and well-wishers.

The Boston fans rubbed their eyes the way their boys scored three runs on the great Mathewson in a jiffy. Hooper led off the Red Sox's first with a scratch hit to Matty which ran up Christy's arm, and Harry promptly stole the first base of the series. Yerkes lined to Fletcher, who in his eagerness to double Hooper off second, muffed the ball and got neither. Speaker singled sharply to center, filling the bases with none out, and the great Boston throng went wild. "So, this is the great Bix Six!" "How are you, Mr. Matty?" "Hey, Muggsy, how do you like it?" were among the cries hurled from the stands.

Lewis hit sharply to Herzog, and the agile Buck's throw to Meyers forced Hooper at the plate. Gardner hit back to Mathewson, who stuck out his hand and deflected the ball to Doyle. The New York Larry retired the Boston Larry at first, but not until after Yerkes had scored the first Red Sox run. Jake Stahl then came through nobly for his side, Hooper and Lewis riding home on his sharp single to left.

Boston fans, however, gloated a little too soon, as the Giants were far from being dead ducks. In the second inning, Herzog, who was hotter than a bowl of chile con carne all through the series, boomed a triple and scored on a single by the Indian, Meyers. It was the old goat of 1911, Murray, who slapped another three-bagger in the fourth, and Herzog's long old-fashioned sacrifice fly to Speaker brought Jack home. That clipped Boston's first-inning lead to one run, but Hooper added a fourth Red Sox tally in the fifth when he singled, stole second, and romped home on Yerkes' triple. The three-bagger was the day's favorite bingle.

It was no longer funny for Hub rooters when the Giants banged in three runs in the eighth to take the lead, 5 to 4. Southpaw Collins had been belted hard and finally succumbed in this inning. Duffy Lewis put the Vermonter in a hole when he muffed Snodgrass' easy fly. Doyle followed with a single and was forced by Becker. Murray also was hot and came through with a double, which sent home Snodgrass and Becker, and Collins to the shower. Charley Hall took over at this stage, and the pestiferous Herzog promptly got to him for another two-bagger, which drove Murray scurrying over the pay-off station.

Artie Fletcher came to the rescue of the depressed Red Sox fans in the Boston half and tied it up again. After Matty set down Yerkes and Speaker, Lewis tried to atone for his muff with a double to center and ran happily home when Gardner's grounder went through Fletcher like a greased pig. Stahl scratched an infield hit, Gardner reaching third. Jake stole second, and Old Man opportunity beckoned loudly to Heinie Wagner. But Mathewson arose to the occasion and struck out the Manhattan Dutchman.

The Giants unscrambled the deadlock in the tenth inning when Merkle led off with a long triple to center. Heinie tossed out Herzog, holding Merkle on third. Hall then walked Meyers, and McGraw sent in Shafer to run for the Chief and Harry McCormick to bat for Fletcher. The Moose made good with a long fly to Lewis on which Merkle scored, but getting Meyers out of the game proved a break for the Sox. The big chunky Indian was replaced by Art Wilson, a second stringer, and another Art—Shafer—went to shortstop.

Speaker wasn't through and tied the score again in Boston's hectic turbulent half, as the crowd turned handsprings in the stands. With one down, Tris belted a terrific clout into deepest center and tried to stretch it into a homer. While the ball was being relayed in by Snodgrass and Shafer, Herzog bumped into Speaker as Tris rounded third, throwing the Texan off his stride. As a perfect throw came into catcher Wilson, he muffed the ball as Tris slid safely over the plate. As the ball rolled away from Wilson, Spoke tagged the plate again to make the run doubly sure, and then started up the third-base line after Herzog.

"You try that again, and I'll drive all your teeth down your throat," barked Tris angrily. Charley, pounds lighter than Spoke, bristled up like a terrier. "Any time, you want to start, cowboy," he said. However, the umpires, Jake Stahl, McGraw, and other players got between the battlers. McGraw growled something at Speaker, and Tris yelled, "You better keep him out of my way, if you don't want him to get hurt."

With darkness setting in fast, Jake sent young Bedient into the game in the eleventh for his World Series baptism. The New York State kid was fidgety and wild, and McGraw's rash coaching probably saved him. Hugh hit Snodgrass, the first man to face him, and later walked Becker, but each time McGraw sent the base runner down, and Bill Carrigan's rifle arm shot the would-be base thief at second. Matty got the three Sox in order in his half, and umpire Silk O'Loughlin dismissed school, saying, "It's too dark for any more baseball today."

3

While the schedule called for the two teams to shift each night between New York and Boston, it also provided that in the event of a tie, the clubs would remain over in the city of the deadlock and play it off before moving on. So the National Commission ordered the third game played at Fenway Park, October 10, and with Boston getting whackier by the minute, the crowd went up to 34,624, Boston's second best of the series.

On the morning of the game, a delegation of New York fans waited on John McGraw at the Copley Square Hotel and made a request that he take Fletcher out of his line-up and put Shafer into the game at shortstop. Telling McGraw how to manage his ball club was one way of making him boiling mad. If he had had any idea of benching Fletcher, the delegation's visit would have been his best reason for keeping Fletcher in the game.

"I have not the slightest intention of doing anything like that," he said with his best McGravian scorn. "Fletcher has played good ball for me all season, and just because he was unlucky in two games, I do not think it is up to me to take him out."

The Sox heard of the visit, and as Fletch's sardonic tongue already was famous in both leagues, they let him hear all about it. "Don't the nasty New York fans want Arthur to play?" they asked with mock sympathy. "We hope Mr. McGraw doesn't listen to 'em; we *like* the way you play shortstop."

However, if there was cutting satire on the ball field, the ballplayers of the two clubs didn't forget they were playing for cash as well as glory. A committee of Red Sox and Giants was named to call on the National Commission and request that the players be declared in on the tie game of October 9 as well as the first four to a decision. "The owners get their cut of this game; why shouldn't we get ours?" was their contention.

It brought up again the question which Herman Schaefer, Tiger second baseman, asked Chairman Garry Herrmann in Chicago before the 1907 series: "Is a tie a legal game?" In that case, the players were declared "in," but after a first-game tie in that series, the Commission decided the players thereafter would share only in the first four games, regardless of the result.

Clearing his throat, Garry told the committee: "We do not make the rules; we only enforce them, and the rules say the players' pool is on the first four games." And that was that!

The third game proved one of the screwiest of all World Series contests, as a good part of the crowd left Fenway Park thinking that the Red Sox had won the game by a score of 3 to 2, whereas the Giants were victors by a count of 2 to 1. The author, then a cub sports writer, almost got a clip on the jaw for trying to set right a fan who also had seen the ball game and already was celebrating a Red Sox victory.

For this game, Stahl used Bucky O'Brien against Rube Marquard, McGraw's sensational nineteen-straight winner of the early season. However, after Rube's brilliant streak had been stopped by Jimmy Lavender of the Cubs in early July, Marquard's performance in the second half of the season was mediocre. From July 4 on, the lanky New York left-hander won only seven more games and lost eleven, and the Red Sox hadn't too much respect for him. "He hasn't been a .500 pitcher since they broke his streak," Stahl told his players. "Everybody's pinning his ears back, so why not us?" But Rube regained his early-season stuff in the series and proved McGraw's toughest pitching nut for the Red Sox to crack.

O'Brien served a strong effort for the Red Sox; each pitcher gave up only seven hits, but the Giants cashed two early doubles off Bucky into as many runs. Murray opened the second inning with a two-base lick to right, was sacrificed to third by Merkle, and scored on Herzog's long fly to Hooper. In the fifth, it was the red-hot Herzog who opened with a two-bagger and reached third on Meyers' infield out. This time the erring Fletcher came through; he lifted a short fly to right, which Hooper just failed to reach. The ball dropped in the well for a single, and Herzog ran home from third.

Marquard had a 2-to-0 shutout going into the ninth, when the Red Sox just missed pulling out the game, and many excited spectators thought they did. An evening mist was coming in from the bay and hung over the outer stretches of the outfield; it contributed to the fans' later confusion. After Spoke lifted to Fletcher, Lewis beat out a hot jab to Merkle for an infield hit. Larry Gardner sent the stands into an uproar with a stinging blow to the right field stands for two bases. The Boston coach momentarily held Lewis at third, but when Merkle messed up the throw-in, Duffy scored. Stahl hit sharply to Marquard's left, but Rube knocked down the ball and got it to Herzog in time to retire Gardner. However, on Wagner's grounder to short, Fletcher's throw to first was a trifle wide, and Merkle dropped it. Heinie was safe, and Jake hotfooted it to third. A moment later Wagner stole second; the Sox had the tying and winning runs in scoring position, and there was bedlam in the stands.

The crowd gave a wild yelp of sheer joy as Cady, who had replaced Carrigan, sent a white streak coursing into deep right field.
It looked like a sure hit, as the ball melted into the late afternoon
haze. But as Josh Devore, Giant right fielder, was on a dead run, he
speared the ball just as it was about to tear past him, and without
changing his direction, continued his sprint for the clubhouse. A good
part of the crowd was in no position to see the catch; they saw Stahl
and Wagner, off with the crack of the bat, dash over the plate with
the runs which they thought won for Boston.

Back in the rest room of the Copley Square, I encountered a joy-
crazed fan, just in from the ball park. Supreme happiness was written
all over his face. "What a game! What a game for the Red Sox to
win!" he exclaimed.

It was a shame to disillusion him, but with youthful impetuosity,
I blurted, "But they didn't win; the Giants won, 2 to 1."

He looked at the young sports writer belligerently and then said
with dignity and emphasis: "I was out there. I'm just back from
Fenway Park, and the Red Sox won, 3 to 2. They scored three runs
in the ninth."

"I'm back, too, from the ball park, but Devore caught that ball
of Cady's, and New York won, 2 to 1," I repeated.

"Are you trying to kid somebody?" he demanded. "I ought to take
a poke at your jaw."

Before he started poking, I suggested we had better take a walk
out to the newsstand. A paper handler was bringing in a bundle of
the latest Boston sports extras. A streamer across the front page
read: *GIANTS TIE SERIES, BEAT RED SOX, 2 to 1*. The man
looked as though he had seen a ghost, and was too dumfounded even
to attempt an apology.

4

Back to New York for the fourth game, October 11, Joe Wood
gave the Red Sox a two-to-one edge with a second victory over Jeff
Tesreau at the Polo Grounds. Though Smoky Joe gave up nine hits,
he was even more effective than in the first game and brought this
one home by a score of 3 to 1. He also made two of the eight hits
which the Red Sox prodded out of Tesreau and Red Ames, and
drove in the last run. While Heinie Wagner went hitless and was
charged with Boston's lone error, his shortstopping was almost un-
believable. Several times he ran over to Yerkes' side of second for
impossible stops. "How can we win with a shortstop like that against
us?" lamented Tom Lynch, the National League president from New

Britain, Connecticut. "That fellow's making plays that aren't human."

The Red Sox pecked away and got their runs one at a time. Gardner brought in the first, tripling to deep right center in the second inning and bolting home on a Tesreau wild pitch. Vermont Larry started it again with a walk in the fourth; he was forced by Stahl, who stole second and took third on an out. Jake scored when Fletcher failed to handle Cady's grounder to deep short, though the scorers awarded the tall catcher a scratch hit.

Gardner was in McGraw's hair by the time the ninth inning rolled around. He opened this one with a single to center against Ames and was sacrificed to second by Stahl. Wagner walked and was forced by Cady, but Wood, a hitting pitcher, slapped Ames for a sharp single to left, scoring Larry.

The Giants tallied their only run on Wood in the seventh. With one out, Herzog got a hit on a hot grounder which even the agile Wagner could not subdue, and scored when Fletcher slashed a long double to left. McCormick, batting for Tesreau, beat out a nasty hopping bounder to Yerkes for an infield hit, but McGraw, coaching at third, wigwagged Fletcher home, and Steve's good peg to Cady shot him down at the plate.

Stahl's red-hosed gladiators then got the big three-to-one jump when the Sox nosed out Mathewson, 2 to 1, in the fifth game, played in Fenway Park on Columbus Day, October 12. Though the crowd of 34,683 topped the third-game turnout by only 59, the unreserved seats were snatched up by noon as thousands of disappointed holiday-bent fans were turned away. They milled unhappily outside as mounted police kept them from the entrances.

With one game to the good, Jake took a real gamble and sent his brilliant youngster, Bedient, against the great Matty. Hits were as scarce as Giant rooters in the bleachers, with McGraw's huskies straightening out young Hugh's curves for only three and the Red Sox getting only two more off Big Six's famed fadeaway. Bedient walked three; Mathewson, with his superb control, none. Giant fans long have muttered over a fumble by Doyle costing Mathewson this game, but it also was a boot by Gardner which made New York a present of its lone run.

All five hits off Matty came in the first three innings, and after Boston hung its two big runs on the scoreboard in the third, the Red Sox never put another runner on base. The Red Hose started this round as though they intended to K. O. McGraw's pitching prince. Hooper led off with a scorching hit to the extreme left-field corner of the arena; the ball rolled through a chute between the bleacher and the grandstand, and by the time little Devore dug it out, Harry had stretched it into a triple. What a kick it was for the New England fans when a few moments later Yerkes rammed another three-bagger to deep center, Harry ambling in! Doyle then made a bad fumble of an easy hopping ground ball, Yerkes scoring, but when Spoke tried to make second, Murray, who had retrieved the ball, nailed him with one of his strong pegs to Fletcher. And then Matty mowed down the next seventeen Bostonians in succession.

The Giants' lone tally off Bedient came in the seventh when Merkle led off with a double and hung around second base as Speaker pulled down fly balls from the bats of Herzog and Meyers. McGraw then called in his dangerous pinch hitter, Moose McCormick, who hit a sharp grounder at Gardner. There was a gasp from the stands as Larry fumbled long enough for Merkle to score and the lumbering Moose to reach first base. Shafer ran for McCormick, but Mathewson gave Gardner a second chance to retire the side. This time the Vermonter pounced avidly on Matty's grounder and easily nailed the big pitcher at first.

5

Everyone on the Boston squad, from manager Stahl down, thought that Bedient's victory meant an easy series triumph. "That was it! That was it!" the happy Sox players yelled as they slapped young Hugh on the back. "Joe will wind it up for us in New York on Monday."

October 13 was a Sunday, and in 1912 there was no Sunday ball in either New York or Boston. The Red Sox took a leisurely Sunday day train to New York, and almost a holiday spirit prevailed. Many of the players were busy with pencil and pad, figuring the winning shares of the spoils. Even without a cutin on the fifth game, it would run around $4,000, more than most of them were paid for the season. A number of the boys already were spending their money. Everyone expected Wood to pitch the next game; certainly Smoky Joe expected to work, and there was a solid conviction on the squad that another day would end everything. Even Stahl made no effort to check this gleeful optimism; he, too, thought his team was in.

However, on the Sunday night, Jimmy McAleer visited Stahl at his New York hotel room, and asked, "Who are you going to pitch tomorrow?"

A little surprised, Jake answered, "Why, Wood, of course."

McAleer, an old player and manager, demurred and continued,

"Do you think that's wise? We're ahead, three games to one, and can afford to take chances, so why not take another chance with O'Brien. He pitched well in the third game and only lost, 2 to 1. McGraw is almost certain to toss in Marquard again, and Buck deserves a chance to get back at him. And if we should lose, Wood will have another day of rest, and we can send him back for a seventh game in Boston."

Stahl argued against such a change in his pitching plans, but McAleer was the president, and his views prevailed. The Boston players were displeased when they heard of it, especially Speaker and Wood. Joe had been all primed mentally to work the game; he never needed more than two full days of rest at that time and was anxious to end the series.

Even New York expected nothing but the worst, as the Polo Grounds crowd of October 14 dwindled to 30,622, a drop of approximately 6,000 from the fourth game, and there were some wide open spaces in the bleachers and the upper stands. It was a dark cloudy afternoon, a perfect day for Joe Wood's smoky delivery. The Giants and New Yorkers who had remained loyal to McGraw perked up when they saw O'Brien, rather than Wood, warm up for Boston against the lean left-hander Marquard. Somehow it seemed to effect a psychological change in the entire picture, and the fans were treated to an early display of Giant power, the New Yorkers belaboring O'Brien for five runs in the very first inning. With two out and runners on third and first, Bucky was guilty of a stupid balk, which gave New York its first run and long remained a sore subject with the Sox. It nettled and disturbed O'Brien, who promptly went to pieces, and the game was wrecked for Boston before left-hander Ray Collins could waste seven strong innings of scoreless pitching on a losing cause.

The inning started harmlessly enough for O'Brien. After he retired Devore on a grounder to Gardner, Doyle beat out a slow squirming hopper to Yerkes and stole second, but Buck swept a third strike past Snodgrass for the second out. Murray then scratched another infield hit, outfooting his roller to Wagner, and Doyle legged it to third.

It was at this point that O'Brien made his fatal balk. He feinted a throw to first, and when he failed to complete his toss to Stahl, his balk was so obvious that everyone in the stands was aware of it. Klem promptly waved Doyle home and sent Murray to second. There was immediate griping on the Sox team against the pitcher, and O'Brien collapsed. Merkle and Herzog followed with doubles, and Meyers with a single. With three runs in, Herzog on third, and

Meyers, one of baseball's slowest runners, on first, McGraw rubbed it in by ordering a double steal. He got away with it, too, when Yerkes made a wild return to the plate, Herzog scoring, while Fletcher's single scored the big Indian. The rally finally ended with the unlucky O'Brien picking the chattering Fletcher off first base.

A pair of Giant errors helped the Red Sox to get two of these runs back in the second inning. Marquard's wild throw to first gave Gardner a life; Stahl followed with a single to left, and when Devore kicked the ball, Gardner pulled up at third, and Jake at second. The Rube fanned Wagner and set down Cady on a foul to Meyers, but Clyde Engle, batting for O'Brien, drove in the two runners with a two-bagger. Hooper then ended the inning with another foul to Meyers.

The Red Sox threatened a number of times thereafter, but Marquard repeatedly was saved by brilliant support, Snodgrass making an especially great play in the fourth inning when after a hard run and last-minute leap he caught Wagner's terrific clout and turned Heinie's bid for a triple into a double play. The Giants couldn't touch Collins' left-handed shoots, Ray giving up only five hits in his seven innings, and the game ended, New York, 5, Boston, 2.

6

There was much bitter feeling and recrimination on the train ride back to Boston following O'Brien's defeat. The players knew McAleer practically had ordered Stahl to pitch Buck, and they asked angrily: "Why the hell don't McAleer run his end, and let Jake run his? If Jake had pitched Wood, as he wanted to, we now would be on our way to our homes with the big checks, instead of coming back to Boston."

O'Brien wasn't the most popular player on the squad; he heard much that was uncomplimentary about his disastrous balk and subsequent collapse. He got into a fist fight with Paul Wood, Joe's brother, who had bet a hundred dollars on a Red Sox sixth-game victory, thinking Wood would pitch. O'Brien wore a shiner back to Boston, though some of the players took his side.

With the team in a none too happy mood, the McAleer-McRoy ownership made a tragic blunder in selling seats for the seventh game at Fenway Park, October 15; it almost cost the Red Sox the series and had many unhappy repercussions. Inasmuch as no one expected more than three games at Fenway Park when the series started, the Royal Rooters had purchased a section of the left-field stands for those games, taking it for granted that these seats would be held out if there were any subsequent games in Boston. But Bob McRoy, in charge of ticket sales, unwittingly had put tickets for these seats on sale at the regular windows on the day of the game.

When the Royal Rooters marched on the field shortly before game time, they found their seats occupied by other customers. There were bitter exclamations of surprise, oaths of indignation and chagrin, and blistering attacks on McAleer and McRoy. Mad as only a group of Irishmen can be mad, they held an indignation meeting on the diamond, and then forming behind their band, they paraded around the field. And despite the pleas of the umpires and foot police, they refused to surrender the field to the ballplayers, insisting the management provide them with seats, but by that time the park was sold out. Eventually mounted police were called in, and wheeling the shoulders of their horses against the irate Rooters, herded them behind the left-field bleacher rail or out of the park.

The day had started out as a wretched one for baseball. Low black threatening clouds hung in the sky, and a wind of almost gale proportions swept across the field. Wood warmed up alongside of Jeff Tesreau, the man he twice had defeated in New York, and just as Joe stepped on the rubber to start the game, the Royal Rooters took over. Wood stood for a while in the cold wind, and then when it became evident that it would be no easy matter to clear the field, he took refuge on the bench with the other Boston players. It was nearly a half hour before play got under way, and by that time Wood chilled and his arm stiffened. The first inning was a cruel repetition of the first round in New York the day before; the Giants lit into Smoky Joe for six runs, the worst drubbing the thirty-four-game winner took all season. And McGraw, now feeling he had the upper hand, ran the Red Sox into the ground with his daring and spectacular base-running attack.

Devore opened the game by beating a slow roller to Wagner, and Doyle slapped the second pitch over second base for another single. Both speed merchants immediately worked a double steal and rode home on Fred Snodgrass' hard double to right. Murray sacrificed Snodgrass to third, and Fred scored on Merkle's fly ball to left, which the wind blew away from an assembly of Boston fielders. Merkle reached second on a futile relay to the plate to get Snodgrass. Herzog hit to Wood, and while Merkle was being run down, Buck made second, from where he scored on Meyers' single. Fletcher slid a single past Stahl, and Hooper's beeline throw to third had Meyers, but Gardner spilled the ball, and the big Indian was safe.

Tesreau hit to Wood, who cuffed the ball around the infield so long that he could get neither Meyers at the plate nor Tesreau at first. Fletcher, in the meantime, romped to third, and the Red Sox were made to look foolish on what started to be a delayed double steal. Tesreau left first base as Cady was returning the ball to Wood, and before the Sox could run down the mastodon pitcher, Fletcher ran home with the sixth run without a play being made on him.

It was a dreary assemblage which sat through the remaining eight innings. Charley Hall faced the Giants in the second, and the men of Manhattan, now confident and cocky, bashed out sixteen hits to coast to an 11-to-4 victory, tying up the series at three victories for each team. The sun came out after three innings, but the wind continued to play queer pranks with the ball, and the rival Larrys—Gardner and Doyle—reached the center-field bleachers with homers. Pitching in the high wind, Tesreau wasn't nearly as effective as in his earlier games in New York, but the Red Sox blew opportunity after opportunity to score a mess of runs. Big Jeff was prodded for nine hits; he walked five, and the Giants tossed in four boots, but to the dismay of the fans a full dozen Red Sox were left on the bases.

Just to save it from being a complete blackout for Boston, Charley Hall, the pitcher, hit a double and two singles in three times at bat, and Tris Speaker executed the only unassisted double play ever made by an outfielder in World Series competition. After Art Wilson, who had replaced Meyers as New York's catcher, reached second base in the ninth on a single and Speaker's wild throw, Tris atoned for the error a moment later. Coming in on a dead run, he snatched Fletcher's short fly, and still running full tilt, tagged second base before the surprised Wilson could return to the bag.

7

Boston felt pretty sick on the morning of the eighth and deciding game. After New York had scored only one win in the first five games, the brash fighting Giants had drawn up to even terms by winning two overwhelming victories. And McGraw had his ace, Mathewson, primed for the crucial game, while Stahl had to bank again on his comparative novice, Bedient. Matty still was gunning for his first victory of the series, and it didn't seem in the cards that a pitcher of his caliber could go through an eight-game series without one triumph.

After the unhappy seventh game, McAleer and McGraw tossed

a coin in Garry Herrmann's hotel room to see whether the deciding game would be played in Boston or New York. The Commissioners and most persons connected with the series hoped McGraw would win the toss. The unfortunate affair with the Royal Rooters and the two crushing defeats had left a bad taste in the mouths of Boston fans, whereas Giant partisans, having seen their prides pick themselves off the floor, were in a high state of excitement. But when Herrmann flipped the coin, McGraw called, "Heads." It was "tails," and the eighth game was played in Boston.

Played at Fenway Park, October 16, it was one of the unforgettable games of baseball and one of the real historic contests of seventy-five years of major league ball. It ran through the entire gamut of human emotions, as victory hung in the balance. But when McGraw was within a half inning of a glorious uphill series triumph, the fickle gods of baseball snatched the victor's cup from his lips and tossed it into the laps of the surprised but receptive Red Sox.

The crowd for the eighth game dwindled to 17,034, only half of what it was for the fifth and seventh games at Fenway Park. The Royal Rooters stayed away, with many of them saying they didn't give a damn what happened to the club so long as McAleer and McRoy remained in charge. Other Boston fans were afraid the tide had turned, and had no wish to sit in on what they believed might be a wake.

After a clubhouse rally, in which some of the players let their hair down, the Red Sox pulled themselves together, and Jake's men waged a courageous, determined, never-say-die fight. Bedient again was good and battled Mathewson for seven innings, when he retired for a pinch hitter, after which Wood, knocked out the previous day, took over, pitched three strong innings, and eventually was credited with a ten-inning 3-to-2 victory, giving him three out of four for the series.

The Giants were the first to score, putting over a run in the third inning when Devore started the round with a walk, reached third on two infield outs and ambled home when Murray clubbed a vigorous double to center.

Harry Hooper unquestionably saved the game and the series for Boston in the sixth inning with one of the greatest of all World Series catches, a play depriving Doyle of a home run and preventing the Giants from winning in nine innings. Larry hit a terrific line drive to the temporary bleacher in deep right center, and it looked like curtains. Hooper ran back as far as he could, and threw himself backward over a low railing, and half-supported by the backs of the crowd, reached upward and caught the ball just as it was about to fall into the stand. It was a magnificent effort, though the Giants claimed it wasn't a legal catch. John B. Foster, former editor of Spalding's *Guide* and later secretary of the Giants, insisted to his dying day that Hooper was entirely off the playing field when the ball was caught and that Doyle's home run should have been allowed. But Boston fans never bothered about such a technicality, and that catch made Harry a hero as long as he remained in Boston.

Stahl yanked another hero off his bench in the person of sturdy little Olaf Henriksen in the seventh inning. That run by Devore in the third was looming bigger and bigger as the game advanced, but thanks to little Olaf, the Red Sox tied in the "lucky seventh." And again Boston got a break! Stahl hit a fly ball to short left, and Devore, Snodgrass, and Fletcher all gathered around it. Fletcher went far enough to balk the others, and then stopped himself, the ball dropping to mother earth for a single. That seemed to unsettle Matty, as he walked Wagner on four successive pitches, but Cady popped to Fletcher for the second out. Jake then sent in Henriksen to bat for Bedient, and Olaf turned in a pinch hit which was as history-making as Hooper's catch of the preceding inning. Mathewson wasted little time with the youngster. Olaf swung and missed the first pitch, and Matty followed with a quick called second strike. Big Six then gave Henriksen a high outside curve, and Olaf, normally a right-field hitter, lined it down the left-field foul line for a double. The drive hit the third base bag, and darted into foul territory, as Stahl tore in with the tying run and Wagner pulled up at third. It gave Hooper a chance to distinguish himself on the offense as well as defense, but he lifted to Snodgrass.

In the first half of the tenth, those two former unlucky New York players, Murray and Merkle, broke the deadlock and put the Giants ahead, 2 to 1. After Snodgrass fouled to Stahl, Murray cracked out his second double and scored on Merkle's single, a low liner to center on which Speaker attempted a shoestring catch. The ball got through Tris for an error, putting Merkle on second, but Wood struck out Herzog and threw out Meyers at first on a hard chance. Smoky Joe knocked down the Indian's hard smash, injured his hand, and could not continue pitching.

The great Mathewson, defeated once and held to an eleven-inning tie, needed to hold the Red Sox in check for only a half inning to give the Giants a spectacular World Series victory. The gloom was so thick on the Red Sox bench and in the Boston stands that one could have cut it with a knife. Then in a jiffy everything changed.

If Wood hadn't been hurt, he no doubt would have batted for himself, but Stahl sent in Engle to hit for the injured pitcher. Clyde lifted an everyday lazy fly to center field, the kind ballplayers refer to as a "can o' corn." Snodgrass had to move only about ten feet to get under the ball, and then waited a few seconds for it to come down. The crowd gulped as the ball filtered through Fred's fingers as though he had lard on his glove, and trickled to the ground, while the happy Engle pulled up at second. The play electrified the stands; the fates had interfered, and here was a gift from the gods. Anything now could happen, and did.

Hooper sent Snodgrass back for his liner, and "Snow" made a really meritorious catch, but there again was bedlam in the stands when Matty walked Yerkes, bringing up the great Speaker. Then came the blow "that killed father," in this case the chesty McGraw. Spoke raised an easy foul—just outside the first-base coach's box, which any schoolboy first baseman could have caught. But the Fenway pixies again took a hand, as Merkle, Meyers, and Mathewson formed a triangle around it. It seemed to be Fred's ball, but the pixies apparently whispered that the Indian would take it, and it fell to the ground in the middle of the triangle. Matty gave the pair a pained look, as much as to say, "What's the use?" picked up the ball, and walked to the mound.

His batting life saved, Speaker promptly made good, stinging Matty's next pitch to right for a long single which sent Engle over the plate with the tying run and Yerkes scurrying to third. The crowd sensed this was the beginning of the end, and thrilled at being in on the kill. As a desperate move, McGraw ordered an intentional pass to Duffy Lewis, filling the bases and making a force play possible at every base, but Larry Gardner was equal to the emergency, driving Devore back for his long fly. Little Josh started a futile relayed throw to the plate, but the play at the plate wasn't even close, as Yerkes dashed in with the run which, after a lapse of eight years, again made the Red Sox baseball's world champions. What the 17,000 crowd lacked in size, it made up in sound, as the fans shouted, shrieked, sang, hugged, and danced in the half-empty stands. There was a triumphal march through Boston's downtown streets, and at a mass meeting at Faneuil Hall, "Honey" Fitzgerald referred to the Red Sox as "the gamest club ever."

If the sudden change of fortunes from the first half of the tenth inning to the second lifted the Red Sox to a seventh baseball heaven, it dropped the Giants from the heights to the pit of despair. Wilbert Robinson, McGraw's heavyweight coach, sagged in a corner of the dugout, and it was fifteen minutes before he could pull himself together, while Harry Sparrow, then McGraw's 275-pound business agent, collapsed in his box near the Giant dugout like Humpty Dumpty falling off the wall. One of the better New York writers, Sid Mercer, then particularly close to McGraw, was so overcome with emotion that tears of chagrin coursed down his handsome cheeks as he dictated the tenth inning to his telegraph operator.

The difference between a Red Sox winning share of $4,024.68 and a losing Giant share of $2,566.47 was $1,458.21. As twenty-two Boston players cut in for full shares, the difference represented around $32,000. As a consequence, Snodgrass' failure to glue himself to Clyde Engle's fly still is known today as Snodgrass' $30,000 Muff, one of baseball's ignoble plays.

McGraw, however, blamed the loss of the game more on the failure of Fletcher to catch Stahl's seventh-inning fly and on Merkle and Meyers messing up Speaker's tenth-inning foul than on Snodgrass' muff. "Mathewson still would have pitched himself out of the hole if Speaker's foul had been caught for the second out," he contended. And to show Snodgrass, who later came to Boston as a Brave, that he harbored no resentment, he gave Fred a raise for 1913.

But no matter what Giants were selected as the top goats by McGraw, the New York fans, and the nation's sports writers, that second half of the tenth inning provided a happy winter for the Red Sox players. The series, which almost got away, still is a pleasant memory to Speaker, Wood, Hooper, Lewis, Carrigan, and the other living 1912 Red Sox world champions.

10

ALONG CAME RUTH!

I

JAKE STAHL'S glory as the world champions' manager and the fellow who beat out Connie Mack and then put it to McGraw was short-lived. The Athletics, one of baseball's greatest teams, bounced back strongly in 1913, winning easily, and such opposition as there was came from Washington and Cleveland. Boston finished an unsatisfactory fourth, winning seventy-nine games and losing seventy-one for a percentage of .527. Even that position was higher than much of the Red Sox's season pace. Running seventh in April and most of May, the Red Sox ran fifth, with the exception of a few days, until September 7, when they finished fairly strong to take fourth place from the White Sox by fourteen points.

Stahl injured his right leg in the spring and played little, Clyde Engle and a kid named Bill Mundy filling in at first. Wood, the thirty-four-game winner of 1912, suffered a broken hand and was out for two months; he took part in only twenty-two games, winning eleven and losing five. The rest of the staff bogged down, and Buck O'Brien, who wouldn't stay in condition, was sold to the White Sox. To top Stahl's troubles, Heinie Wagner, who dazzled Tom Lynch with his shortstopping the fall before, had a sore arm and other miseries and played in only 105 games.

When a world champion and 105-game winner topples from the heights to an also-ran in little over half a year, there usually are repercussions in the way of cool relations between the club president and manager. And the 1913 Red Sox were no exception. Boston writers hinted at friction, and fans spoke of two factions on the club, the Masons and the K.C. There had been such rumblings the year before, but they were drowned out in the din as the club galloped to its spectacular pennant. A story was bruited around Boston that Stahl would succeed McAleer to the presidency.

Angrily McAleer called Stahl to his office and in an accusing tone said, "Jake, the story is that you spilled it around town that you expect to succeed me as president of the club."

Stahl, taken by surprise, replied, "Jim, I'm too much your friend to say or think a thing like that. Besides, I have troubles of my own."

However, McAleer was not satisfied and in early July announced that he had displaced Stahl as manager of the Red Sox, "for the good of the club," and turned the management over to Bill Carrigan, the Holy Cross catcher.

That sudden move got Ban Johnson, Stahl's sponsor, hot under the collar; in Chicago he said that Jake had "been publicly humiliated" and that "we don't do things like that in the American League." He called McAleer to Chicago, and according to press accounts of the day, "administered a stinging rebuke."

In Boston there was speculation as to how Speaker and Wood would click with Carrigan. They were called "pro-Stahl men," leaders of one group, whereas "Rough" Carrigan and Heinie Wagner, both forceful characters, were leaders of the other. But there need have been no worries on that score. Spoke and Smoky Joe were too good ballplayers to let personal feelings interfere with their play, and both always gave Holy Cross Bill their best. Speaker hit .366 in 1913, and again ran third to Cobb and Jackson, while Wood was good when his hand permitted him to pitch.

Most of the players respected Carrigan, not only as an intelligent chap but as an aggressive, inspiring ballplayer. He didn't get his nickname, "Rough," playing tiddlywinks. And he had several ways of being persuasive.

Billy Evans, the Detroit club's executive vice-president and former crack American League umpire, once told of a little conversation he overheard while in Boston. The umpire's dressing room was near the Red Sox clubhouse, and no one at the time had thought of putting in soundproof boards.

Carrigan was in an argument with one of the team's top stars. "You're no better than anyone else on this club," Bill roared. "When I issue an order for morning practice at ten, you're supposed to be here, just like anyone else.

"I don't care how well you are playing. The fact that you won three or four games last week doesn't mean a thing to me. There is going to be discipline on this club, and I'm the guy to enforce it."

Conversation grew more heated; soon Billy heard sounds of scuffling; then everything became quiet.

Curious as to what had happened, Evans asked one of the players to let him know confidentially what the rumpus had been about. "Nothing much," replied the player. "Bill just grabbed one of the boys who wouldn't listen to reason and shook him up a bit. He'll behave from now on."

By the following winter, Bill Carrigan had a new boss. There were repeated rumblings that McAleer wouldn't last long after the Stahl episode. He didn't, even though in late October, Francis Eaton of the Boston *Journal* wrote that stories of Jim's retirement were a joke; McAleer had no thought of selling his team and was busy planning to regain the world championship.

But Ban Johnson had other ideas. While McAleer was on the Comiskey-McGraw round-the-world baseball mission, Johnson made the announcement in Boston that the McAleer-McRoy interests had been sold to Joseph J. Lannin, Boston and New York hotel and real-estate man. Lannin paid $200,000, even though the Taylor interests supposedly offered $220,000 to regain this half. The Taylors still retained a big interest, as well as the bonds on Fenway Park. A Boston sports writer, A. H. C. Mitchell, succeeded McRoy as the business head of the club.

"There is some regret in Boston over the passing of McAleer," reported Francis Eaton, "but little over the departure of Bob McRoy. In fact, at one time Mayor Fitzgerald had called on the club, or the league, to dismiss McRoy. Bob never lived down that unfortunate business with the Royal Rooters at the 1912 World's Series."

Joe Lannin, the new owner, was born in Quebec, and at the age of fifteen he came to Boston, where he obtained a job as a bellhop. Lannin had a good French-Canadian sense of thrift and an acute business sense; tips also must have been pretty good, because at the time that Joe bought the Red Sox, he owned the Great Northern in New York, the Garden City Hotel, and several golf courses at Garden City, Long Island, the Massachusetts House at Shelter Island, and the Arborway and Fordham Court Apartments in Forest Hills, Boston. The latter were immense structures and covered acres of ground. In those early days Lannin let Carrigan and some of the other Red Sox players have two-room apartments for as little as eighteen dollars a month.

Lannin was a deeply religious man and a great checker enthusiast, helping to promote national tournaments. He had been a baseball fan since his bellhopping days, and after getting into the chips, he had a yen to own a big league club. He had a chunk of the Braves, which he sold, and he bought into the Red Sox only after a deal to buy the Phillies fell through. Joe Lannin later got his family pretty well fixed in the club. His son Paul became secretary; Tom Lannin, a brother of Joe, did a general supervising job, and another brother handled the concessions.

2

Lannin, the fan-owner, ran immediately into the Federal League war, and he soon was speaking of ballplayers as "unreasonable" and "grasping." Just around the time that he closed for the Red Sox, Joe Tinker, the former great Cub shortstop and Red manager, jumped to the Federal League and started the dive of a flock of other National and American Leaguers into Federal League waters.

Comiskey and McGraw had an aggregation of rich talent on their world trip, Tris Speaker, Sam Crawford, Lee Magee, Buck Weaver, Larry Doyle, Hans Lobert, Fred Merkle, George Wiltse, Mickey Doolan, Otto Knabe, and others, and when they docked at the Cunard Line pier in New York, March 6, 1914, there was a small regiment of Federal League agents, with pockets bulging with bills, at the dock to tempt the returning athletes.

The agents only landed Magee and the Philly double-play pair, Knabe and Doolan, but Lannin had to boost the ante for Speaker, who drew $9,000 in 1913, to a two-year contract calling for $36,000. "What did I get into?" Joe asked in dismay.

However, if pay checks were high, the 1914 Red Sox produced for the new owners. The new manager, Carrigan, proved a genius, especially in getting the best out of pitchers, and the 1914 club rebounded to second and gave the Athletics, winning their fourth flag in five years, a scare in the late season. The Athletics' lead over the Red Sox at the finish was eight and a half games, but Boston took the year's series from the A's, twelve to nine, and wiped up the famous Philadelphians in the latter part of the season.

"When we took eight out of our last ten games from the Athletics that year, I knew we had the coming club of baseball," said Carrigan.

The great outfield never was better than in 1914; this time

Speaker's average dropped to .338, but he tied Joe Jackson for third.
Heinie Wagner was out for most of the season with a sore arm, but
the club came up with another great shortstop in Everett Scott, a
smooth-fielding Hoosier obtained from St. Paul. Never much of a
hitter, Scottie developed into the Marty Marion of his day and a
player who had a remarkably high fielding average for his position.
"Scottie never misses one," Fenway Park fans used to chant. Mike
McNally, another great defensive infielder, but not too heavy with
the bat, came from Utica. Mike, now the barrel-shaped president of
the Red Sox farm club in Wilkes-Barre, was so skinny in those days
that they nicknamed him "Slats."

First base, Stahl's old position, remained a trouble spot, as Engle,
Hal Janvrin, Dick Hoblitzel, and Del Gainer all played the position
that season. Janvrin was one of John I. Taylor's last scouting
pickups; he was a local boy, plucked by Taylor off Boston's English
High School team in 1911 and developed in Jersey City. Hoblitzel,
known as Hobby, was purchased from the Cincinnati Reds, and
Gainer was obtained on waivers from Detroit.

Wood was bothered with a lame arm, took part in only eighteen
games, but still had enough cunning to win nine games while losing
three. The burden which the young Kansas Cityite put on the arm
in the late teens and early twenties already was beginning to tell.
But other pitchers, notably Hubert "Dutch" Leonard, a left-hander,
and George Foster, a stocky little right-hander, jumped into the
breach. Both had been with the team in 1913 and under Carrigan's
skillful guidance developed into stardom overnight.

Leonard was a California collegian from St. Mary's College, who
had a brief tryout with Mack in 1911. Foster, a ranch hand from
Lehigh, Oklahoma, was a chunky little sidearm pitcher who was
procured from Houston, Spoke's big league steppingstone. In 1914
Dutch led American League pitchers with an amazing earned-run
average of 1.01 and won nineteen games out of twenty-four; Foster
ranked second in earned runs with 1.65 and won fifteen games out
of twenty-three.

3

About the time that Lannin bought the Red Sox, he also acquired
the Providence International League club. With the Federal League
putting clubs into two International League strongholds, Baltimore
and Buffalo, and later Newark, the big minor league of the Atlantic
seaboard, presided over by Ed Barrow, was in sore straits and almost
went under. Its angel during those harrowing years was Joe Lannin.

In trying to protect his Providence investment, Joe also had to help the clubs hardest hit, Baltimore and Buffalo, and at one time supposedly carried the three clubs.

The Orioles started the 1914 season with one of the greatest minor league clubs ever assembled, but Jack Dunn, the Baltimore owner, couldn't stand the Federal League competition and in midseason broke up his club and sold his stars piecemeal to the various major league clubs.

His particular prizes were a young left-handed pitcher, George Herman "Babe" Ruth; a six-foot 4½-inch right-hander from Guilford College, North Carolina, Ernie Shore, who in 1912 had had a brief tryout with the Giants; and their catcher, Ben Egan. Dunn had given Connie Mack first crack at Ruth and Shore, but Mack, going through what he since termed his toughest season, told Jack, "Sell them to somebody who can pay you real money for them." So on July 8, 1914, in recognition of the help that Lannin had rendered the league and his club, Dunn sold the trio to the Red Sox for $8,000, of which Ruth's cost was listed at $2,900.

Catcher Egan soon was passed along to Cleveland, along with pitchers Rankin Johnson and Fritz Coumbe, for a veteran left-hander, Sylvanus "Vean" Gregg, already suffering from arm trouble but a great pitcher when he was right.

Ruth, of German parentage and product of the Baltimore water front, then was a rather scrawny-looking kid twenty years old. He already had grown to his six feet two inches but hadn't started to fill out. As a small boy he had been sent to St. Mary's School in Baltimore, an industrial school for orphans and boys who needed discipline. At St. Mary's they taught Babe to pitch, catch, and be a tailor. One of the instructors, Brother Mathias, became convinced that Ruth had unusual baseball talent, and recommended the left-hander to Jack Dunn. Dunn signed the kid for a trial contract, calling for six hundred dollars for the 1914 season, after getting permission from a Baltimore court to take Ruth out of the institution before Babe was of legal age. It led to reports that Dunn legally had adopted George.

Ruth was an immediate sensation in the International League, and scouts rated him as a sure bet but looked at him solely as a fast-ball pitcher. Carrigan worked Ruth into four American League games after he joined the club, and Babe was credited with two victories and one defeat. Then, as Lannin's Providence team was in the International League race, Joe sent the big Baltimore boy over to Rhode Island to help Bill Donovan and his Clam Diggers win the pennant.

Between Baltimore and Providence, Ruth won twenty-two games that season and lost nine. In forty-six games, he hit .231 and smacked one homer. No one then had the faintest idea that this rookie would develop into baseball's number one all-time slugger.

Having been obliged to toe the mark at St. Mary's, Babe was bursting with inhibitions and pent-up desires when he first reached league baseball. Many amusing stories still are being told of Ruth's first few weeks in the American League. Inasmuch as both Ruth and Shore came from Baltimore in the same deal, Eddie Riley roomed his two Oriole recruits together. The partnership of Shore and Ruth was of short duration.

Shore called on Carrigan and announced he was returning to North Carolina. "Why, what's the matter, Ernie; aren't we treating you all right?" asked Bill.

"Yes, Mr. Carrigan, but I can't live with that man Ruth."

"Why, I thought you and Babe were friends," added Bill.

"That's right; we are," said Ernie, "but there's a place where friendship stops. I told him he was using my toothbrush, and he said, 'That's all right; I'm not particular.' But that isn't all, Mr. Carrigan; a man wants some privacy in the bathroom."

The season of 1914 was a good one for the Red Sox to come in second, as the Braves, for years the underdog in Boston baseball patronage, provided unexpected and spectacular competition. It was the year of George Stallings' miracle team, when the Braves climbed from last place in mid-July to a "four straight" World Series in October, in which they spread-eagled the vaunted Athletics. Joe Lannin loaned Fenway Park to his friend Jim Gaffney for the 1914 Boston World Series games, as the old Columbus Avenue National League grounds were no place to stage such a show.

There also were gay days in the Boston press box, as the "Three Musketeers," Ralph McMillin of the *Journal*, Nick Flatley of the *American*, and Johnny Moran of the *Journal*, later of the *American*, went through their zany capers. McMillin, a really gifted writer, might have become a Boston Ring Lardner or Damon Runyon if he had not died of influenza four years later. Paul Shannon continued his puckish ways; handsome and versatile Burt Whitman was doing clever pieces for the *Herald* and *Traveler*, and that lovable old soul of the Baseball Writers Association, Jim O'Leary, made the natural conversion from a baseball telegraph operator, who knew all the answers in the press box, to a full-fledged baseball writer.

4

As Carrigan predicted, that strong second-place finish of 1914 was an augury of still better things to come. In 1915, the Red Sox again stormed the pennant heights, winning Boston's closest American League race, with the exception of 1904, against the spirited opposition of Hugh Jennings' slashing Tigers. The Crimson Hose really had to bear down to win that one, as Detroit won 100 games and lost 54 for a percentage of .649. But the Carrigans won 101 and lost 50 (they had three unplayed games at the finish) for .669. The 1915 Tigers were the only American League club which ever hit the century mark in wins and still failed to win the pennant.

Detroit led most of the time until May 15, when the Yankees set the pace for a week. A strengthened White Sox team was in front from May 22 to July 18, with Boston running second, but after the Red Sox took the lead on the nineteenth, they never were headed. Several times Detroit managed to get uncomfortably close for Back Bay fans, but the Tigers never could quite nudge the Red Sox out of the front seat.

Reach's 1916 *Guide* describes Boston's fourth pennant winner in the pithy paragraph: "The Red Sox possessed the finest pitching staff in the league, both in point of numbers and exceptional ability; a strong catching department; a well-balanced infield; and a grand outfield." How could they lose?

What's more, the Red Sox won the pennant by smacking down the ears of their closest rivals, the Tigers. Though the fifth-place Yankees constantly were in Carrigan's hair, winning the year's series from the new champs, twelve to ten, the Red Sox rolled back the superior Tigers, twelve games to eight.

The Red Sox really won their 1915 pennant in the final two series between the two clubs, both stormy, hectic affairs. In Detroit, August 24, 25, and 26, the Red Sox won two out of three. Ernie Shore took the first game from Harry Coveleskie, the burly left-hander, 3 to 1. Ruth and Leonard next were victors in a thirteen-inning 2-to-1 duel with James and Boland, and Harry Salsinger, the Detroit writer, was peeved that the winning run should be driven in "by that weak-hitting Everett Scott." The Tigers finally got away with the third game, 7 to 6, in twelve innings, after the Red Sox had thrown a big scare into the Tigers and their fans by scoring four runs in the ninth. Tim Murnane did a little gloating and said the Red Sox "nailed a slander that they only can win at home, and aren't a good road team."

Jennings and his snarling Tigers still were on the necks of the Red Sox when the clubs met again at Fenway Park, September 16, 17, 18, and 20. After the Tigers' George Dauss won the first game from Foster, Collins, and Mays, 6 to 1, the Red Sox grabbed the next three, 7 to 2, 1 to 0, and 3 to 2. The 1-to-0 tilt was a spirited twelve-inning pitching duel between Shore and Coveleskie, and in the final game, young Ruth, getting a little late-inning help from Foster, downed the formidable Dauss.

Both teams played rough; Boston pitchers had reputations, deserved or otherwise, of driving batters back from the plate with "bean balls"; the Tigers rode into bases with spikes high.

Tim Murnane reported some more little pleasantries:

Boston players had complained that the Tigers treated them roughly in the series between the two teams in Detroit and the newspapers took up the cue and made rather much of it. The result was the crowd was ready for the visitors when they came here, and they got a warm reception. Ty Cobb seemed to be a special "attraction" and the fans rode him until he lost his temper and threw his bat at Pitcher Mays. That was a bad break considering the temper the fans were in and it was considered necessary for a squad of policemen to escort the fiery Georgian off the field for fear he might be roughly handled.

The 1915 Red Sox were a solid ball club all the way down the line. While the Tigers outhit them, .268 to .260, and Tris Speaker, by now called the Gray Eagle, was the only Boston regular hitting .300, the club had a lot of good clutch hitters, Lewis, Gardner, Hooper, Hobby, and Jack Barry. The latter, the Athletics' former crack shortstop, was more or less a gift from Connie Mack. After Chief Bender and Eddie Plank, the Athletics' pitching aces, jumped to the Federal League, Connie tore apart his club by selling Eddie Collins and Eddie Murphy to the White Sox. As the Athletics already had nose-dived to the cellar by July 4, Mack sold Jack Barry, black-haired Holy Cross boy from Meriden, Connecticut, to Lannin for $7,500. Black Jack relieved Heinie Wagner, with his aching arm, at second base and played the position as well as he ever had played shortstop.

However, the great strength of the Boston club was its pitching. Young Babe Ruth, in his first full season as a big leaguer, was the loop's won-and-lost leader with eighteen victories and six defeats for a percentage of .750. Though Wood's sore arm forced him to knock off in the latter part of the season, Joe won fourteen and lost five and had the league's best earned-run average, 1.49. But there were arguments with Joe Lannin, who thought Wood was nursing his arm too much. Foster won twenty games and lost nine, and Ernie Shore, the tall boy who came up with Ruth from Baltimore, had a nineteen-and-seven record. The Carolinian pitched a deceptive sinker. Dutch Leonard won fifteen and lost seven. Carl Mays, a stocky underhand pitcher, was advanced from Providence, and Carrigan employed him mostly as relief, while Herb Pennock, promising kid southpaw, was picked up from the Athletics on waivers.

Young Ruth, feeling his oats as he rose early to stardom, gave Carrigan a few headaches. Babe was getting hold of money for the first time in his life, and money was something to spend. Released from the strict discipline of St. Mary's, he found life in the outside world a gay, exciting, and amusing adventure.

Before they had Sunday ball in Washington, the Red Sox had an idle Sunday in the capital, and Ruth asked Carrigan's permission to run home to near-by Baltimore to spend the day with his folks. Like the good guy he is, Bill promptly granted permission. Everything might have come out all right if Ruth's father hadn't decided to attend the following Monday game in Washington. Spotting Ruth from his box seat near the Red Sox bench, he called at Babe: "You're a fine one, George. Down this way, and never came home to see us."

Rough found one way of solving his Ruth problem. He and Wagner occupied adjoining double rooms on the road. He had Dutch Leonard, a left-handed pitcher, bunk in with him, and gave Babe to Heinie as a roommate. Between them, they kept a pretty good eye on Ruth and rather crimped Babe's early style.

11

☹

BILL CARRIGAN WINS THREE
2-TO-1 GAMES

I

THE shuffle of the baseball cards called upon the Red Sox to play
the Phillies in the 1915 World Series. Led by Pat Moran, who had
been a Boston National catcher early in the century, the Phillies won
the lone pennant of their sixty-five year National League history.
As pennant winners go, Pat didn't have much of a championship outfit, and his team's percentage of .592 was the lowest to win a
National League flag up to that time.

Nevertheless Moran, a native of Fitchburg, was one of the cagiest
chaps ever to handle the reins of a big league ball club, and he was
especially smart with pitchers. For his trump ace he had the famous
Grover Cleveland Alexander, rightly known at that time as the
"great Aleck" or "Alexander the Great." Grover won thirty-one
games that season, twelve of them shutouts, suffered only ten defeats,
and had the uncanny earned-run record of 1.22 while pitching 376
innings. Fitchburg Pat also coaxed many winning games out of a
Jewish pitcher, Erskine Mayer; George "Dut" Chalmers, a former
New York sand lotter; and a tall left-handed bean pole from Cul-
peper Court House, Virginia, Eppa Jeptha Rixey.

Gavvy Cravath, who was with the Red Sox for a spell in 1908,
played right field and supplied much of the team's power, hitting
twenty-four home runs, which was the pre-Ruthian high for the
century. First baseman Fred Luderus, who was to be quite a nuisance

124

for Red Sox pitchers during the series, also packed a lethal punch. The club had a skillful first-string catcher, Bill Killefer, but an injury kept him out of the series, and Moran's second stringer, Eddie Burns, turned in a neat job. George Whitted, who had played center field for Stallings' miracle Brave team the year before, was in left field; Dode Paskert, an antelope, galloped in center, and Dave Bancroft, a later-day Brave shortstop-manager, was the team's rookie shortstop and one of the finds of 1915. Milt Stock, a former Giant, was on third, and Bert Niehoff on second.

Bill Carrigan privately had no great respect for the Phillies, but the Braves' four straight victories over the Athletics a year before had won new respect for the National League, and Bill wanted no overconfidence on his ball club. Confidentially he told Speaker, Lewis, Hooper, Gardner, and a few other veterans of the 1912 world champions that he didn't think the Phillies were half the club McGraw had three years before, but he expected no pushover.

"That fellow Alexander could be awfully tough," he told his players in a pre-series clubhouse bull session. "He's one of the best in baseball, and every time we face him our pitcher will have to pitch a shutout or hold them to one run to win. If the series goes long enough, we're sure to see him three times, so we've got to keep bearing down all the time."

The Phillies still were playing at their cigar-box ball park, Baker Bowl, and some temporary box seats in left and center field, raising the limited capacity to 20,306, made it even more of a home-run orchard. As the Braves had used Fenway Park because of its larger capacity in the 1914 World Series, the Red Sox now availed themselves of the newly built Braves Field, which had seats for around eight thousand more than the Boston American League park. In a way that was a break for the Phillies; having played eleven games in the Allston plant in 1915, they were more familiar with the lights and shadows of Braves Field than the resident Red Sox.

The practice of tossing a coin for the opening game still was followed, and William F. Baker, the Philly president and a former New York City Police Commissioner, won the first two games for his cigar box. The schedule then called for two in Boston, next, one in each of the rival cities, with another coin to be flipped for a possible seventh game. But the Red Sox made no such procedure necessary.

The first game was played on October 8, and the Boston players were heartbroken when Ernie Shore lost to Alexander by a score of 3 to 1. The Phillies had reached Shore for only five hits, all singles, while Boston made eight off Alexander, but at the finish Philadelphia had two more runs. The Sox blamed themselves for letting Ernie down in the eighth, when Moran's team scored two runs without getting a ball out of the infield. The game was played on a soggy field, still heavy from several days of rain. Most of the hits likewise were of the soggy variety, balls which failed to take the customary bounce when drilled into the soft infield.

Shore took the defeat in good spirit, but other players griped: "What the hell does a pitcher have to do to win a World Series game if the kind of game Ernie pitched can't win." At the time, there was a pretty well-founded superstition that the winner of the first game also took the series. In the nine series played after the National Commission took charge in 1905, the winner of the first game won on eight occasions. But Rough Carrigan was quick to beat down such a defeatist complex. "We lost one, so what of it?" he said. "We've got lots of others to win, and the hell with what the first-game winner did in the past."

The Phillies had picked up the first run of the series in the fourth inning of the opener, and it was a rather cheesy run. Paskert dropped a short fly in right field, which fell at Hooper's feet for a Texas Leaguer when Harry couldn't come in fast enough on the wet turf. On Cravath's sacrifice bunt, it looked as if Shore had a chance for a force play on Dode at second, but Ernie played it safe and tossed out Gavvy at first. Paskert reached second on the play, advanced to third on Luderus' infield out, and scored when Whitted beat out a slow bounder to Barry for an infield single. It was a close decision, but Silk O'Loughlin, the American League umpire gave Philadelphia the benefit of the doubt. Whitted stole second but got no farther, as Scottie tossed out Niehoff.

Most of the action of the game was crowded into the eighth inning, when the Red Sox tied the score, only to have the Phillies promptly untie it with two runs in their half. After Alexander retired Scott, Moran told him not to give Speaker anything good to hit, and Tris walked on four straight bad ones. Stock fumbled Hoblitzel's hot sizzler long enough to miss a double play, but he got Hobby at first, Spoke taking second. With two strikes on Lewis, Duffy came through with a sharp single to left, and the happy Gray Eagle danced home with the run which made the scoreboard read Boston, 1, Philadelphia, 1. On Whitted's futile throw home, Duffy sprinted to second, and Gardner made a gallant effort to keep the rally going, only to have Paskert pull down his long fly after an acrobatic running catch.

It was bad news for the Sox in the second half of the eighth, when everything seemingly went wrong. After Barry tossed out Alexander,

Stock worked Ernie for a pass. It looked as though Bancroft's poke would get through for a hit, but Barry made a sensational running one-handed stop of a difficult bounce. Scott apparently didn't think Black Jack could make the play, and was slow in covering second for a sure out and possible double play. Barry had to delay his throw a fraction of a second, and by the time he threw, Stock had beaten the ball to second. This served to unsettle Shore, and he walked Paskert, filling the bases.

The Philadelphia fans called on big Cravath to break it up, but the hefty slugger's best was a grounder back at the box, which eluded Shore. Scottie came in for it; there was a possible force play at the plate, but Everett played it safe and threw Cravath out at first, Stock scoring. Shore then cuffed Luderus' poke around the infield, and Bancroft pranced home with the second run of the inning.

The Red Sox had a final spasm left in the ninth. After Barry struck out, Olaf Henriksen, the hero of the final game of the 1912 series, batted for Cady and reached first when Luderus momentarily fumbled his grounder. Carrigan then gave Babe Ruth, his pitcher-slugger, his World Series baptism, sending up the big Maryland boy to bat for Shore. The Baltimore youngster whizzed one like a bullet down the first-base line, but Luderus atoned for his previous error with a clever put-out, and Hooper ended the game with a pop fly to Luderus.

With the last put-out, admiring Philadelphia fans from the boxes, grandstand, and bleachers thronged on the field and blocked the path of the players to the clubhouse. They weren't content until they carried the happy victors, Alexander, Luderus, Cravath, Whitted, Stock, "Banny," and Paskert, off the field on their shoulders. It was well they did their rejoicing then; there was little opportunity for the sons of William Penn to throw out their chests after that.

2

The second game, played in Baker Bowl on Saturday, October 9, was a historic occasion, as it marked the first time that the President of the United States attended a World Series game. Woodrow Wilson, accompanied by his fiancée, Mrs. Edith Galt, came up from Washington to take in the game. President Wilson, who was a good fan despite his austerity, threw out the first ball, and after one pitch, umpire Rigler returned it to the chief executive for a souvenir.

Babe Ruth wanted a chance to tie up the series for Boston, and asked Carrigan, "Are you going to let me pitch this one, Bill?"

"No, I'll save you for one of the games in Boston," Carrigan replied.

Rough picked George Foster as his pitcher, and the choice was popular with the team. He had pitched great ball all season when the chips were down. Moran opposed George with Erskine Mayer, who had an odd season in 1915. Up to July 4, when he was married, he had matched Alexander victory for victory, but in the second half of the season, Ersk stumbled frequently and eventually wound up with twenty-one victories and fifteen defeats. Mayer did well, keeping ten Boston hits well distributed, but Foster flung one of the classics of World Series competition—George gave up only three hits, struck out eight, walked none, and only thirty Phillies faced him. He matched the three Philadelphia hits himself, smiting a double and two singles, and won a well-deserved 2-to-1 decision from Mayer.

The Red Sox speed boys picked up a tally in the first inning by fast flying around the bases. Hooper led off with a pass, and after Scott fouled to Luderus, attempting to sacrifice, Rough put on the hit-and-run play, and Harry sped to third on Speaker's sharp single to right. Carrigan then put on the sign for a double steal, and while neither Hooper nor Speaker was credited with a steal, the play accomplished its purpose. Burns's throw to Bancroft nailed Spoke at second, but Banny's return throw to the plate was a little low; it got there in time to retire Hooper, but when Burns made an excusable muff, Harry slid safely over the home plate. Hoblitzel followed with a single, but Carrigan still was trying out Burns's arm, and Hobby was shot down on another attempted steal.

Philadelphia managed to bunch most of its scant ammunition in the fifth inning when Fitchburg Pat's boys tied the score. After Foster had retired the first twelve men to face him, Cravath, with two strikes on him, doubled to the left corner of the field and scored when Luderus followed with a second two-bagger to right. That brought the Quaker City crowd to its feet, but its thrill was brief, as Foster set down the next three batsmen without Luderus moving off second base, and the Phillies put only one more runner on base, Bancroft hitting a harmless single with two out in the sixth.

However, that fifth-inning run kept the game tied up, and it looked as though it might go into extra innings, when Foster, getting tired of the way the thing dragged along, poked in Boston's winning run with his third hit in the ninth. Gardner led off with a screaming single to left, but Barry, after two unsuccessful attempts to sacrifice, raised a long fly for Paskert. Janvrin, who had succeeded Scott at short in the seventh inning, hit an infield tap to Mayer on which Gardner reached second, bringing up Foster.

"You can bring in that run yourself, George," yelled Carrigan as the pitcher left the bench. Foster did it, slashing a clean single to center which fetched in Gardner.

While the Phillies failed to get on in their half, they set off a few parting fireworks and came within inches of tying the score. While Stock was at the plate, he was hit by a pitched ball, but umpire Cy Rigler, insisting Milt hadn't been sufficiently agile in getting out of the way of the pitch, refused to let him take his base. That stirred up a furious argument, in which Stock, Pat Moran, and Luderus fumed and the Philly fans booed Rigler. Forced to bat over again, Stock let out his injured feelings with a terrific line drive to left, but Duffy Lewis managed to drag it down.

After Bancroft struck out, Paskert hit a long line fly which seemed on its way to the center field bleachers for a home run and a tie score. A high wind made it difficult for Speaker to judge the ball, but Tris, making a desperate last moment lunge, leaned over the bleacher rail and snatched the ball almost from the lap of a Philadelphia fan.

3

The day after the "President Wilson game" was a Sunday, and that gave Rough a chance to plan for the new week ahead. "Are you going to pitch me in Boston tomorrow?" asked Babe Ruth on the train.

"No, Babe, I guess it'll have to be Leonard," said Bill. "Alexander is going to go again for Moran, and I want somebody with a little more experience to face him, but you'll get your crack at them."

The Babe was cast down over Carrigan's decision, but Leonard was pleased with the nomination, as were most of the Red Sox players. "I'll take care of those babies for you, Bill," said Leonard.

As for Carrigan, he radiated confidence. Before the Boston game of October 11, he said half jokingly to a bunch of reporters on the field, "You know I'm a devil in my own home town," and then added with a little more seriousness: "We got into our stride in that second game in Philadelphia, and we intend to keep it up. If I say it myself, the Red Sox can play ball as few ball clubs can, and I haven't the slightest doubt now that we'll take the series."

Brand new Braves Field, which Jim Gaffney and George Stallings hoped would be the setting for their Braves in this 1915 series, was jammed to the runways for the third game. The throng reached

42,300, more than the first two Philadelphia crowds combined and a figure that was a stunner, not only for the fans but for the baseball people of four decades ago. It knocked the previous attendance record, 38,281 for the first game of the 1911 Giant-Athletic series at New York's Polo Grounds, out of the book by a margin of 4,019. At the time, they hadn't moved in the distant Braves Field fences, and the National League ball park was an outfielders' paradise, in which the great Red Sox trio really could roam and show itself to its best advantage.

As Carrigan had expected, it was Aleck against Dutch, and though the great Philly right-hander yielded two less hits than in his first winning effort, he lost by the same score as did Mayer on the preceding Saturday—2 to 1. In many respects the game was a carbon copy of the last affair in Philadelphia; the Red Sox again broke a 1-to-1 tie by scoring in the ninth, and again the winning Boston hurler held the feeble Philly hitters to three hits.

This was Duffy Lewis' day as the chunky little Californian cracked out three of the six Boston hits, drove in the winning run, and helped Leonard out of his worst jam in the third inning with the game's best catch. All six of the Red Sox hits off Aleck went to the Red Sox outfield; in addition to Duffy's three, Spoke had two, and Hooper, one.

The first of Philadelphia's three hits, a double by third baseman Stock, the opening hitter of the game, was an out-and-out gift by Spoke. Milton raised an ordinary fly to center field, only about fifteen feet from where the great Tris was standing. A loud oh went up from forty thousand throats when the Gray Eagle never moved for the ball, and it fell safe almost at his feet. Unaccustomed to Braves Field, the Texan had lost the ball completely in the sun and didn't even know it was headed in his direction. But Dutch pitched himself out of this early hole. After Bancroft sacrificed Stock to third, Leonard retired Paskert on a foul to Gardner and then whizzed a third strike over on Cravath.

The Phillies poked Leonard for their only run in the third, and it wasn't Cravath's fault this time that only one Quaker tally was posted on the scoreboard. Eddie Burns opened with a single to right, Barry making a desperate but vain effort to bring down the ball. Alexander tapped a sacrifice bunt to Gardner, but when Hobby muffed Larry's perfect throw, both runners were safe. Stock sacrificed the pair along, and Bancroft followed with a single to center, on which Burns scored. Aleck also rounded third for a break for the plate, but Moran, coaching at third, seized him, and Grover

Everett Scott

(Insert) Larry Gardner

© *Charles M. Conlon*

© *Sporting News*

Hubert "Dutch" Leonard

Carl Mays

scrambled back to third. Speaker in the meantime had thrown home for an anticipated play on Alexander, and that gave Banny a chance to scamper down to second.

Paskert then hit a ball to short right, which looked like a hit until Barry seemed to come right out of the ground to make the catch. There was one big wallop left in the Philly rally, when Cravath hit his longest ball of the series. It was a tremendous drive to deepest left. Lewis, running with his back to the plate, looked like a small boy running under a flying bird. Duffy turned at the correct moment and caught the ball in front of the left-field bleachers, then about four hundred feet from the plate.

The Red Sox tied the score in the very next inning when Speaker felt he had to square accounts for making Stock a present of the first-inning double. With Scott down on a fly to Paskert, Tris hit the first pitch for a drive down the right-field foul line, and by the time the Phillies ran it down, Spoke had run the hit into a triple. He didn't tarry long at third, as Hoblitzel drove him home with a long fly to Paskert.

Carrigan, the Red Sox, and the Boston fans did a lot of yelping at umpire Silk O'Loughlin in the seventh inning. Speaker led off with a single, and Hoblitzel tapped in front of the plate for an attempted sacrifice bunt. Catcher Burns dove for the ball, fired it to Bancroft for a force play on Speaker at second, and when Hobby didn't run, claiming the ball was foul, Banny's relay to Luderus doubled him at first.

Rough was at the plate in a jiffy as though hurled from the dugout by a catapult. "That ball was foul! Everybody in the park could see it was foul," roared Bill. "What was the matter with you? Didn't you see it?"

"It was a fair ball," said O'Loughlin in his silken tones.

"It was foul! It was foul! It was foul!" Bill fairly shrieked.

"All that yelling won't get you anywhere, Mr. Carrigan," said Silk. "I said it was fair."

And Silk's version stood; it was fair.

But the Red Sox won again in the ninth, when Carrigan had better tools than Moran and also outguessed Pat on the managerial chess board. Hooper had two strikes on him when he brought thunderous yells from the stands with a single to right. Scottie tried twice to sacrifice, and each time bunted foul. It was the conventional play for Scott to take his full cut at the next pitch, but he bunted again. His sacrifice shoved Harry to second, and his unexpected bunt just missed being a hit. The ball squirmed by Alexander, but second baseman Niehoff, coming in fast, just barely got Everett at first base.

Moran then ordered an intentional pass for Speaker. Hoblitzel also got a tap past Alexander, but Niehoff made another good play and retired Dick at first by a whisker for the second out. On the play, Hooper reached third and Speaker second.

Moran, Aleck, Burns, and Luderus went into a huddle as to whether Alexander should pitch to Lewis, or walk him and take a chance on Gardner. Moran finally decided to try again against Duffy, even though the Californian already had two hits. It proved a poor gamble; Lewis straightened out Alexander's first pitch and stabbed it to center for a clean single, and Harry Hooper came in with the run which sent home 99 per cent of the crowd with beaming faces.

4

The fourth game also was played at Braves Field on Columbus Day, October 12, and though the crowd was 41,096, it fell under the record throng of the previous afternoon. For the fourth straight day it was a pitching duel, and for the third successive time the Red Sox emerged a 2-to-1 victor. In fact, the 1915 World Series became known as the "Two-to-One" series.

Ruth put in his daily plea to pitch, but Carrigan came back with Ernie Shore, his first-game loser. "Ernie won the right to get another crack at them," Rough explained. "If he goes as well as he did in the first game, we're bound to win and get that big three-to-one jump."

Duffy Lewis again was a terrific pain in the neck for Fitchburg Pat and his Phillies. The doughty little man from the far west again drove in Boston's winning run and twice ran into deepest left for two more fine running catches of fearsome clouts by Cravath, balls which would have been easy homers in Philadelphia. Each of the rival first basemen, Dick Hoblitzel and Fred Luderus, made three hits, and an oddity of the game was that Dave Bancroft, shortstop for the National Leaguers, did not have a single fielding chance, the only time that ever has happened in World Series competition.

George "Dut" Chalmers, the New Yorker, was Moran's boxman. He was a tall spitballer who learned his baseball on the lots of Harlem, was subject to arm trouble, and was known as the hard-luck pitcher of the Phillies. And this time his luck again was running bad, as he pitched well enough to win nine games out of ten.

The Red Sox scored their first run in the third, an acrimonious inning in which even the umpires from the rival leagues battled each other. Barry, first Boston batter, walked on a fourth ball, which had half of the Phillies swarming around Billy Evans and asking how a man with his reputation and supposedly good eyesight could see a "perfect strike" as a "fourth ball." Cady bunted past Chalmers and got an infield hit when both Luderus and Niehoff scrambled after the ball and left first base unguarded.

While Shore was at bat, Billy Evans called a balk on Chalmers, and both Barry and Cady advanced a base. But Rigler, the National League umpire on the bases, didn't see a balk. The two arbiters talked it over, and the runners eventually were returned to their former bases. Shore then shoved them along anyway with a sacrifice, and Hooper scored Barry with a high hopper which jumped over Chalmers' head. Niehoff wrestled with it, but by the time he subdued it, it was too late for a play on Black Jack at the plate or Harry at first. That put Cady on third with only one out, but neither Scottie nor Spoke could bring him in. The former fouled to Whitted, and Tris slapped back a harmless tap to Chalmers.

Boston got its second run, the tally necessary for the third 2-to-1 win, in the sixth; with one out, Hobby singled to center for his second hit and scored on Lewis' powerful smash to the left-field fence, which only sharp fielding by Whitted held to a double. No one could bring Duffy home. He languished on second when Gardner flied to Paskert, and Barry expired on a weak grounder to Chalmers.

The Phillies side-stepped a shutout in the eighth, when Cravath scored Pat Moran's daily run. After Bancroft had lifted an easy chance to Lewis and Paskert popped to Gardner, Cravath carried his count with Shore to two strikes and three balls, when Gavvy hit what looked like a hard single to center. However, the ball took a high hop over Speaker's gray thatch, and by the time Hooper retrieved it, Cravath had pounded his way around to third. Luderus brought in Cravath with a hard smash to center, which Speaker knocked down and held to one base. Oscar Dugey ran for Luderus and promptly stole second. It put the Quakers' tying run in scoring position, but Shore was equal to the occasion, retiring Whitted on an infield tap.

Boston had a chance for a big mess of runs in its half, something which would have changed the daily 2-to-1 routine, but what looked like a lot of explosive TNT flickered out as a dud. With one out, Speaker bounced a hot single off Stock's shins and raced to third when, on the hit-and-run, Hobby singled to right for his third hit. At this juncture, Pat Moran wanted no more of Lewis and ordered a walk for Duffy, filling the bases. The stands were in an uproar, as

Larry Gardner came up to the plate, but the noise abated as though a great silencer had been clamped down on Braves Field. Larry tapped Chalmers' first pitch back to the pitcher; Dut's toss to Burns forced Tris at the plate, and Eddie shot the ball down to Whitted, by this time playing first base, ahead of Gardner, retiring the side on a fast double play.

However, the extra runs really weren't necessary, as Shore blotted out the Phillies in order with almost ridiculous ease in the ninth. Four pitched balls retired the side. Niehoff hit the first pitch to Gardner for an out at first; Burns popped a little fly to Everett Scott; and Bobbie Byrne, batting for Chalmers, swung at the first pitch and sent a fly ball out to Lewis. And a one-run lead again had sufficed!

5

It was back to Philadelphia for the fifth and final game on Wednesday, October 13, and all the bad luck of the day went to Bill Baker, headman of Baker Bowl. The Red Sox finally changed the score on Bill, winning the grand finale by a count of 5 to 4, as Harry Hooper bounced two home runs into Baker's temporary bleachers in center field, and Duffy Lewis smashed a third into the regular left-field bleacher. Without Hooper's so-called "Chinese homers," the Phillies would have won the game, and Baker was given a terrific razzing. Probably it was a little undeserved, as Baker had tried to take care of a few more fans by putting in the extra seats. But the nation's press and Philadelphia fandom jumped on him with both feet. He was accused of playing for a few extra nickels, with his temporary seats, and he thereby lost his share of an $83,000 sixth-game in Boston.

Much to the disappointment of Ruth, Carrigan again passed him by and picked George Foster for the final game. Bill really intended to find a spot for Babe in the series, but it never came. Bill says today that if there had been a sixth game in Boston, Ruth would have pitched it for him. By the fifth game, he figured he had the Quakers on the run, and that by pitching Foster again, he was pressing his advantage. He remembered well how the 1912 world championship almost got away from Jake Stahl by his failure to pitch Joe Wood when the Red Sox had a similar three-to-one lead.

As a matter of fact, Foster wasn't nearly the pitcher that he was in his first attempt, and he was lucky to win. Far from pitching a three-hitter in which only thirty batters faced him, he was constantly in trouble. The Phillies closed the series with their only display of power; they got nine hits, including Luderus' homer and double, while George walked two Phillies and hit two others.

There was a general idea that Pat Moran would call again on Alexander, even though Grover had worked only two days before, but this was one of the few times in Aleck's career that he complained that his arm wasn't right. Moran started Erskine Mayer but shifted to Eppa Rixey, his bean-pole left-hander, in the fourth inning. Pat was holding Alexander back for a possible sixth game; even with his ailing arm, Grover probably could have won the fifth game.

Hooper started his greatest World Series hitting afternoon by lining Mayer's first pitch of the game for a single, but languished on first. The Phillies, however, showed early that they wouldn't be hypnotized by Foster's magic this time, attacking George for two runs in the first inning. The Boston right-hander got off to a shaky start when the Phillies filled the bases with none out. Stock was hit by a pitched ball; Banny lined a single to left; and Paskert beat out a bunt on a first-base decision by O'Loughlin which had Carrigan, Foster, Hobby, and Thomas protesting as though Silk had robbed them of their eyeteeth.

For a spell, the Red Sox then were saved by one of the strangest plays ever attempted in a World Series. Cravath, the clean-up batter and twenty-four-homer man, carrried the count with Foster until it was two strikes and three balls. As all runners were in motion on the next pitch, and the Red Sox were expecting Cravath to swing from the hips, Moran tried to cross them by signaling the big slugger to bunt on a squeeze play. But Philadelphia fans had a sinking feeling in the pits of their stomachs when it was over. Foster scrambled after the swinging bunt, and his peg to Thomas at the plate just barely got there ahead of Stock, while Chet relayed it down to Hoblitzel at first in time to get the slow-moving Gavvy on a lightning double play. "Now, I've seen everything," yelled Hugh Fullerton, the baseball dopester, in the press stand.

The play still left Bancroft on third and Paskert on second, and the big Philadelphia tough guy, Fred Luderus, sent them both tearing home when he pumped a hard double to left. Speaker retired the side when he pulled down Whitted's line fly.

The Red Sox got one back in the second inning, when with two out, Gardner tripled to center, the ball barely escaping a bound into the bleachers, and came home when Barry stabbed a sharp single to left. Thomas followed suit with another safety to the same field, but Foster, batting hero of the second game, popped weakly to Luderus.

However, the Red Sox quickly tied it up when Harry Hooper, first up in the third, hit a ball to center out of Paskert's reach, and the sphere hopped into the convenient temporary seats for the first home run of the series. After Speaker singled in the same inning, Moran pulled out Mayer, substituting the left-hander Rixey, and Carrigan countered the move by sending Del Gainer to hit for Hoblitzel. Pat won, for the moment, in this battle of wits, as Del grounded to Bancroft for a double play.

Philadelphia had its last real chance to shout in the fourth, when the Quakers again pulled two runs in front. Luderus gave the crowd a real thrill, when he hammered a home run over the high right-field wall into Broad Street, and the fourth run followed on singles by Niehoff and Burns, and Hooper's wild throw to head off Niehoff at third, which bounced over Gardner's head into the stand.

Rixey was doing quite well, and it looked as if the series would move back to Boston, when things happened fast and furious in the last two innings to change completely the complexion of the ball game. With none out in the eighth, Boston tied the score in the twinkling of an eye when Gainer beat out a slow grounder to Stock, and Lewis lined a home run deep into the left-center-field bleachers. Big Eppa staved off the inevitable for a few minutes by getting the next three Boston hitters.

There was quite a rumpus in the second half of the eighth when Foster walked Cravath with two out. Moran sent Dugey to run for Gavvy, and the entire crowd shouted for Luderus, who already had a homer, double, and single, to "do it again." "You can do it, Ludy, you can do it, another one over the fence," they implored. However, with two strikes on the slugger, Dugey, a fast man, went down to second on an attempted steal, and Cady, who had succeeded Thomas behind the plate, apparently shot him down. At least, O'Loughlin waved Oscar out, and the Red Sox started to scamper to their dugout.

But Bill Klem reversed Silk and called the Boston players back to their positions. He said that Foster's pitch had grazed Luderus' uniform, and sent the broad-shouldered German down to first, while Dugey was called safe at second. That didn't suit Rough, who did a lot of grousing, but Whitted, one of the "busts" of the series, helped lower Carrigan's blood pressure with an easy tap to Foster, retiring the side.

Harry then was Hero Hooper when he toppled Pat Moran's house of cards with another one of those "Chinese homers" after Foster had fanned to open the ninth. It was almost a duplicate of Harry's earlier effort; again the ball struck on the ground and went into the open seats on the first bound. It's still a mystery today why the managers didn't agree to make such hits ground-rule doubles. In justice to Rixey, he played out the string, retiring Scott on a hot grounder to Banny and striking out Speaker.

Foster hadn't pitched a particularly brilliant game up to this point, but propped up by that 5-to-4 lead, he now put every ounce of remaining energy behind each pitch in the bottom half of the ninth. George quickly snuffed out the side, as Philadelphia hopes became deader than a mackerel on a Gloucester dock. He whizzed a third strike past Niehoff and retired Eddie Burns on a grounder to Gainer. As his last forlorn hope, Moran trotted out Bill "Reindeer" Killefer, out of the series with an injury, as a pinch hitter for Rixey, but Foster promptly got rid of the limping Reindeer on a grounder to Scott, and the Red Sox again were world champions.

Everybody rushed to embrace Foster, Duffy Lewis, Harry Hooper, and Carrigan, and Ban Johnson, shouldering his way into the Boston clubhouse, shouted above the din, "We've squared accounts for 1914; now I again can look any man in the eye." Ban was referring to his humiliation of a year before when the Braves had cleaned up his Athletics in four straight games.

The big Boston heroes were Duffy Lewis, Harry Hooper, and the three winning Red Sox pitchers, Foster, Shore, and Leonard. With eight hits in eighteen times at bat, Lewis hit a magnificent .444; Harry wasn't so far behind him with seven in twenty for .350. Foster came out of a low-hitting series with a .500 batting average, four bingles in eight times at bat; Spoke hit .313, and Hobby .294.

Outside of Fred Luderus, who almost equaled Lewis with .438, and Bancroft, who hit a satisfactory .294, the rest of the Philly regulars were pretty sad. The high efficiency of the Red Sox staff was attested by the anemic team batting average of .182 for Moran's players and such joke individual averages as Paskert's .158, Cravath's .125, Stock's .117, and Niehoff's .063.

Tim Murnane, the old gladiator of the Boston *Globe*, went into superlatives in praising the all-round performance of Duffy Lewis. "Duffy Lewis was the real hero of this Series, or of any other," wrote Tim. "I have witnessed all of the contests for the game's highest honors in the last 30 years, and I want to say that the all-around work of the modest Californian never has been equalled in a big Series."

However, Ty Cobb, the perennial American League batting champion, who had attended the series as a "reporter," stressed the Red

Sox's airtight defense. "The figures show how the Boston players outhit the Phillies," said Ty, "but there is a general tendency to overlook the Red Sox's tight defense. To my way of thinking, this 1915 Red Sox team is the greatest defensive club that has been put together in baseball in many years."

Despite the limited capacity of Baker Bowl, the individual Red Sox fared well in the series, the winning shares running up to $3,780, only a few hundred less than the Boston checks in the adventure with the Giants three years before. Jack Barry had become a plutocrat, and the players considered him "filthy rich" with five World Series pickings in six years for a total of $14,841. The Phillies didn't do so badly either, getting $2,520 per man for their puny batting averages.

Mayor Curley tried to keep the new world champions in Boston long enough for the city to throw a banquet in their honor, but the players were anxious to get away to hunt, be lionized in their home towns, or just sit down somewhere and relax. Even Hal Janvrin, the native Bostonian, ducked several Boston victory celebrations to skip to Bill Carrigan's camp in Maine.

And on his return to Winston-Salem, North Carolina, Ernie Shore encountered a neighbor who inquired: "Been away, Ernie? Ain't seen you around in some time."

As for Duffy Lewis, capitalizing on his great series play, he took a fling in vaudeville. Part of his act was to answer baseball questions, especially pertaining to the recent World Series, which were asked by his audiences. While Lewis was playing a theater in Los Angeles, where Cravath resided and had played minor league ball, a big fellow bellowed, "At what park, Duffy, did you catch those long flies hit by Gavvy Cravath?"

"Why, those balls were hit at Braves Field, Boston," Lewis replied courteously.

"Well, lucky for you, Duffy, they weren't hit at Baker Bowl, Philadelphia," shot back the questioner, "or he would be up there now, instead of you."

12

⊖

SPEAKERLESS RED SOX STILL
ARE GOOD

I

OPENING day of the 1916 season was a gloomy one for New England fans. Bostonians going to work rubbed their eyes with amazement—and some indignation—as they read streamers across the front pages of the Boston *Globe* and Boston *Post*: "Tris Speaker Sold to Cleveland for $50,000 and Two Obscure Players." The players tossed into the deal were two Cleveland rookies, pitcher Sad Sam Jones and infielder Fred Thomas. The former later developed into stardom and became one of the most durable pitchers in the league.

At that time, Boston fans still were accustomed to their club's buying stars, rather than selling them. Tris Speaker had been a determined holdout all spring, and though he trained with the club at Hot Springs, Arkansas, and played in the exhibition schedule, he was not under contract. Peace had been made with the Federal League the preceding winter, and salaries were cut all down the line. Spoke had been set back to $9,000, the pay he drew in 1913, and half of his $18,000 stipend for 1914 and 1915. One of Lannin's excuses was that Tris had had a steady batting decline since hitting .383 in 1912—.366, .338, and .332. Of course, the cowboy reared on his hind legs and refused to take the cut.

Speaker's pal, Joe Wood, also had been cut to $5,000. Smoky Joe wasn't at the training camp, saying he wouldn't play ball for such a "measly salary." To which Lannin replied, he couldn't pay Joe more fter what he termed "Wood's measly victories of 1914 and 1915."

Despite the argument, Boston fandom felt that sooner or later the owner and his great outfielder would patch up their differences. Speaker then was topped only by Cobb among the game's ace players and was to Boston baseball what Ty was to the game in Detroit and Mathewson in New York. That such a player would be sold or traded never occurred to any of the fans or writers. Yet a few days before the Red Sox opened their home season, the observing reporter might have got a hint of what was in the wind when Lannin purchased center fielder Clarence "Tilly" Walker, a fairly hard hitter, from the St. Louis Browns.

The Speaker deal was one of those inside affairs put over by the astute Ban Johnson, whose friend Jim Dunn had recently taken over the Cleveland club. Johnson also had a chunk of the club, as both Ban and Comiskey advanced loans to Dunn to help him buy out Charley Somers, the original American League angel, who now was in financial hot water. The deal was sprung so quickly that only a few insiders had any knowledge of it until it was announced on the eve of the opening of the 1916 season. It infuriated the two new New York owners, Colonels Ruppert and Huston, who were spending money lavishly to build up the Yankees. They never were given a chance to bid on Tris and never forgave Ban for this oversight.

It speaks volumes for the inherent strength of the Red Sox and for Carrigan's skillful guidance that the club repeated its 1915 honors with the great Tristram in Cleveland. However, it was fortunate the 1916 Red Sox did not have to beat out a hundred-game-winning Tiger team, as the new champions won ten less games than they did the preceding year. They brought home the fifth Red Sox pennant with ninety-one victories against sixty-three losses, winning by a scant two-game margin over a fast-coming White Sox club, which won eighty-nine games and suffered sixty-five defeats. Detroit, regarded by the Red Sox as their leading rival most of the season, finished two games behind Chicago.

Boston's class eventually told, but the Carrigan athletes knew all the time they were in a fight. It was a well-matched field, as every club but the Athletics and Browns led at some time or other, and even the latter club put on a fourteen-game late-summer winning streak. Boston and New York alternated for the lead in April, and then Detroit, Washington, and Cleveland all took a crack at it. In fact, Tris's new team, the Indians, with which he won the batting championship from Cobb with a .386 average, amazed baseball by leading the pack from June 1 to June 27. Then a greatly strengthened Yankee aggregation set the pace to July 28. This club might have won, but an unparalleled series of injuries knocked Bill Donovan's luckless team out of the race. The Red Sox, running second to the Yanks, moved to the top, and though the White Sox and Tigers each shoved their noses in front for a few days in August, Carrigan's team had the greater resilience and each time snapped promptly back.

There was a splendid *esprit de corps* on this 1916 club; Boss Bill held frequent meetings, and everybody down to the lowliest substitute was invited to put in his two cents in the way of suggestions. Tilly Walker was no Speaker, but he was a dependable fielder with a good arm and for that period was considered a dangerous extra-base hitter. He hit .265 in 128 games, whacking out 29 doubles, 11 triples, and 3 homers. To add more outfield power, Chick Shorten was brought up from Providence in midseason, and he hit .295 for 53 games. After Chick joined the colors, he played center field against right-handers, Walker against the southpaws.

Shorten's .295 was second only to Larry Gardner's .308, and Speaker's departure was reflected in the club's reduced batting average; the Red Sox slumped to fourth with an average of .249. The mediocre hitting put a heavy strain on the pitching staff and made it necessary for the club to fight desperately for those one-run victories. It also explains why Carrigan defended the plate so zealously against the spikes of Cobb, Bush, and Moriarty. Single runs in that era were most precious.

Those who have a notion that Ruth, the 1916 pitcher, was just a strong left-handed young thrower may get a different slant by examining his record. The Bambino, now starting to fill out, won twenty-three games and lost twelve, his twenty-three wins tying Harry Coveleskie for the league's high in victories. Ruth this year was the earned-run leader with 1.75; he just barely nosed out Cicotte, who rose to real stardom in Chicago. And Babe had that unforgettable thrill of fanning Cobb, Crawford, and Veach with the bases full.

There also was a pinch-hitting incident which in later years became the big moment of Mike McNally's life. Feeling that a right-handed pinch hitter might keep a rally going against a southpaw, Rough Carrigan sent the light-hitting Michael to the plate to hit for Ruth. After Babe later became the game's great home-run king, McNally carried a clipping of that box score until it fell apart from usage. But Mike laughs today, "What is so strange that the great McNally should have batted for Ruth?"

Following Ruth in that 1916 Red Sox pitching parade were Shore with seventeen and nine; Leonard, eighteen and eleven; Mays, seventeen and thirteen; and Foster, fourteen and eight. George was ailing a good part of the season and did not work as often as in 1915. That gave Mays, the sturdy young ox from the northwest, a chance to work regularly. After his spring holdout, Wood did not report to Carrigan until July 25, and then took part in only a few games. Eventually he joined Speaker on the Indians, the Cleveland club purchasing him the following February for $15,000. But Smoky Joe was through as a pitcher and in his Cleveland years played along-side Spoke in the outfield.

Sparkling among other Boston pitching gems of 1916 were a pair of no-hit games, the first hurled by Foster against the Yankees, June 21, and the second by Dutch Leonard against the Browns, August 30. Boston fans had ringside seats for both masterpieces, as both no-hitters were pitched at Fenway Park.

Hal Janvrin, the Boston high-school kid, was the busiest utility man in nineteen states. Though he hit only .223, he took part in 117 games, filling in most ably at various times for Scott, Barry, and Gardner. Jack suffered an injured leg in late August, and Janvrin played second base in the difficult hand-to-hand fighting in the clos-ing month of the season. Scottie played in 121 games, and once he got over some spring mishaps, he launched the 1,307 consecutive-game streak, the record until Lou Gehrig, the Yankees' old Iron Horse, ran off 2,130 games.

Late in 1916 Bill Carrigan tossed a real bombshell into the Boston camp with the announcement that regardless of the outcome of the American League race, he would call it quits after the 1916 season. In his earlier years Bill had helped his father with his grocery busi-ness in Lewiston, Maine; now Bill was following the footsteps of his managerial predecessor, Jake Stahl, and stepping into a lucrative Lewiston banking job. Furthermore, Mrs. Carrigan liked baseball well enough but wanted a husband who spent more time at home.

There were many skeptics, in Boston and elsewhere, who took Carrigan's talk of retirement none too seriously. "He's going to make Joe Lannin come across with some real dough if he wants Carrigan to manage his club in 1917," they said. But Boss Bill really meant it.

2

For quite a stretch it looked as though Carrigan again would tangle up with Pat Moran and his Phillies in the 1916 World Series. There also was the possibility of playing the neighboring club in

Allston, the Braves. And a sensational twenty-six-game September winning streak on the part of the Giants, finally halted by George Tyler of the Braves, made McGraw's men another possibility. However, in a turbulent, ill-willed finish, in which John McGraw walked out on a game in Brooklyn, saying, "I won't be a party to this," and Pat Moran yelled for an investigation, the Dodgers, under the leadership of Wilbert Robinson, won the National League pennant, followed closely by the Phillies, Braves, and Giants. It was Brooklyn's first flag since 1900, and the genial Uncle Robbie was furious at McGraw, his old Oriole side-kick, for what he termed "throwing mud on his [Uncle Robbie's] parade."

Carrigan and the Boston players observed the 1916 National League race with mingled feelings. A good many preferred playing the Giants, because that promised to build up the richest World Series pot, but everyone knew McGraw's club was hotter than a St. Louis day in August. Some thought it would be fun to play the Braves; no one wanted to play the Phillies again. There was the matter of Baker's cigar-box park and Alexander with his greatest season, winning thirty-three games, sixteen of them shutouts. And rightly or wrongly, the general feeling in the Boston camp was that the Brooklyns, often now called the Robins, would be the softest World Series touch. The Red Sox hadn't much respect for Ivan Olson, the Brooklyn shortstop, a stouthearted but erratic player. They had seen plenty of Olson when he was with Cleveland in the American League, and one of the wisecracks on the Red Sox bench was, "When in doubt, hit to Ivey."

Though Robbie and Bill Dahlen, his managerial predecessor, developed a lot of good players in Brooklyn, the hard-hitting Zack Wheat, the irrepressible Casey Stengel, Hi Myers, Jimmy Johnston, Georgie Cutshaw, Nap Rucker, Jeff Pfeffer, and Sherry Smith, Robinson had filled out his club with discards from other clubs, Rube Marquard, Chief Meyers, and Fred Merkle from the Giants, Larry Cheney from the Cubs, Mike Mowrey from the Pirates, Jack Coombs from the Athletics, Ivey Olson from the Indians. Even Jake Daubert, the club's regular first baseman and twice National League batting champion had failed to make the grade as a rookie with Cleveland. The club frequently was spoken of as the "castoffs." One reason the Sox did not hold the Robins in greater respect was that Napoleon Rucker, at one time the National League's greatest left-hander, was pretty well washed up by 1916. Nap now had only a slow ball which hurt his arm every time he pitched. He made only one brief appearance in the 1916 series, as a relief pitcher, but even then had enough cunning left to stop the Sox for two innings.

"We'll take them," said Rough, "but that means everybody has to play his game. You beat them out there, not in the newspapers." He was referring to the near unanimity with which the nation's sports writers picked the Red Sox. He knew, too, that the team would miss Barry, though all of the players had great confidence in Janvrin.

"Hal's a great kid," said Duffy Lewis, "and won't let us down, playing in Jack's place."

The Red Sox again played the Boston games of the series at Braves Field, with its better than forty-thousand capacity, while Ebbets Field in Brooklyn held only a little more than did Baker Bowl in 1915, even though Charley Ebbets also built in some extra seats as did Baker the fall before. And Ebbets, the white-haired Flatbush Squire, was the first club owner who had the temerity to charge five dollars for a World Series grandstand seat. No club prior to that had charged more than three. Ebbets caught plenty of hell about it, too, and was accused of being everything from a "chiseler" and profiteer to a "stick-up man." Heckled by a group of angry fans, Charley stood on his stool in back of the grandstand and shouted back: "We haven't the capacity of the Red Sox in Boston, so we've got to charge more to get somewhere near Boston's receipts. We can't approach the Red Sox in attendance, but after all, Brooklyn has some civic pride in its gate receipts." It worked out that way, too; with Brooklyn crowds only half the size of those at Braves Field, Ebbets' gates ran within $10,000 of Joe Lannin's.

The first game was played at Braves Field on a Saturday, October 7, before a crowd of 36,117, which fell some 5,000 below expectations. The explanation for the empty seats was that the game was played on the Jewish Day of Atonement, keeping away Red Sox rooters of that faith. The game started like a Boston joy ride but ended with the Red Sox winning by the bare margin of the skin of their teeth— 6 to 5. The Dodgers even outhit the Sox, ten to eight. Uncle Robbie had been on McGraw's bench as coach in 1912, saw Marquard defeat the Red Sox twice in that series, and was possessed with the idea that the way to beat Carrigan's club was to shoot left-handers at them. He started Marquard, and Rough opened with Ernie Shore, as he had in Philadelphia the year before.

Boston was the first to score, getting a run in the third inning on Hoblitzel's triple and Lewis' double.

"There's that Lewis again; is he never going to stop picking on us?" asked John K. Tener, the National League president, in the

National Commission box. "I'm afraid Duffy is about to give you another bad series, Governor," said Ban Johnson with feigned sympathy.

Brooklyn tied the score in almost the same manner in the fourth frame, on Stengel's single and Wheat's triple. Hooper stopped further scoring when he converted Cutshaw's line drive into a double play with a beeline peg to Cady at the plate. The American League champs then regained the lead at 2 to 1, when the Sox scored a second run in the fifth on a double by Hooper, Janvrin's sacrifice, and Tillie Walker's single. The Dodger infield gave a good imitation of a sieve behind Marquard in the seventh when the Red Sox tallied three gift runs. Janvrin opened with a double and scored on successive bobbles by Olson and Cutshaw on grounders hit by Walker and Hobby. Lewis sacrificed, and when Gardner hit to Cutshaw, the second baseman threw to the plate too late to get Walker, and Tillie tallied. Hobby took third on the play and came home on a long fly by Scott.

Jeff Pfeffer faced the Red Sox in the eighth, and Rough's boys scored a sixth run, which proved a most valuable tally within the next fifteen minutes. Hooper walked with one out; Janvrin singled to right, and when Casey Stengel threw wildly to Mowrey at third, Harry never stopped running until he had crossed the plate.

With the Red Sox ahead, 6 to 1, and Ernie Shore apparently having the situation in hand like the Marines, many fans started to edge toward the exits, to get a jump on the crowd for the street cars and taxis. But those who stayed saw Brooklyn's most spirited rally of the series; four runs scored, and the bases were full when Scott checked the rally with a great stop and throw.

Daubert opened the inning with a walk; Stengel followed with a single, but Shore pounced on Wheat's bounder and forced Jake at third for the first out. However, Cutshaw also drew a pass, filling the bases, and then young Janvrin was guilty of a most unfortunate boot. In his eagerness to make a double play on Mowrey's grounder, Hal not only fumbled the ball, but kicked it twenty feet away, and both Stengel and Wheat scored. Olson then almost took a leg off Larry Gardner with a savage drive which again filled the bases. With a chance to break up the game, Chief Meyers, the former Giant, smashed several murderous fouls and then raised a gentle foul to Hoblitzel.

It looked as though the big danger was over, but Fred Merkle, batting for Pfeffer, drew a walk, forcing in Cutshaw. By this time Carrigan decided he had given Ernie Shore every chance to extricate himself, and called in Carl Mays from the bull pen. Myers quickly beat out an infield splash to Janvrin, scoring Mowrey with the fourth run, and such Brooklyn fans as were on hand went into a delirium. It brought up Daubert, Robbie's best batter, again, and this time Jake drove to Scott in deep short, but Everett made a beautiful stop and long throw to first just in time to nip Daubert by half a step.

The play started Uncle Robbie moaning about that "trolley line, Scott to first." "Whenever things start going good for us, we go out on that trolley line," he complained, pantomiming Scottie's long throws. Everett handled four assists and two put-outs, but Janvrin was the real busy boy of the infield, as he had eight assists, two put-outs, and his one error.

3

After waiting a year, Babe Ruth finally got his chance to pitch a World Series game, as Carrigan sent his big Baltimore left-hander against the Dodgers in the second contest, played at Braves Field the following Monday before a more satisfactory crowd of 41,373. Still believing "left-handers ought to be bad medicine for that Carrigan," Robinson pitched Sherry Smith, his stocky Georgia southpaw, and the result was the longest World Series game ever played. The Red Sox and Babe finally triumphed in fourteen innings by that magic World Series score of 1915—2 to 1. It was a grand duel, with the Babe giving up only six hits and Sherry, seven; both sides fielded brilliantly, with Lewis and Hi Myers making especially thrilling running catches.

The Bambino was scored on early, Myers hitting a first-inning drive to center field which hopped over Walker's head, and before the other Red Sox could run it down, the deer-footed Hi had stretched it into a home run. "Damn that bounce; that only oughta been a single," said Ruth, but it was to be a long time before Babe's World Series pitching slate again would be sullied.

Ruth took a hand in tying the score himself in the third inning when Scott lashed a line drive to deep left center for three bases and came home on Ruth's infield out to Cutshaw, which George fumbled long enough to prevent a play at the plate. Cutshaw followed with a fumble on Hooper, but Harry was forced by Janvrin. From there on, it was a grueling struggle until the game was ended in semi-darkness with a Red Sox run in the fourteenth. In fact, the veteran National League umpire Bill Klem, who was not working in this series, always has insisted that the fourteenth inning never should

Signing Contracts in 1918.
Seated: Ed Barrow and Harry Frazee; *Standing:* Babe Ruth and
Stuffy McInnis

Herb Pennock

"Sad" Sam Jones

have been started. "I'd never have started it, if I had been callin' 'em that day," Bill has maintained. "It gets dark quick in Boston once the sun goes down at that time of the year, and anyone could tell it would be dark before the inning was over."

Smith opened the historic inning by walking Hoblitzel, and Lewis shoved Dick down to second with a sacrifice bunt. Carrigan then sent Mike McNally to run for Hobby, and Del Gainer, a right-handed batsman, to hit for Gardner. Del hit the third pitch for a double to left, and it was so dark it was difficult for Wheat to follow the ball, but the happy Boston fans saw the slender McNally streak down the third-base foul line with the winning run.

The Babe's face was beaming when he ran into the clubhouse. "I told you I could take care of those National League so-and-sos," he quipped to Carrigan.

"Well, you surely took care of them," said Bill, slapping Ruth on the back. "They never saw such left-handed pitching as you gave them in their league all season."

And on the train back to New York, Wilbert Robinson was still talking of "that damned trolley line—Scott to first." In this game, Scottie had eight assists and one put-out; Janvrin five assists and four put-outs.

The series shifted to Brooklyn on October 10, when the picturesque Ebbets played host to his first World Series crowd. It was an arctic day; fans bundled up in heavy coats and steamer rugs, and the turnout was only 21,087. Charley's extra boxes and bleachers weren't needed. A lot of the Squire's best customers declared a sit-down strike, in their homes, and gave his World's Series the absent treatment. And to the great amusement of Brooklyn and New York, some of the speculators, who at first had been asking twenty dollars for the five-dollar tickets, were glad to unload at game time for four dollars—and didn't sell them all at that price. It made good Flatbush burghers weep when they thought of the "specs' " suffering. Even so, Ebbets and Brooklyn could take civic pride in his gate, as Charley's receipts were $69,762 against $76,489, Lannin's first-game receipts in Boston.

4

Having won with Ruth, a hitherto untried World Series pitcher, in the second game, Carrigan decided to give his submarine-ball pitcher, Carl Mays, who had rescued Shore in the opening tilt, his first big series starting assignment. After pitching two left-handers, Marquard and Smith, Uncle Robbie finally pulled a right-hander out of his deck, old Jack Coombs, the farmer from Kennebunkport, Maine, who had gone direct from Colby to the Athletics in 1906 and pitched that historic twenty-four-inning game against Joe Harris. Jack had won four World Series games for Connie Mack and lost none, and his World Series escutcheon still was unsullied after his first effort on the National League side. With some help from big Jeff Pfeffer, Colby Jack bagged his fifth blue-ribbon win, 4 to 3.

Mays didn't do as well as Carrigan had anticipated. Chunky Carl hadn't developed the World Series *sang-froid* he showed in later years; his fast ball didn't break properly after it rose, and the Robins feasted on it for seven hits and all their runs in the five innings the Oregonian toiled. Foster, the hero of the 1915 series with the Phillies, made his only appearance of the series when he swept up after Henriksen batted for Mays in the sixth.

The Dodgers had all their runs in before Boston even started. Carl wiggled out of a hole in the very first, when the Brooklyns let down their Flatbush admirers. They filled the bases with one out, but Cutshaw forced Myers at the plate, and Mike Mowrey, behaving like a real "Bum," struck out, leaving the "full house."

The Dodgers had better luck in the third, when Wheat scored after he, Stengel, and Cutshaw straightened out Mays's submarine delivery for clean singles. In the fourth, Robbie's boys tallied again, and the Red Sox looked none too good. Olson beat out a bunt and took an extra base when Gardner threw the ball away. On Miller's sacrifice bunt, it looked as if Mays had a play on Olson at third, but he played it safe and threw out Otto at first. Coombs, always a good man with the willow, singled home the Swede.

Two more runs scored on Mays in the fifth and brought about Carl's recall. He couldn't get the ball over for Wheat and Mowrey; both walked, and Olson had the laugh on the Red Sox who were riding him when he fetched in the runners with a triple to deep center.

Coombs had shut out the Red Sox with three hits during this time, but the Boston bats became active in the sixth, and the Sox cut the lead in half. Henriksen, batting for Mays, started it with a walk, and Hooper drove Olaf home with a triple past Myers. Coombs got Janvrin on a fly to Cutshaw, but Shorten, who had had no trouble hitting Coombs, rapped Jack for his third successive hit, driving in Harry.

When Larry Gardner pumped a homer over the right-field fence for a third Boston run in the seventh, Robbie decided Coombs had gone long enough, and called in Pfeffer. Big Jeff clamped down hard on the Boston rally; he gave no hits and struck out Thomas, Foster, and Janvrin in his two and two-thirds innings.

The Red Sox had one great play left, which prevented Brooklyn from winning by a greater margin. Daubert hit a long drive to left center off Foster in the eighth and tried for a homer, only to have a fast relay, Lewis to Scott to Thomas, cut him down at the plate, as Chet had the scoring dish blocked off completely.

Scottie's part in the play was especially commendable. Everett had had a collision with Olson the day before, and when he showed up in Brooklyn his left shoulder was so sore he couldn't raise his left arm. However, with already one substitute, Janvrin, in the infield, Scott insisted on carrying on. "I'll play as long as the arm hangs on," he told Rough.

5

For the fourth game in Brooklyn, October 11, Ebbets enticed 575 more fans into his refrigerated arena and jacked up his receipts to $72,800. Brooklyn's honor and fair name were being upheld; the Robins were losing the series, but Squire Ebbets wasn't too far behind in gate receipts.

Speculators still were selling reserved grandstand tickets below face value, and as far as Brooklyn fans were concerned those who bought marked down ducats at four dollars still paid too much. The National League champions became the fumbling Dodgers again, and four Brooklyn errors helped Boston to a comfortable 6-to-2 victory. The Red Sox, however, helped matters themselves with ten lusty hits. Rough had been holding Dutch Leonard for just this spot, and the left-hander gave him that big three-to-one edge. Robbie still stuck to the idea that Marquard could again beat the Red Sox, but this time the Carrigans finished the Rube in four innings.

After scoring only one run off Ruth in fourteen innings, Robbie put Merkle on first base in place of his captain, Jake Daubert, and sent Jimmy Johnston to the outfield instead of Stengel, in an effort to put more right-handed power in his line-up. For a few minutes in the first inning, it looked as though Uncle Wilbert had a good idea, as Brooklyn scored two runs on Leonard in a jiffy. Johnston greeted Dutch with a triple and came home on Myers' single. Then Leonard walked Merkle, the husky ex-Giant, and Wheat forced Fred for the first out. Janvrin fumbled Cutshaw's hot roller, Myers scoring and Wheat tearing around to third. Brooklyn fans were wild-eyed at this display of scoring power, but the rally quickly burned itself out.

Robbie gave the sign for a double steal, but Wheat was nipped at the plate, and Mowrey again fanned in the clutch.

Leonard was only teasing the Dodgers and their fans in that inning, as Brooklyn made only three more hits in the remaining eight frames. Beginning with the second, Dutch retired fifteen of the Robins on weak pop flies.

Brooklyn fans didn't even have long to enjoy their early lead, as the Red Sox promptly sprang in front with three runs off Marquard in the second inning. The Rube had started off like a world-beater, tossing out Hooper in the first inning and striking out Janvrin and Walker. But it was a different story in the second when Hobby walked, Lewis poled a double to left, and Larry Gardner, who seemed to like the Ebbets Field architecture, hit to the center-field wall for his second homer in successive games.

Carrigan, who was catching Leonard as usual, banged in the fourth run scored off Rube, in the fourth, driving in Lewis, who had singled to left and been sacrificed to second by the busy Gardner. A fifth run was scored on Larry Cheney in the fifth inning. Hooper walked and stole second as Meyers dropped a third strike on Janvrin. Walker popped to Olson, but Hoblitzel sent Hooper home with a roaring double to right. Larry yielded a sixth run in the seventh, when Hooper walked and was forced by Janvrin; Hal scored all the way from first when Cheney threw Hoblitzel's bunt into right field.

Rucker made his long delayed World Series appearance in the last two innings, held the Red Sox to one scratch hit, and struck out Janvrin, Carrigan, and Leonard with his delivery, which according to Nap had three speeds, slow, slower, and slower'n 'at. Incidentally, Rough's strike-out marked his last appearance as a batsman in organized baseball.

6

The fifth and final game was played at Braves Field on Columbus Day, October 12, and this time the crowd really packed the place, as a new record was established for attendance, 42,620, and receipts, $83,873. Even so, the Boston police turned other holiday-bent fans away from the park by the thousands. That attendance mark stood as a World Series record until Yankee Stadium was opened in 1923. It was a historic Columbus Day, as the Red Sox–Dodger World Series headlines vied with those of the greater global World Series as the nation was inching its way into World War I. A German submarine pack which was lurking off Nantucket and Block Island,

Rhode Island, was sinking a fleet of British and French merchantmen which had just left New York harbor.

Carrigan came back with Shore, his first-game hurler, and Robbie finally started his number one pitcher of the league season, Jeff Pfeffer, who had appeared twice in relief pitching roles and once as a pinch hitter. But Brooklyn was washed up by this time; everybody sensed it, the officials, the players, and the writers. And the big Columbus Day crowd was in a Roman holiday mood; it was there to be in on the kill. The partisan American League fans weren't disappointed, as Shore hurled his best game of his two World Series, a three-hitter, and after Brooklyn tallied a tainted run in the second inning, he had the Dodgers eating out of his hand. In fact, Brooklyn didn't get a clean hit until Mowrey singled with two out in the seventh inning. Pfeffer pitched well enough to win an ordinary game, but again the Dodger infield bogged down. On the Boston side, Scott's pole left the trolley wire twice, as Everett, still suffering with the stiff shoulder, bungled two chances.

Brooklyn enjoyed a momentary lead when the Robins scored a cheap run without the aid of a hit in the second inning. Cutshaw drew big Ernie's lone base on balls and got around to third on Mowrey's sacrifice and Olson's infield out. While Shore was pitching to the Indian Meyers, a fast pitch drilled through Cady's glove for a passed ball, and Cutshaw scored.

The Dodgers more or less handed that run back to the Red Sox in the bottom half of the second. Wheat played Lewis' ordinary single so amateurishly that it skipped by him for a triple. Then on Gardner's rather short fly to the same player, Zack threw wide to the plate, and Duffy scored after the catch.

Good old Ivey was of a lot of help in the third, when the Red Sox gained a two-run lead. Cady bounced a single over Daubert's head, and Shore fouled to Meyers trying to sacrifice. Hooper then walked, and Olson not only fumbled Janvrin's grounder, a double-play ball, but followed up the boot with a wild throw to first. It enabled Cady to score and Hooper to scoot around to third base. Janvrin was nailed on an attempted steal, but Shorten plunked a single to center, which scored Hooper standing up.

Just to make the game a little safer, Hooper tallied a fourth run, in the fifth, when he singled with two out and scored on Janvrin's double to left center, a fly ball which Hi Myers misjudged. That made the scoreboard read Boston, 4, Brooklyn, 1, and that remained the final score.

With the exception of the Cubs of 1907 and 1908 and the Athletics in 1910 and 1911, no other modern club had won two successive World championships before. The victory was followed by the usual wild celebration at Braves Field. Some of the younger element, and what remained of the old Royal Rooters, massed behind the band and danced joyously around the infield. When they made the circuit for the first time, they grabbed Joe Lannin and pushed him to the head of the parade. And when they came around again, they got hold of Squire Ebbets, pulled him into line, and the rival owners, with locked arms, led the Red Sox's victory dance.

Mayor Curley again tried to get the team to stay for a public banquet, but as in 1915, the players wanted to get away. And Carrigan's insistence that he was "through with baseball for all time" put a sort of pall on the celebration. In shaking hands with his players and wishing them Godspeed, Joe Lannin told them, "I am still hopeful that Bill will change his mind."

The players also had lined up in the clubhouse to say, "Good-by, Bill; good luck!" some sadly, others with the mental reservation they would see him again next spring. They couldn't conceive of a manager of thirty-three retiring from baseball while riding the very crest of the wave. However, Bill quickly was off for his camp at Lake Annabessacook, Maine, saying he wanted a rest before plunging into personal business, while a group of other Red Sox World Series heroes formed a hunting party which took to the bush out of Plymouth, New Hampshire. Others stayed around long enough for a Sunday exhibition game in New Haven.

Along with Bill Carrigan, pitcher George Foster also announced his retirement. Even though he had pitched three scoreless innings in the game in which he relieved Mays, George said he had been sick a good part of the season and that his back had given him hell whenever he tried to pitch. Besides, his ranch at Bokoshe, Oklahoma, needed his attention. Nap Rucker also told Brooklyn friends that his tight relief job in Ebbets Field was the swan song of his illustrious pitching career.

The Red Sox World Series heroes again were the stars of 1915: Duffy Lewis, who led the players that were in all five games with a .353 average, and Harry Hooper, who was right under Duffy with .333. While Gardner hit only .176, two of his three hits were home runs. With Robbie sticking to left-handers, Chick Shorten was in only two games, but he hit .571, collecting four hits in seven times at bat. And good old Rough went out with a series average of .667, getting two hits in three times at bat in the game in which he caught Leonard. Many nice things were said and written about the three winning pitchers, Shore, Ruth, and Leonard. And plenty of praise went to Scottie for his fielding; he handled nine put-outs and twenty-five assists.

The Boston players were quite liberal with their World Series division, which thanks to Charley Ebbets' five-dollar grandstand seats, set new records for the players' pool. Twenty-two regular Red Sox drew shares of $3,826, while the Dodgers, less liberal in their divvy, pulled down $2,834 a man. Even their league president, John Kinley Tener, criticized their division, which left out some deserving men, and said his champions played all through the series as though they were satisfied with their losers' cut. The Boston players voted three-quarters of a share each to Heinie Wagner and Vean Gregg, who had been in few games; a half share to each of the young Athletic pitching pickups, Herb Pennock and Weldon Wyckoff, $1,000 to outfielder Jimmy Walsh, and $500 each to road secretary Eddie Riley and Charley Green, the trainer.

There was an unfortunate aftermath of the series as far as Riley was concerned. Lannin fired Eddie while he was sick in one of Joe's Forest Hills, Massachusetts, apartment houses, the secretary having caught a cold at one of the Brooklyn games. Eddie had many newspaper friends who defended him, men who remembered him when he first went to work for John I. Taylor in short pants and took one of Jimmy Collins' teams west when he was only a few years older. Eddie quickly caught on with the rival Boston baseball outfit, the Braves.

And Lannin admitted to newspaper friends that if he got his price for the Red Sox he wouldn't be averse to selling while he was on top. He admitted baseball was a lot of fun, but it had plenty of headaches, even if a man was owner of a world championship club.

13

⊖

EVIL GENIE FROM PEORIA
ENTERS PICTURE

I

A BLACK shadow fell across the Boston baseball picture a few
months after the winning of the second straight world championship.
Joe Lannin had intimated he was going to withdraw while his team
still was on top. He gradually had taken over the Taylor interests,
including the park, though the Taylor family still held onto preferred stock and the bonds. Lannin's health wasn't good; he had a
heart condition, and though in three years he had two blue ribbons
and a runner-up, baseball hadn't been all joy. Joe had his share of
vexations, and he hadn't always seen eye to eye with Ban Johnson,
the league's dictatorial president.

There were rumors in November that Lannin was selling out to
some New York theatrical men, though Herman Nickerson of the
Boston *American* treated it as a bolt from the blue when he wrote,
December 4:

The big excitement for the fans of this city was the startling announcement that the World's Champion Red Sox had been sold to two New
York theatrical men, Harry Frazee and Hugh J. Ward. It came as a
surprise for there had been little talk of a sale although it was well
known that Joseph J. Lannin was willing to dispose of his property if he
could get the figure he set upon it.

Ban Johnson's friends later said that Joe Lannin caught Ban quite unawares in selling the valuable baseball property to Frazee and Ward, and that Joe made the sale to the theatrical men knowing it would pique Johnson. However, Ban retained his almost czarlike powers in 1916, and it still is difficult to understand how he ever permitted Frazee to get into the American League. Nickerson gave the purchase price for the ball club and Fenway Park as "more than $1,000,000," though it later developed that Harry bought the club on the proverbial shoestring, giving notes for the better part of the purchase price, which he expected to pay off from profits. Lannin's three-year profit on the club was given as $400,000. The deal was put through at Lannin's Garden City, New York, hotel after a week of negotiations, and the name of Willie Collier, a prominent actor at the time, at first appeared as one of the purchasers. Jimmy Callahan, former White Sox manager, headed a Chicago syndicate which also had been bidding for the property.

Frazee later was to be the evil genie of the Red Sox, but when Harry and Ward first were received by the Boston press in middle December, they made a favorable impression on the town's sports scribes. Both were friendly and affable and promised Boston nothing but the best. There was a report in circulation at the time that the new owners had offered the Washington club $60,000 for Walter Johnson. Frazee didn't deny it, nor would he confirm it, but added, "Nothing is too good for the Boston fans." That had a strange sound in subsequent years. Ward had the zeal of a baseball missionary; he wanted to popularize baseball all over the world. The two theatrical men even agreed to "take out papers" and become citizens of Massachusetts, provided they were given permits to celebrate New Year's eve in New York.

Frazee was born in Peoria, Illinois, and left the town against the counsel of his parents, who told him, "Harry, you'll find it hard out of Peoria." Eventually, he made things plenty hard for New England fans. Like Lannin, his presidential predecessor, he once was a bell-hop but later did quite well in the theatrical business as a producer; he also owned the Frazee Theatre in New York and had a piece of the Cort Theatre in Chicago. In fact, he brought Larry Graber of Chicago, assistant treasurer of the Cort, along to Boston as the Red Sox secretary.

Frazee's former fling into the sports world was as one of the promoters of the not-too-savory heavyweight championship fight between Jack Johnson and Jess Willard in Havana, April 5, 1915, in which Jack was counted out while shading his eyes from the Caribbean sun.

Harry's first problem was to sign his manager. One report in the *Sporting News* at the time had Bill Carrigan in "a receptive mood," and said that Harry could have signed Rough had he gone high enough. However, discussing that phase of his career, Carrigan told the author it was no question of money; he was through with baseball in the winter of 1916–17, and there was no attempt to hold up the new owner. The best that Holy Cross Bill could give the Boston fans was that if he ever really was needed, he would be back.

Convinced he couldn't get Carrigan, Frazee elevated the Red Sox's quick-thinking second baseman, Jack Barry, to the management, January 5. Black Jack was another Holy Cross alumnus and his first question after his appointment was, "Am I to be a real manager like Bill Carrigan?"

"Absolutely, Jack," replied Frazee. "Whatever you say goes."

The appointment was hastened by the fact that Hugh Ward, Frazee's early associate, was sailing for Australia. "Now that Jack Barry has been named manager, I can sail with my mind at ease," said Hugh. "Jack is one of the smartest fellows we have in baseball, and I am sure the club can win another pennant under him."

In the February 10, 1917, issue of *Sporting Life*, there appeared a story on Frazee's new holdout problems from the facile pen of Tim Murnane:

President Frazee of the Red Sox now is convinced that at least two-thirds of the players on the champion Red Sox have decided to ask for salary increases this season. The latest from Carl Mays, saying that he must have a raise of $1,400, was the last straw.

Three days before the date of this issue, Boston was shocked at the sudden death of genial Tim, its most beloved sports writer.

2

Giving the devil his due, Frazee, in his early years as Boston owner, did not show the ruinous proclivities of his later tenure. In both 1917 and 1918, he was trying to give Boston the best club he could put on the field. The United States entered World War I in April 1917, but big league ball was little affected that season. Barry had most of the players that Carrigan employed in 1916, and fought a good race, though eventually losing by nine games to the White

Sox, the club which had finished so strongly in 1916. Oddly enough, Barry's second-place 1917 team finished one point higher than did Carrigan's 1916 champions, .592 to .591.

Boston led most of the time up to June 8, when the White Sox overtook Barry's gladiators. The two clubs ran neck and neck for weeks, but after the Red Sox snatched the lead for a day, August 17, the White Sox really started rolling and ran away from Boston in September.

Nine years later, two of the players expelled in the Chicago "Black Sox" World Series scandal of 1919, shortstop Swede Risberg and first baseman Arnold "Chick" Gandil, created a stir when they charged that the 1917 Detroit Tigers "sloughed off" a series to the White Sox during the crucial days of that race. There was a mid-season 1917 series in which the White Sox defeated Detroit four straight, and Chicago stole seventeen bases on the Tiger catchers, mostly on Oscar Stanage, which had Barry's players blue in the face when they read the box scores. However, the late commissioner, Judge Landis, made a thorough investigation, held an open hearing in Chicago, to which he summoned thirty-five players, but eventually cleared everybody. Landis did find that the White Sox got up a purse from their 1917 World Series money to reward Detroit pitchers and Stanage for winning games from Boston, but that was a not uncommon practice at the time, though now strictly prohibited.

Even though Barry finished with practically the same percentage as Carrigan in 1916, there was a feeling that with Rough at the helm, the Red Sox might have made it three straight. Writing at the end of the season, Ralph McMillin had this to say: "Now, that all is over, there is something of a reaction, and it is extending even to the point of grumbling at the way Jack Barry handled the team. Fans are reminding each other that Bill Carrigan said he would return if the team needed him. Well, they are saying: 'It's plain the team needs Bill, and the best thing Frazee can do is bring him back.'" But Ralph doubted Bill would be back, since he was running a string of theaters as well as his bank.

Ruth matched his 1916 record and again checked in with twenty-three victories, while losing thirteen games. Mays, now a full-time regular, became the club's right-handed ace with a twenty-two-and-nine record, while Shore won thirteen and lost ten. The loss of the pennant was blamed on the slumps of Leonard and Foster. With a midseason losing streak of seven straight, Dutch had a .500 record with seventeen and seventeen. Foster changed his mind about retiring, but again was beset with miseries, and won eight games and lost seven. Duffy Lewis led the regular Red Sox hitters with .301, while Boston fans were remarking of Ruth, "Say, that big guy can hit as well as pitch." Babe hit .325 in fifty-two games, his hits including six doubles, three triples, and two homers. The Great McNally no longer batted for Ruth against left-handers.

Two 1917 Red Sox games which still are fresh in the memories of Boston fans are Ernie Shore's perfect game against Washington, June 23, and the Tim Murnane benefit game with the All-Stars, September 27.

Shore's game was all the more remarkable as Ernie wasn't Barry's starting pitcher. It was the first game of a Saturday double-header, and Ruth was Barry's pitching selection. The Babe walked Eddie Foster, the Washington lead-off man, or at least Brick Owens, the umpire behind the plate, called a fourth ball.

Babe stormed in to the plate and demanded, "What was the matter with that last one? Can't you see, you blind bat?"

"Get back to your position, you big ape," said Brick.

After a few more exchanges of compliments, Ruth hauled off and socked Brick on the neck. Of course, Babe immediately was tossed out of the ball game, and Boston writers were afraid it might be for the season. Ralph McMillin later complimented Ban Johnson for his leniency in letting Ruth off with a hundred-dollar fine and a week's suspension.

Having to dig up a pitcher in a hurry, Barry summoned Shore from the bench. Only a week before, Ernie had been suspended, along with Heinie Wagner, for a rumpus in Chicago, after which Frazee wired Johnson, "Why do you punish my men and let off the Chicago player who caused all the trouble, Buck Weaver?"

Owens gave Ernie a little time to warm up in the box. Foster, the man who was on base, was nipped on a steal, and Ernie retired the next twenty-six men as fast as they came up. Despite the fact that Ruth permitted the first man to reach base, baseball statisticians and historians always have termed it a perfect game for Shore, as no one reached base on Ernie. Along with the Grand Old Man, Cy Young, he is one of the six pitching immortals credited with this performance.

Some seventeen thousand fans turned out for the Tim Murnane benefit game, and Ralph McMillin, the chairman, turned a check for a little over $14,000 to Tim's widow. The Red Sox won a valiant 2-to-0 tussle from the greats of the American League, plus Rabbit Maranville, the crack Brave shortstop. The All-Stars were one of the greatest teams ever assembled and took the field with Maranville at short; Ray Chapman, second base; Ty Cobb, center field; Tris Speaker, left field; Joe Jackson, right field; Buck Weaver, third base; Steve O'Neill, catcher; Urban Shocker, Howard Ehmke, and Walter Johnson, pitchers.

Ruth and Foster pitched for the Red Sox, the Babe giving up only three hits in five innings and Foster none in the last four. Duffy Lewis won the game with an eighth-inning triple off Walter Johnson. John I. Taylor, the former president, was so pleased with "his boy," that he handed Lewis a check for $25, saying, "Duffy, you never made a better hit in your life." In pregame field events, Ruth won the prize for hitting the longest fungo, and Mike McNally won the bunt and run to first base contest.

And the Babe, by now an affluent young man of twenty-two, took to himself a bride, Helen Woodring, an attractive Nova Scotia waitress from Landers' Coffee Shop, in the neighborhood of Copley Square. "Do I know how to pick them?" said the Babe.

3

One more pennant was in the bag for the Red Sox before the great post–World War I plunge into the sea of despondency. The club won the 1918 flag in the curtailed war season of that year, Secretary of War Newton Baker and his draft director, General Enoch Crowder, having ordered the big leaguers to shut down on Labor Day, September 2, or be subject to the drastic "Work or Fight" order. It was an urgent invitation for the athletes to get into war plants or put on Uncle Sam's khaki or navy blue.

Of course, a lot of big leaguers had gone into the services, either by enlistment or the operation of the draft, long before Secretary Baker's order. A whole raft of Red Sox joined the colors in the winter of 1917–18, and as Boston is on the sea, most of the Red Sox warriors, headed by manager Barry selected the Navy. Red Sox servicemen included Duffy Lewis, Ernie Shore, Del Gainer, Mike McNally, Chick Shorten, Herb Pennock, Hal Janvrin, Jimmy Walsh, Fred Thomas, and lesser lights.

Dick Hoblitzel started the season at first base but played in only nineteen games, when he went into the Army and won a captain's commission. Incidentally, Ensign Ernie Shore was the only ball-player to win a navy commission in World War I. Dutch Leonard pitched in sixteen games in 1918 before he, too, went into the Navy.

To fill Barry's managerial post, Frazee named that doughty base-ball warrior of the major and minor league trails, Edward Grant

Barrow, as Black Jack's successor. As International League president, Barrow had safely piloted the loop through the stormy Federal League war, and as a reward he had his salary sharply slashed when the circuit ran into the bigger war. Ed snatched Frazee's offer. Barrow was no managerial novice, having formerly directed the Detroit Tigers, Toronto and Montreal Internationals, and Indianapolis Indians, and as owner-manager of the Paterson, New Jersey, club of the old Atlantic League he had developed the immortal Honus Wagner and sold him to Barney Dreyfuss, then the owner of the Louisville National League club. In later years, Barrow was the highly successful business manager and president of the New York Yankees.

He was a big two-fisted guy, and in his Red Sox days he still swung two formidable dukes. Once as manager of the Toronto club, he knocked out an umpire with a powerful right at the home plate in the Springfield ball park. Several times during the 1918 season, Babe Ruth, feeling his oats, became obstreperous. Once when Ruth didn't like Barrow's way of doing things, he threatened to join the shipyard team in Fall River. Barrow dismissed the other players, locked the clubhouse door, and said, "Now, Babe, let's have it out; we'll see who is a better man, you or me." When the door was opened, Ruth was much more amenable.

Yet strange as it may seem, there would have been no war pennant for the Red Sox if the later-day seller, Frazee, hadn't been a buyer in 1918. Frazee was flush with war money; he really opened the till and paid Connie Mack handsomely for the only players of caliber Connie had left of his old champions, first baseman Stuffy McInnis, center fielder Amos Strunk, catcher Wallie Schang, and pitcher Joe Bush.

In an earlier deal for Bush, Schang, and Strunk, Frazee gave up pitcher Vean Gregg, the sore-armed southpaw, catcher Chet Thomas, and outfielder Merlin Kopp, who was ticketed for the Army. According to 1918 reports, Frazee sweetened the deal with $60,000, which may have been a little exaggerated, but the check the theatrical man handed Connie was not for chicken feed. However, Harry, the trader, had to give up some pretty good material to get McInnis—third baseman Larry Gardner, outfielder Clarence Walker, the fellow purchased from St. Louis to fill Spoke's shoes, and catcher Forrest Cady.

McInnis was an especially popular acquisition at Fenway Park, as he came from Gloucester and was only eighteen when he jumped from the Gloucester High School to a utility infield role with the Athletics in 1909. Originally a shortstop, Stuffy became Harry

Davis' first-base successor on Mack's greatest Philadelphia teams. To fill Jack Barry's vacant spot at second base, Frazee and Barrow swung a smart interleague deal with the Reds, giving up pitcher George Foster for second baseman Dave Shean, a native of Arlington, Massachusetts, and product of Fordham University. Herrmann, the Red owner, was bilked on that one, as Foster never reported to Cincinnati. George Whiteman, the outfielder who was purchased from Houston with Speaker in 1907 and had a tryout with Chance's Yankees in 1913, was acquired from Toronto as a war replacement for Lewis.

Oddly enough the Red Sox won this flag with a percentage of .595, the club varying only four points in its closing days' figures in 1916, 1917, and 1918. On the Labor Day dead line, Barrow's club had seventy-five victories and fifty-one defeats. The second place Cleveland Indians had seventy-three wins and fifty-six defeats, finishing a half game ahead of Washington. While Boston's lead at the finish was only three and a half games, the Red Sox showed the way during most of the curtailed season. The Fenway boys led from April 20 to May 9, when Cleveland, sparked by Speaker, went to the fore for three days. But Boston sprang back in front on May 12 and showed the way until June 25. The Yankees and Indians enjoyed a few days of the rarefied first-place atmosphere around the July 4 holidays, but after the Red Sox regained the lead on July 6, they never were headed.

Barrow didn't exactly do it with mirrors, but he turned in a swell managerial job with a club which finished seventh in team batting with an average of .249. To bolster his offensive, Barrow made a daring move, and the Kaiser must be given a large assist on the play. If Wilhelm hadn't involved Uncle Sam in a war, no sane manager would have tried to make an outfielder out of Babe Ruth, a twenty-three game winner in both 1916 and 1917, especially to play him in place of Duffy Lewis, one of the great left fielders of all time.

But with Duffy in the Navy, and Whiteman, a right-handed hitter, batting .267, Barrow tried to find use for the sturdy bat of his big left-handed pitcher on days when the Babe wasn't pitching. He began playing Ruth in left field against right-handed pitchers, Whiteman playing the position against the southpaws, and the experiment exceeded Ed's fondest anticipations. In ninety-five games, Ruth hit an even .300, and knocked out ninety-five hits. However, what opened the eyes of the baseball world to Ruth's slugging potentiality was the big fellow's high percentage of extra-base hits, twenty-six doubles, eleven triples, and eleven home runs. His eleven round-trippers tied Tilly Walker, the former Red Sox, for the American League lead.

However, the 1918 club won largely on its tight defense. Barrow is as proud of the way he nurtured Sam Jones into a winner in 1918 as he is of converting Ruth into a wartime outfielder. Sad Sam was one of the players tossed into the Speaker deal in 1916 as a "little something extra." "I found Jones just another pitcher on the club," said Barrow; "no one had paid any attention to him. I quickly saw he had a most baffling delivery, made him one of my regular starters, and he rewarded me with sixteen victories against only five defeats. And from that season on, Sam was one of the league's best right-handers."

In between his outfielding, Ruth still had time to win thirteen games out of twenty decisions. Mays had a big year in that short season, winning twenty-one games and losing thirteen. Joe Bush, still suffering from Athletic tail-end habits, broke even in thirty games, and Dutch Leonard won eight and lost six before he went into the Navy.

Barrow's big trouble spot was third base. He started the season with Stuffy McInnis, the old Gloucester High shortstop, at the hot corner and Hoblitzel on first, but by May Hobby was off for the Army. Stuffy then moved over to his regular position at first, as Fred Thomas (who also went into the Navy during the season), Jack Stansbury, George Cochran, and Jack Coffey, now graduate manager of athletics at Fordham, all took a crack at third base. "Everybody plays third base on the Red Sox," said Scottie. "Just as soon as I know the name of the guy who's playing alongside of me, somebody else turns up to play the bag."

14

⊖

BARROW WINS WORLD WAR I
TITLE

I

WITH the regular league season clamped down for the duration on
Labor Day, it looked as if the 1918 World Series might be a war
casualty. But Garry Herrmann, chairman of the old National Commission, took a chance and wrote Newton D. Baker, Wilson's Secretary of War, asking for permission to play the series after the
holiday. He said a percentage of the receipts would go to war charities. Baker had been a former Democratic mayor in Cleveland and
was active in Democratic politics in north Ohio. Garry, on the other
hand, had been one of the leaders of the old Republican machine
in Cincinnati. Whether politics helped or hindered, Baker gave his
consent without any direct answer to Herrmann.

The Commission chairman received a wire from General Enoch
Crowder, who was in charge of the draft machinery in World War I
as follows:

The request contained in your letter of Aug. 21, asking for the extension of the application of the work or fight order to professional ball
players of the National and American Leagues is granted by the Secretary of War. The period of extension will be until Sept. 16. Necessary
instructions have been issued by telegraph. Crowder.

The order made possible the historic 1918 war series between the
Red Sox and the Chicago Cubs, one of the most unusual of the long

163

stretch of games played between the champions of the two major leagues. The Cubs were led by Fred Mitchell, the former Cambridge and Allston man who had been a pitcher under Jimmy Collins in 1901, the year the Red Sox came into Boston, and who was passed on to the Athletics in 1902. Fred also was a former Harvard baseball coach.

Mitchell's name really was Fred Yapp, which he had changed for obvious reasons. In the slang of that day, a yap was equivalent to the present-day "jerk." And Mitch was anything but that! He was one of the few players who switched from the sending to the receiving end of a battery, as he became a catcher under George Stallings on the New York Highlanders, the Rochester Internationals, and Boston Braves. He was Stallings' coach on the miracle Braves of 1914 and received credit for the development of the Big Chief's strong pitching staff. His smartness around pitchers and general baseball acumen led to his selection as Cub manager in 1917, when he succeeded the great shortstop of the old Chance machine, Joe Tinker.

Late in the season, Barrow had sent pitchers Joe Bush and Carl Mays and catcher Sam Agnew to Pittsburgh to scout the Cubs when they were playing there. "They're a good ball club," "Bullet Joe" reported, "but we can take 'em."

In a war move to strengthen the Cubs, the Chicago president, Charles H. Weeghman, had acquired the crack Philadelphia battery of Alexander and Killefer for $60,000 and some lesser players, but the Red Sox were not being asked to face their 1915 World Series foe. Uncle Sam had taken care of that; he drafted Aleck after he had pitched only three 1918 games.

Even without Alexander, Mitchell had a good wartime club, strong enough to finish with a percentage of .651, ten and a half games ahead of the second-place Giants. And Mitch still was strong in pitchers with a formidable pair of southpaws, Jim Vaughn, former Yankee, and George Tyler, a member of Stallings' great trio of 1914, and two sturdy right-handers, Claude Hendrix, a former Pirate, and "Shufflin' Phil" Douglas, a giant Alabamian, who could do as much with a spitball as Chesbro or Walsh when his manager could keep him on the reservation. However, Mitchell had such respect for Ruth's extra-base prowess that his strategy throughout the 1918 series was to keep Babe from playing the outfield. His two lefties, Vaughn and Tyler, pitched virtually the entire six games; Hendrix and Douglas each worked only one inning for the Cubs.

By an odd twist of the baseball fates, Fred Merkle, who had played against the Red Sox in a Giant uniform in the series of 1912, and again with Brooklyn in 1916, now bobbed up as the first base-man for the Cubs. Charley Pick, the former Athletic, was on second; Charley Hollocher, a miniature Honus Wagner but a hypochondriac who later committed suicide, was the Chicago shortstop, and Chuck Deal, Stallings' 1914 third baseman, was stationed at the hot corner. The Cub outfield was made up of three speed boys, Les Mann, Dode Paskert, and Max Flack, while the Chicago catcher also could carry the mail, Bill "Reindeer" Killefer. Paskert and Killefer were vet-erans of the 1915 Philly–Red Sox rumpus.

Following the precedent of the Boston clubs, who took advantage of their rival league parks because of their greater capacity in 1914, 1915, and 1916, the Cubs moved their World Series down to Comis-key's ball yard in Chicago's South Side and played to a lot of empty seats. In the language of Dizzy Dean, they might as well have "stood" in their own twenty-thousand capacity park on the North Side. Frazee was smarter; he didn't transfer his games to Braves Field as in the two Carrigan series, feeling his own Fenway Park could take care of all the business, and he was very right.

Because of war travel conditions, the old National Commission decided to play the first three games in Chicago, September 4, 5, and 6, and then finish the series in Boston, which meant the Hub would get anywhere from one to four games. With a good part of the public apathetic toward the series, and some openly critical, it was decided not to raise the general admission prices, which invariably is done at World Series. As a result the gate was most meager—only $179,619 for six games, and when the players learned they were playing for peanuts, they almost broke up the series.

The Navy gave the Red Sox a break when they furloughed third baseman Fred Thomas so that he could play in the series. It enabled Barrow to patch his weakest position.

That Boston's chances were not considered too good prior to the opening of the series was apparent from Burt Whitman's Boston letter to the *Sporting News*:

Odds, outside of Boston, favor the Chicago Cubs in the Series. If the Cubs win the opening game the odds will be long and will favor the Mitchellmen more than ever. But long odds will spur on the Red Sox. The psychology of being the underdog is great medicine. If the Sox can win one of the three games in Chicago, they ought to even it up right off the reel when they get back to Boston and then go on ahead.

Burt's observations tell the story of what confronted Barrow when he faced the Cubs in the postponed first game, September 5, before

a rather disappointing crowd of 19,274. Rain had delayed the start
of the series a day. Ed Barrow knew the importance of winning that
first game, also that Mitchell would open with Jim "Hippo" Vaughn,
a 215-pounder who won twenty-two out of thirty-two games and was
the National League's earned-run leader with 1.74. As this would
keep Ruth out of the outfield, Barrow had the happy hunch of starting the Babe on the mound against Hippo. Barrow, at seventy-eight,
still chuckled on how he crossed the writers, who felt sure he would
open the series with a right-hander, Bush, Mays, or Jones.

The Bambino got off the Sox on the right red-stockinged foot with
a 1-to-0 shutout victory, holding the Cubs to six hits, while his Boston mates made only five off Vaughn. Big Jim had only one slip, and
that proved fatal. He walked Dave Shean to start the fourth, and
Strunk popped a fly to Vaughn trying to sacrifice. However, Georgie
Whiteman stabbed a single to center, his second hit, and drove
Shean to third. Stuffy McInnis came through like the grand little
campaigner that he was. He was a dead left-field hitter, and
Mitchell tried to place his fielders accordingly, but Mac lined a
single over third baseman Deal's head, scoring Shean. It was the last
hit Boston made off Vaughn that day.

Ruth was in two tough spots, and each time he picked on the
Athletic discard, Charley Pick, to get him out of the hole. With two
down in the first inning, Mann's grounder took a lucky hop over
Shean's head for a single, and Les ran to third on Paskert's single to
center. Ruth pitched gingerly to Merkle, a right-handed hitter, and
eventually walked him, filling the bases. But Pick left the full house
with an easy fly to Whiteman.

Scottie made one of the historic World Series shortstopping plays
in the seventh inning, but it was only possible because the batter
was the slow-moving Hippo Vaughn. The burly southpaw shot a hot
grounder between short and third, and no one even suspected a play
was possible until Everett made a flying leap and stabbed the ball
with his bare hand. Without even looking up, he whirled completely
around and pegged the ball to McInnis at first in time to beat
Vaughn by a step. Even the partisan Chicago fans arose almost to a
man to cheer the brilliant play. Boston writers compared it to a
similar play Scott had made on Jake Daubert in the second game of
the 1916 Series when Ruth also was the beneficiary.

Ed Barrow loves to tell a little story on the Babe's pitching that
day. In various clubhouse sessions, he had gone over the Cub line-up
with his players, and especially had stressed that Leslie Mann, a

right-handed hitter, could be particularly tough on left-handers. Mann was a little fellow, but stocky and well built.

Several times, Ed reminded Ruth: "Never let up on that Mann; keep bearing down on him all the time. And loosen Leslie up the first time you face him."

The Chicago lead-off man was Max Flack, a chap about Mann's height but not quite so sturdy and a left-handed batsman. Giving it everything he had, Ruth whistled three fast balls over on Max for a quick strike-out.

Grinning from ear to ear and quite pleased with himself, Babe yelled over to Barrow, "Well, I guess I took care of that guy Mann for you, eh?"

2

"We've got that big first one," Barrow told his players in the clubhouse before the second game, September 6. "Joe Bush is going to do our pitching. We're sure to get Tyler; he's a good left-hander, and we won't make many hits off him, but he isn't as fast as Vaughn, and if we wait for our chance, we can beat him."

However, Tyler was too good; he yielded only one clean hit in the first seven innings, weakened a little at the finish, but had enough in reserve to defeat Bush by a score of 3 to 1 to tie up the series. A somewhat larger crowd of 20,040 was out, but there still were rows of empty seats in Comiskey's big park. The game was lost to all intents and purposes by the Barrowites in the second inning, when Chicago scored its three runs, two hammered in by Bush's pitching rival, Tyler.

Bullet Joe lost Fred Merkle after a count of two strikes and three balls, and the former Giant walked. Pick rapped what appeared to be an easy grounder at Thomas, but instead of waiting for the longer bounce, Fred came in fast to field the ball on a short hop, and it hopped past him for a single. Bush set down Deal on a pop fly to Shean, but Reindeer Killefer came through with a two-base wallop to right, scoring Merkle, and it took a great throw by Hooper to hold Pick on third. However, the beautiful peg went to waste, for with the infield playing in, Tyler rifled a single through the box and Pick and Killefer scampered home.

After Tyler had the Red Sox hypnotized for seven innings, they did a little hitting in the last two frames. Schang, batting for Agnew, singled in the eighth, and Hooper also punched a safety to right, but Flack, the Chicago right fielder, shot down Wallie at third with the kind of play baseball men term a "perfect strike." The throw came to third baseman Deal on a beeline—smack into his glove, and Deal just had time to stoop and tag Schang as Wallie came sliding into the base.

The Sox had a little dynamite left for the ninth, and Mitchell had Douglas and Hendrix working furiously in the bull pen after Amos Strunk and George Whiteman hit successive triples. However, Tyler worked himself out of the hole at the expense of one run, striking out pinch hitter Jean Dubuc and getting rid of the dangerous Schang on a fly to Hollocher.

This game was no Sunday school strawberry festival, and several times it threatened to develop into a free-for-all. The feud really had started in the first game, when Heinie Wagner, the Boston coach, used his jockey's whip on Vaughn, who during his New York Yankee career was known as one of the "lazy'nest" men in the league. In the second game in retaliation, Otto Knabe, the former Philly captain and utility infielder on the Cubs, gave Bush the works, especially in the second inning when the hits were whistling past Joe's ears. "You're not ducking fast enough; you'll be killed if you stay out there," taunted Otto.

The argument then shifted back to Wagner and Vaughn, when Heinie came out to the coaching lines for Boston in the third inning. The Texan shouted something from the bench which got under the New Yorker's skin, and Heinie charged into the Cub dugout after the 215-pound left-hander. Several of the Red Sox followed in Heinie's wake, and with the help of the umpires pulled apart the battlers. When Wagner emerged, it was evident he had been put through the mill. His face was bruised and his back was covered with mud and water, but the umpires, Hildebrand, Klem, Owens, and O'Day, took no action against the fighters.

The war almost broke out again a few innings later, when Les Mann had to duck quickly to avoid being hit by an inside pitch, and getting up, he stormed at Bush and accused Joe of pitching a bean ball. Mann hit the ball down to McInnis, and when he saw that Bush was going to cover the first-base bag, bumped heavily into the Boston pitcher. Both soon were sputtering and swinging, but Klem, the first-base umpire, quickly sprang between the pair and preserved the peace for the old National Commission.

3

Burt Whitman had written that if Boston won one of the three games in Chicago, the Red Sox would be in good position for a strong finish in Boston. They did even better, as chunky Carl Mays, with his tricky submarine delivery, sank the Cubs, 2 to 1, in the third game of the set, September 7. By this time Saturday had rolled around, and a pleasant early fall day brought out 27,054 fans, the best crowd of the series.

Mitchell crossed the writers, who had named right-hander Hendrix as his pitcher, by coming back with his big southpaw Hippo Vaughn, after only one day's rest, and though the huge Texan pitched another fine game, he again finished on the wrong side. In eighteen innings, the Cubs scored only one run for him. "What the hell does one have to do to win one of these things," he wailed. And Reach's 1919 *Guide,* reports: "There was continued bitter feeling between the rival players."

Each pitcher gave up seven hits, but as in the first game, the fourth inning was Boston's lucky frame and Vaughn's hoodoo round. Jim got into difficulty when he plunked Whiteman with a pitched ball, and George scored on successive line singles by McInnis and Schang. Then Scottie's single drove Stuffy over the scoring dish with what proved to be the winning run. After the fourth, Boston put only two more runners on base.

Mays was in hot water several times, but Carl had the benefit of brilliant support, and the Cubs penetrated his defense for only one run in the fifth when Pick drove through Scott for a two-bagger and raced home on Merkle's single to left.

In the preceding inning, Whiteman, who was getting more and more into the Cubs' fur, robbed Paskert of a two-run homer with a spectacular running catch. Reach's *Guide* records: "The shift in pitching selections broke well for Boston, for had Ruth been covering left field instead of Whiteman, Dode Paskert would have had a home run in the fourth inning and two Chicago runs would have crossed the plate. Ruth could not have made the catch Whiteman did, one of the best of the Series."

One of the thrills for the Saturday crowd was reserved for the ninth inning, when in the last second of the game the Cubs almost tied the score. It all started with two out, when Charley Pick beat out an infield single to Dave Shean on a hairline decision. And in a jiffy Charley was on third; he stole second and then made third when one of Mays's tricky uphill shoots jumped out of Schang's mitt for a passed ball.

The ball rolled only a few feet away from Wallie, who quickly recovered and threw down to Thomas at third. The play was close, and umpire Hildebrand had raised his hand to wave the runner out, when he observed that Thomas had failed to hold the ball and that it had trickled away.

Pick and Thomas both were mixed up on the ground, and it was a play similar to a "loose ball" in football. Thomas finally was the first to get on his feet, while the wild Chicago crowd was beseeching Pick to get up and score the tying run. Had Charley been free-footed after the spilled throw he undoubtedly could have done so, but by the time he started for the plate, it was too late. Schang was waiting for him with Thomas' return throw, and Wallie had the plate well blocked off. Pick tried his best to dislodge him, but Charley bounced back from the collision and rolled over on the ground, while Wallie stood like a statue as he watched Bill Klem give the signal that Pick was out, ending the game.

4

As the players of the two teams traveled to Boston on the "National Commission Special" on Sunday, the eighth, there was plenty of grousing in the athletes' cars over the failure of the Commission to schedule a game in Chicago on the Sunday. Since the first game, the series had picked up considerably in enthusiasm and attendance and a Sunday game unquestionably would have taxed the 1918 capacity of Comiskey Park.

The players had an even greater beef. The winter before, John K. Tener, the former National League president, who resigned in July 1918, had put over his plan for having all the first-division players of both major leagues share in the World Series players' pool. Prior to 1918, the pool had gone only to the players of the contending teams, but at Tener's insistence, the second-, third-, and fourth-place players now also had been declared in for smaller cuts of the series melon.

It was unfortunate that this worthy plan should first have been tried out in a war year. With crowds under capacity, and no increase over the regular season prices, the players figured their shares would be the smallest in years, so despite the bickering and feuding on the ball field, the Red Sox and Cubs declared a truce long enough to select Captain Harry Hooper and Les Mann, the Chicago left fielder, as their spokesmen to wait on the National Committee. Harry and Les made a request that the Commission withhold the Tener plan until peacetime and give the contending Boston and Chicago players the entire players' pool, as was the custom for years.

"I'm sorry, boys," explained old Garry Herrmann, "but the Commission is only an enforcement agency. We don't make the rules. Voting in those other first-division players was done by the National and American Leagues, and the Commission has no power or authority to change their action."

The players grumbled but went on with the fourth game which was played at Fenway Park on Monday, September 9, before 22,183. Mayor Peters, still wearing his summer straw hat, threw out the first ball; "Honey" Fitzgerald rallied some of the old Royal Rooters, and Boston fans left the park in a joyous mood when the Red Sox gained that big three-to-one edge by winning another tight, thrilling game, this time by a score of 3 to 2.

Barrow came back with Ruth, hero of the Chicago first-game shutout, and Mitchell threw in George Tyler, his left-handed second-game winner. However, where Barrow had Ruth batting ninth in the first game, this time he had Babe swinging from the seventh notch in the batting order, with Everett Scott eighth and Sam Agnew ninth. The Bambino eventually was replaced by Joe Bush in the ninth, but Ruth was credited with the victory, and before Chicago scored on him in the eighth, Ruth had pitched twenty-nine consecutive scoreless World Series innings (including thirteen in 1916) and taken the record from the former Giant pitching master, Christy Mathewson, who formerly held the top mark with twenty-eight. And today, as Ruth sits at ease in his dressing gown in his New York apartment and chats of big moments of his great career he would rather talk of those twenty-nine World Series innings with Boston and of the time he fanned Cobb, Crawford, and Veach with the bases full than about his sixty homers with the 1927 Yankees.

Ruth also made his first World Series hit in this game; it was a glorious affair and largely responsible for the Red Sox victory. As in games numbers one and three, the "Lucky Fourth" was the big inning. Shean started it with a walk and stole second, helped by Killefer's short passed ball. After Strunk flied out, Whiteman walked, but McInnis forced Tyler at third. A roar went up from the Boston rooters, when Ruth toted his piece of lumber to the plate.

"Hit it out, Babe!" "Win your own game!" "You can do it!" were among the cries of encouragement.

But it looked as if Tyler had no intention of giving the big fellow a good ball to hit. Anyway, the left-hander pitched three straight balls, all wide of the plate, and then changing his tactics, slipped over a slow curve which the eager Babe bit at and missed for a first strike. Brick Owens called a second strike; and then Tyler made his fatal mistake; he tried to sneak over a third strike. Babe met the ball waist-high and sent the sphere spinning far over Flack's head in right field for a triple, bringing in Whiteman and McInnis. Tyler then retired Scott, leaving Ruth to languish on third. Manager Mitchell was sorely criticized for not walking Ruth, as Scott was hitting .071 at the time, also for not playing Flack deeper in right field.

Two double plays and Max Flack's wanderings off first base helped Babe to keep his slate clean until the eighth. Max apparently was having day dreams; once catcher Agnew's peg to McInnis caught him off his base of supplies, and later it was Ruth who picked him off first.

The Cubs finally scored on Ruth in the eighth, tying the score with two tallies, the first National League runs recorded on the Bambino since Hi Myers hit that trick home run in the first inning of the second game of the 1916 series. Killefer opened with a walk, and Claude Hendrix, batting for Tyler, lined a pinch single to left. Both runners advanced on a wild pitch. On an attempted squeeze play, the unlucky Flack bunted a pop fly to McInnis. It looked as if Stuffy missed a chance for a double play, as Hendrix had run almost to third, and the Gloucester boy held the ball and permitted Claude to scuttle back to second.

Killefer then scored on Hollocher's infield out, and McCabe, who was sent in to run for the intrepid Hendrix, fetched in the tying run on Mann's single. But Ruth got rid of Paskert for the third out on a grounder to Thomas.

Phil Douglas, the big spitball pitcher, took the hill for Chicago in the second half of the eighth, and the Red Sox promptly regained the lead by jolting a run out of the Shuffler. Schang, batting for Agnew, banged out a pinch single and landed on second a moment later when one of Phil's moistened shoots slipped through Killefer's glove. Hooper sacrificed, and when Douglas threw the ball into right field, trying to throw out Harry, Schang scored, and Hooper pulled up at second. Harry hung around the bag, while Shean and Strunk went out on outfield flies and Deal tossed out Whiteman.

Barrow did his best to let Ruth finish what he started, but after Babe walked Merkle and Zeider, the first two men to face him in the ninth, Ed yanked him off the rubber, sent Ruth to left field, and called in Bush from the bull pen. A great play by McInnis on Wortman brought the crowd to its feet. The batter tried to sacrifice, but Stuffy, anticipating the play, ran almost to the plate for the ball, and without steadying himself, whipped the pellet to Thomas for a force play at third. Turner Barber then batted for Killefer, and his grounder to Scott was converted into a fast double play, which ended the game and gave Ruth his third World Series triumph.

5

A strike of the World Series gladiators almost prevented the fifth game at Fenway Park, September 10, and well nigh gave baseball one of its worst black eyes. With the end of four games, the players had ceased sharing in the receipts, and they believed this was the time to thresh out the dispute with the Commission about their individual shares.

Fans, reaching the Boston baseball orchard, were surprised to see no sign of activity on the diamond, while the players, in uniform, huddled sulkingly in their dressing rooms, engaged in animated conversation. A crowd of 24,694 was on hand, and there were angry murmurs when game time approached with no pitchers warming up or other signs of action. The Boston police chief, having been tipped off that something was in the wind, had several hundred extra policemen on hand. He feared there might be a riot when the fans learned there would be no game, which was the outlook at two o'clock.

While these murmurings were going on at the park, Ban Johnson, the American League member of the Commission, was at a convivial drinking party at the Copley Plaza. Ban was with Taylor Spink, then the young publisher of the *Sporting News* and an official scorer of the series, and several congenial companions. A fishing-tackle manufacturer from Bristol, Connecticut, Charley Riley, joined the group, and soon Ban and Charley tried to match each other with high tales of their piscatorial accomplishments.

In high good humor, and about three sheets to the wind, Ban reached the park about five minutes before scheduled game time to learn the entire park was waiting on him. The other two commissioners, August Herrmann and John Heydler; manager Ed Barrow of the Red Sox, and former Mayor Fitzgerald of Boston all had pleaded with the players to go on, but with an obstinate persistency they refused to budge.

Herrmann and Heydler were in the umpires' dressing room with the spokesmen for the players, Harry Hooper and Les Mann. The players, turned down in their request that no money be paid the other first-division players, offered a compromise. They would agree to take the field if the Commission promised to pay each of the winning players $1,500, and the losers, $1,000. That, too, was rejected, and Hooper said, "Then, let nobody get anything out of it; let's give the entire receipts to the Red Cross."

That was the situation when Ban came blinking into the room. Other baseball officials and about two dozen sports writers had crowded into the little chamber. "What is all this? Why aren't these players on the field?" asked Johnson. In as few words as possible, Herrmann and Heydler tried to give him the low-down.

Assuming an air of grave if unsteady dignity, Johnson turned to Hooper and boomed in pontifical tones: "Harry, do you realize you are a member of one of the greatest organizations in the world—the American League? And do you realize what you will do to its good name if you don't play?"

Before Harry had a chance to reply, Ban flung a heavy but affectionate arm around his shoulder, and leaning heavily on the Red Sox star, he importuned: "Harry, go out there and play. The crowd is waiting for you."

Hooper turned to Mann, and both shrugged their shoulders. It was evident that Ban was in no condition to talk serious business. Both emissaries returned to their respective dressing rooms; there was more excited conversation, but in another ten minutes the players charged on the field amid the cheers of the crowd. They had won no concessions, and Hooper and Mann gave out a statement that they "agreed to play for the sake of the public, and the wounded soldiers in the stands." "Honey" Fitzgerald, without his silk hat but in good voice, informed the crowd he had been authorized to make the statement for the players.

However, the incident brought much unfavorable publicity for the players. A baseball strike in wartime was called the last word in baseball lunacy, while there were uncomplimentary references to the "greed" and "commercialism" of the athletes. Yet it had its amusing, even ludicrous, side. The backdown of the players might never have taken place but for the hopelessness of dealing with the exhilarated Johnson.

The fifth game finally got under way nearly an hour late, and Mitchell threw in big Jim Vaughn for the third time. On this occasion the huge left-hander pitched a 3-to-0 shutout, and he kept the series alive with a decision over Sam Jones. Vaughn held the Red Sox to five thin hits, seventeen for the three games in which he faced them, but young Jones also turned in a steady job, and it was anybody's game until the Cubs iced it with two runs in the ninth. Hollocher was especially troublesome for Jones; Charley wasn't feeling so well, so he prodded out three of the seven Cub hits and scored two of their three runs.

Chicago scored its first run in the third, when Hollocher completely outwitted Stuffy McInnis. With two out, Hollie worked Sad Sam for a pass and took a long lead off first base. Agnew snapped the ball down to first, and it looked as though Hollocher was a dead duck. McInnis groped with the ball for a phantom Hollocher, only to look up and see the flesh-and-blood Hollocher scampering into second. While the crowd still was laughing at Stuffy's discomfiture, Mann slashed a double down the left-field foul line, driving in Hollocher.

That one run would have sufficed for Vaughn, but the Cubs propped Hippo Jim with two more in the ninth. Sad Sam put himself in a hole by passing Flack, and fortune smiled again on Hollocher. He tapped a bunt down the left-field foul line. Fred Thomas stood over it, watching it wriggle down the chalk mark. Fred hoped and prayed it would roll foul, but eventually it came to rest a half inch in fair territory. Paskert brought in Max and Hollie with a double to the left-field fence.

6

Vaughn's fifth-game win only delayed the Red Sox's fifth world championship by a day. Barrow's players terminated the series on the eleventh, Carl Mays winning his second 2-to-1 game of the series, this time gaining the verdict over George Tyler. The near strike of the previous day soured Boston's stomach for the series, as the crowd for the finale dipped to 15,238.

Max Flack came out of the sixth game with the goat's horns, which Fred Snodgrass wore in 1912, but Mays won the new crown for the Red Sox by pitching a brilliant three-hitter. The Bostonians made only five hits themselves off Tyler, but George also walked five, and with Flack's help that proved enough for the Sox. Mays walked only two, and two of the Cubs who reached base were picked off on neat throws by Carl and Schang. Only two Cubs were left on base in the nine innings.

Tyler's wildness beat him in the third inning when the Red Sox scored twice without a hit. Tyler began the inning by walking his pitching rival, Mays, and Hooper sacrificed Carl to second. Then Shean worked the Cub left-hander for another pass. Strunk, a batting weakling during the series, expired on a grounder to Pick, and then came the blow which slew the Cubs. Whiteman met a curve solidly and sent a stinging line drive to right field. Flack judged it perfectly, but he couldn't close his hands around the ball, and as it slipped through his nervous fingers, Mays and Shean dashed home with the big runs.

The Cubs had a chance to even things in the fourth, but got only one run out of a promising opening. Trying to atone for his error, Flack opened with a single to center, and after Hollocher rolled out, Mann was nicked on the ankle with a pitched ball. But while Mann was woolgathering off first, perhaps thinking of the strike settlement of the previous day, Schang snapped the ball down to Stuffy and caught Leslie off the bag. The nap proved especially painful for the Cubs when Paskert followed with a walk, which would have filled the bases, and Merkle followed with a single which scored only Flack. The round ended with Hooper spearing Pick's line drive, and from there on Mays blew down the Cubs as fast as they came up.

There was no wild demonstration such as followed the previous world championships won by the Red Sox. Some even said the better team didn't win, which got quite a rise out of Burt Whitman, who wrote: " 'The Cubs were the better team and should have won.' That, my dears, is the backwash of the old disgruntled prophet, the unvarnished bunk."

After the National Commission took out the 10 per cent for war charities, and the other first-division teams were given their cuts, there wasn't too much left for the gladiators. As the players realized, their checks were most modest. The winning Red Sox pulled down $1,108.45 a man, and the losing Cubs, $671. Captain Hooper requested that the Red Sox's war charities deductions be turned over to him so the Boston players could give the money at their discretion. Herrmann acceded, and sent Harry a check for $2,083.75.

The Red Sox won their fifth series with the anemic team batting average of .188 against .210 for the Cubs. The generally acknowledged hero of the series was Georgie Whiteman, the thirty-two-year-old war replacement from Toronto. He had fielded brilliantly throughout the series and did potent damage with his .250 batting average. McInnis also hit .250. Schang was tops with .444, getting four hits in nine times at bat, but Wallie caught only two complete games. Mays and Ruth each scored two victories, and the Babe did a lot of damage with his one triple.

Ed Barrow always has been proud of the 1918 Red Sox world champions. "We were a war team, and we didn't hit much," said Ed, "but we hit enough to win. But there's one thing about that 1918 series that often has been overlooked, and that is our fielding. I've attended most of the World Series, but I think the Red Sox fielding in 1918 was the greatest I've ever seen. We made only one error in the six games, for the remarkable fielding average of .996. As all of our victories were by one run, two 2-to-1 games, one 1-to-0, and one 3-to-2, you can realize what that near-perfect fielding meant to the manager sitting on the bench. There were probably a half-dozen times in each of these games where a boot would have changed victory into defeat. But my 1918 boys never faltered."

And Harry Frazee still wasn't such a bad kind of a guy in Boston. After congratulating the New Yorker on winning his first world championship, and his handling of the tickets in Boston, Burt Whitman wrote: "He's still batting high in the Put-it-Over League. People who think Harry is a boob can have their little fun, but he'll be there with bells on when a lot of them will be eating hay."

15

⊖

THE RAPE OF THE RED SOX

WHAT happened in the years after the 1918 pennant has been described as "Boston baseball's dark ages," "Harry Frazee's crime," and some other niceties which wouldn't pass Boston's book censors. Burt Whitman, who suffered through it all, terms it "the Rape of the Red Sox."

Harry Frazee once told the author the rape wasn't premeditated. He didn't plan it that way; it just happened. He needed money, and the Yankee colonels, Ruppert and Huston, hungry for a winner, had plenty of it. At the time, the Yankee office on Forty-second Street was only two doors from Frazee Theatre, where Harry had his office. So Red Sox stars gravitated to the Polo Grounds, where the Yankees were still playing then, and Ruppert-autographed checks helped Frazee's depleted checking account.

Though Harry later produced one of musical comedy's biggest hits, *No! No! Nanette*, with its tuneful "Tea for Two," which had five companies on the road at one time, there was a period after the war when flop followed flop. Frazee used to put posters advertising his shows on the entrances to Fenway Park, and one of his fairly successful shows was *My Lady Friends*. A disgusted Boston fan looked at the sign and said none too kindly, "Well, they're the only friends the so-and-so has." And when Harry would sell another ballplayer to the Yanks, Johnny Drohan of the Boston *Traveler* would exclaim, "Well, another of Frazee's road companies will eat for the next few weeks."

Yet when the war ended, and Frazee's service players came tumbling back, Harry was really in pretty much the same position as was Sam Breadon, of the present-day Cardinals, in the winter of 1945–46. Harry had a world champion team and more good players than his man Ed Barrow knew what to do with. Having purchased McInnis, Schang, Strunk, Bush, and Shean in 1918, Harry felt he could afford to unload a little of the higher-priced members of Carrigan's old champions and pick up a tidy check in the bargain. He disposed of the two prewar pitching aces, Ernie Shore and Dutch Leonard, and Duffy Lewis to the Yankees in a deal for catcher Al Walters, pitchers Ray Caldwell and Slim Love, and outfielder Frank Gilhooley. A $50,000 check also went to "Frazz," as Huston affectionately called him when the pair were drinking companions. Caldwell brought more cash in a subsequent sale to Cleveland.

The deal wasn't of a great help to New York; neither Lewis nor Shore returned to their prewar stardom, while Leonard injured Ruppert's feelings during a salary dispute and was passed on to Detroit. However, the trade started the evil Frazee practice of selling star players "down the [Hudson] river," and had many subsequent ramifications.

Babe Ruth had quite a salary wrangle with Frazee before he signed his 1919 contract; he got himself a manager and even threatened to take up pugilism and go after John L. Sullivan's old heavyweight crown. That made Barrow laugh. Even though Ruth electrified the baseball world by hitting twenty-nine homers that 1919 season, the world champions of 1918 fell kerplunk into sixth place with a percentage of .4818, the Browns beating them for fifth with .4820. That was a terrible comedown, but Ruth kept the eyes of the nation on the once mighty Red Sox.

As far back as the training season, the hefty Baltimore boy made history by hitting a home run of over five hundred feet off George Smith in a Red Sox–Giant exhibition game in Tampa. Paul Shannon, Frankie Graham, the author, and other enterprising Boston and New York reporters diligently measured it out on the old Tampa fairgrounds with a tape measure.

In 1919, twenty-nine homers was considered the very stratosphere of home-run hitting. The American League record was sixteen, established by Socks Seybold of the 1901 Athletics, and the generally accepted major record was twenty-five by Buck Freeman, the early Red Socker, with the Washington National League club of 1899. As Ruth's magic bat spouted forth home runs, they dug up a mark of twenty-seven made by Ed Williamson, early Chicago White Stocking, in 1884, but the Babe tied that one, September 20, with a hefty belt off Lefty Williams, chunky White Sox left-hander, at Fenway Park.

Ruth always could save his greatest feats for the biggest crowds. On this occasion, the Père Marquette Council of the Knights of Columbus was having a day for Ruth at the Boston orchard. Despite the fact that the Red Sox were going nowhere, the Council went to town and filled the park in Ruth's honor, and the Babe did his stuff, tying Williamson's ancient record.

Johnny Drohan asked Ruth, "What did Frazee give you for drawing all those people to his park?"

"Oh, a cigar," replied Babe.

Ruth didn't stop with twenty-seven home runs but hit his twenty-eighth off Bob Shawkey of the Yanks, September 24, and his twenty-ninth off Jordan of Washington on the twenty-seventh. People then said that new mark probably would stand for another fifty years. Ruth almost doubled it the next season.

Babe hit four grand-slam homers in 1919, the most picturesque being the one which knocked Lee Fohl right off the managerial bench in Cleveland and made the Gray Eagle a big league pilot. In a clutch situation, Fohl pulled out his southpaw Fritz Coumbe, a former Red Sox, and sent in Hi Jasper to face Ruth with the bases full. George Herman knocked his first pitch over the right-field screen at Cleveland's League Park, and that night Jim Dunn, the Cleveland boss, fired Fohl and put Tris Speaker, Boston's old star, in command.

Ed Barrow never liked golfing ballplayers, but two of the Red Sox, Harry Hooper and Everett Scott, played daily matches on the road with Burt Whitman. "And Barrow couldn't say a word about it," said Burt, "as Harry and Scottie were playing the best ball on the club." Scott also was the card wizard of the league, and it made no difference whether the game was bridge, hearts, poker, or blackjack. The Red Sox had one refrain: "Even though Scottie comes up with deuces, he never loses."

Carl Mays ran out on the 1919 Red Sox and precipitated one of baseball's worst feuds. Carl wasn't gifted with an angelic disposition, and when, after winning twenty-two games in 1917 and twenty-one in 1918, he went into midseason with five games won and eleven lost, he got the idea some of the boys weren't trying too hard on days when he was on the hill.

After several errors had been made behind him in a game at Comiskey Park, Chicago, on July 13, he left the contest in a huff between innings, saying, "I'll never pitch another game for the Red Sox."

Barrow didn't take it too seriously at first and sent another player to the clubhouse, saying, "Tell Carl to forget about it and get back in the game." The player brought back word that Carl had dressed, and was about to leave the park. Mays's last words were, "Tell Barrow I've gone fishing."

Mays took a train back to Boston, ignored telegrams which Frazee and Barrow sent him to return to the club, and went on that fishing trip. In the meantime, the Yankees, White Sox, Indians, Tigers, and Browns all made offers to the Red Sox for Mays. Ban Johnson passed word around that he wanted no Mays deal until the submarine expert made peace with the Boston club, and thought there was a general understanding to that effect. He also expressed his displeasure with Frazee for not putting Carl under suspension.

Then, on July 29, sixteen days after Mays walked out on Barrow in Chicago, the stocky pitcher was sold to the Yankees for $40,000, the New York club also tossing in pitchers Allan Russell and Bob McGraw. Johnson was incensed at Frazee and the Yankee owners, tried to block the deal, and instructed his umpires not to permit Mays to play in a New York uniform. He issued the following statement to the press:

Baseball cannot tolerate such a breach of discipline. It was up to the owners of the Boston club to suspend Carl Mays for breaking his contract and when they failed to do so, it is my duty as head of the American League to act. Mays will not play with any club until the suspension is raised. He should have reported to the Boston club before they made any trade or sale.

The Yankee owners, however, procured an injunction restraining Johnson and his umpires from interfering with Mays's pitching for New York. The league broke up into two factions, with Frazee, the Yankee colonels, and Comiskey of Chicago called the "Insurrectionists," and the owners of the other clubs, Navin of Detroit, Griffith of Washington, Mack and Shibe of Philadelphia, Dunn of Cleveland, and Ball of St. Louis, termed the "Loyal Five." There were suits and countersuits, with the Yankees eventually suing Johnson and his "Loyal Five" for $500,000. They brought up the Speaker deal of 1916, in which they hadn't had a chance to bid for Tris, and charged that Ban had tried to manipulate things so that Mays also would land in Cleveland.

Johnson wouldn't recognize the games Mays, protected by the court order, pitched for New York, and issued two sets of averages. In one, he tossed out the games Carl pitched for the Yankees. The third place World Series shares also were held up, as the Yankees were third with Mays's New York victories, fourth without them. The "Insurrectionists" formed an alliance with the National League and prevented the re-election of Garry Herrmann, Johnson's pal, to the chairmanship of the old National Commission.

Johnson eventually had to swallow a bitter peace. The Yankees called off their big suit, and Mays was reinstated as a member of the Yankees; his 1919 games with the Yankees were recognized, and third-place money was awarded to the New York players. The peace was only a truce, for the following November, the same alliance of anti-Johnson American Leaguers and the National League forced the naming of Judge Landis as baseball's dictator-commissioner over Johnson's head, using the threat of a new twelve-club National League, with two clubs in Boston, New York, and Chicago, as their most potent weapon.

2

The sale of Carl Mays to the Yankees in the summer of 1919 was followed by a deal with New York which made even greater headlines. Harry now was selling in a big way, and this was a deal which really knocked Boston fans right out of their chairs. On the blustering morning of January 9, 1920, Jake Ruppert, president of the Yankees, called the New York reporters to his office and announced, "Gentlemen, we have just bought Babe Ruth [Ruppert always pronounced it "Root"] from Harry Frazee of the Boston Red Sox." Frazee's Red Sox office gave out the stunning news at the same time in Boston.

"No, I can't give the exact figures, but it was a pretty check— six figures. No, no players are involved. It is strictly a cash deal," said Ruppert.

The New York brewer-owner didn't tell all. The straight cash involved was $100,000, but that was only a minor factor. The big consideration, which only became known some years later, was that Ruppert granted Frazee a $350,000 mortgage on Fenway Park. As was said before, Harry had purchased the club from Lannin on a shoestring which could stretch only so far. He had taken on the ball park, as well as the ball club, and both the Taylors and Lannin now were pressing him for the payment of unpaid notes. "The Ruth deal was the only way I could retain the Red Sox," Frazee once told the author in a moment of confidence.

Barrow at first fought the deal with all of his usual zeal. "You can't do this to me, Harry," he bellowed. "Why, Ruth is the biggest attraction in baseball."

"I'm sorry, Ed; I've just got to do it," Frazee replied apologetically.

"Well, then don't insult me by having the Yankees toss in a couple of second raters like they threw in McGraw and Russell in the Mays deal. If you've got to make the deal, make it for straight cash."

The deal naturally raised a terrible stench in Boston, and Back Bay no longer found anything cute about Hairbreadth Harry, the producer. Ruth had been guilty of his foibles and failings, but Boston liked the big guy; he had acquired a farm in the outskirts, and the town considered the Bambino as its own. Frazee promised Boston he would use his newly acquired cash in rebuilding the team, and said rather belligerently, "Ruth's twenty-nine homers were more spectacular than useful; they didn't help the Red Sox get out of sixth place."

However, Frazee, the theatrical man, looked even worse as a showman when Ruth, in his first season with the Yankees, hit the undreamed total of fifty-four homers, almost batted the Yankees into their first flag, and enabled the New Yorkers to set an American League home attendance record of 1,289,422, which stood until the flush year of 1946.

As to the Ruthless 1920 Red Sox, they fared just about the same as the club of the year before—finishing fifth with a percentage of .471. Barrow had swung a few pretty good deals, acquiring the versatile Ossie Vitt, later manager of the Cleveland "Cry Baby" Indians, from Detroit for Chick Shorten, pitcher Slim Love, and catcher Eddie Ainsmith. In another deal with Griffith of Washington, Ed obtained outfielder Mike Menosky, southpaw hurler Harry Harper, now a Hackensack, New Jersey, millionaire, and the veteran third baseman Eddie Foster, for outfielder Bobbie Roth and infielder Maurice Shannon. Pitcher Elmer Myers was purchased from Cleveland.

The club was seventh in batting, but stouthearted pitching enabled the Red Sox to give a reasonably good account of themselves. They even made possible the 1920 pennant of Speaker's Cleveland club by knocking off the strong second-place White Sox (who lost the pennant by two games), twelve games to ten. Herb Pennock, the frail left-hander picked up from the Athletics back in 1915, now was

coming into his own and won sixteen games for the second successive year. Bush broke even in thirty games, and Sam Jones, pitching in uncanny tough luck, won thirteen and lost sixteen, just
reversing Pennock's record. Waite Hoyt, Brooklyn high-school no-hit
star, who had a brief trial with the Giants and had pitched for the
strong Baltimore Drydocks team during the war, showed a crackling
fast ball but was held back by injuries and was credited with six
victories and as many defeats.

3

Barrow bade farewell to Boston at the end of the season and was
glad to get away. Harry Sparrow, the Yankee business manager,
had died during the 1920 campaign, and Barrow moved on to New
York to take his place. It was a pleasant change for Ed, as he was
on the receiving end of Frazee's subsequent deals rather than on the
sending end. Ed's successor as Boston pilot was loyal, likable, faithful Hughie Duffy, now head Red Sox scout, who was one of the
pioneers in bringing Boston into the American League in 1901 and
was mentioned as a possible manager then and again after Stahl's
suicide in 1907.

Frazee got Hughie off to a good start by making another of his
infamous deals with the Yankees. This time it was catcher Wallie
Schang; the promising New York schoolboy pitcher, Waite Hoyt;
Harry Harper, the Hackensack left-hander; and utility infielder
Mike McNally, for catcher Harold "Muddy" Ruel, pitcher Herb
Thormahlen, second baseman Derrell Pratt, and outfielder Sammie
Vick, Ruth's New York right-field predecessor and famous to this
day for his fabulous appetite.

Huggins made that deal primarily to get the battery of Hoyt and
Schang, especially the hard-hitting, hard-working catcher. He later
termed the inclusion of Ruel in the deal as his "biggest mistake."
He figured Muddy to be a promising kid but not big enough to stand
the gaff of daily catching. Ruel fooled him by working 113 games
for Duffy that season, and then caught over 100 games for eight
successive seasons, going up to 149 with the Washington champions
of 1924.

Hughie Duffy really did a swell job with that club, finishing fifth
with an average of .487, the Red Sox's best percentage since the 1918
pennant winner. Hugh lost only four more games than he won—
seventy-nine defeats to seventy-five victories. The Red Sox still
weren't disgraced. Stuffy McInnis led the regular Boston hitters with

.307, while Joe Bush had a great season, hitting .325, while he won sixteen games and lost only nine. Sam Jones was the league's work horse and had a brilliant season with the fifth placers, winning twenty-three and losing sixteen.

In the meantime, the Yankees had won their first flag, with Ruth boosting his home-run output to fifty-nine, with Mays winning twenty-seven games, and young Hoyt nineteen. But they couldn't pitch the Yankees into the world championship, the Ruppert-Huston entry losing to the Giants, five games to three.

What, therefore, was more natural than for the Colonels again to reach into their Boston "farm" for replacements? Bush and Jones were too good in 1921 not to escape the attention of the avid New Yorkers. This time they acquired Duffy's 1921 pitching aces, Bullet Joe and Sad Sam, along with the durable Red Sox shortstop, Everett Scott, for three New York pitchers, Jack Quinn, the ancient spit-baller; Warren "Two Gun" Collins, and Bill Piercy, and shortstop Roger Peckinpaugh, the former Yankee captain.

But there was a catch in it for Boston fans. Peck remained with the Red Sox for only a few minutes, as he was sent to Washington for the former Athletic shortstop, Joe Dugan, a former Holy Cross star. Griffith had procured temporary title to "Jumping Joe" by sending Connie Mack outfielder Bing Miller and a Cuban pitcher, Acosta.

Even so, Boston fans were to enjoy Joe Dugan's shortstop play for only a few months; by early August, the St. Louis Browns were leading the Yankees by two games, and the Colonels had to do something about that—and immediately. So this time they snared Dugan and outfielder Elmer Smith from Boston for a bunch of Yankee second stringers, infielders Chick Fewster and Johnny Mitchell, out-fielder Elmer Miller, and pitcher Lefty O'Doul.

After each deal, Hughie Duffy would say loyally, "They say there was *no other* consideration." The other consideration this time was another $50,000 check for Frazee, and this late-season deal raised such a stink that the St. Louis Chamber of Commerce and the Mound City civic clubs vied with each other in sending resolutions to Judge Landis and the major league presidents, and in yelling their indignation to the high heavens. The deal was so raw, making the Yankees another winner, that Landis recommended the passage of the present rule whereby no player deals, except waiver price transactions, are permissible after June 15.

And before the unhappy season of 1922, the Red Sox also lost the last regular of the world champions of 1912, 1915, and 1916, the old favorite, Harry Hooper. With Ruth in right field, the Yankees never seemed to want Harry's services, and he was traded to the Chicago White Sox for outfielders John Francis "Shano" Collins, of Charlestown, Massachusetts, and little Nemo Leibold. "Now that Harry's traded Harry, he's batting 1.000 as a wrecker," said a disconsolate Back Bay fan.

With Bush, Jones, Scott, and Hooper gone, what followed was inevitable. The Red Sox went right through their hose and plummeted through the trap door into the cellar. Reach's *Guide* for 1923 tells a little of the suffering endured by Boston fans in its brief summary of the 1922 Boston situation:

Boston last season reaped the fruits of four years' despoliation by the New York club, and for the second time in American League history this once great Boston team, now utterly discredited, fell into last place —with every prospect of remaining in that undesirable position indefinitely.

The former Yankee pitchers, Collins and Quinn, did fairly well with records of fifteen and fourteen and thirteen and fifteen. Dragged down by his support, Pennock won only ten games while losing seventeen. A few other bright spots were the peppery young backstop, Ruel, catching 112 games, and George Burns, the new first baseman, hitting .305.

If there was any balm in Gilead for Boston fans in that distressing season it was that Frazee's scrubs almost knocked the New York varsity out of the pennant. It was the year the Yanks nosed out the Browns by one scant game. Oddly enough, the powerful New Yorkers could knock the whey out of the second-place St. Louisans, winning that series fourteen to eight, but they had a peck of trouble with their old castoffs, leftovers, and misfits now parading in Boston uniforms. The tailenders beat the league champs, fourteen games to eight.

In fact, in the last few days of the race, the Red Sox almost K.O.'d Huggins, Ruth, Meusel, and the other Ruppert men. The Yanks came to Fenway Park for a three-game series, September 28. They had four games left to play, the three in Boston and one in Washington, and needed only one to clinch the flag, but they had a heck of a time winning it. Bush dropped the first one to Rip Collins, 3 to 1, and the next day Jack Quinn won a 1-to-0 duel from Shawkey. Huggins was getting apprehensive, and Ruth was bellowing, "What the hell are those guys trying to do to us?"

The next day, a Saturday, Duffy wanted to pitch Pennock, but Frazee, who was enjoying it, said: "Let's use Alex Ferguson. [He was another New York castoff.] Those former Yankees are knocking them off, so why not stick to the system?" Hughie deferred to the boss and started "Fergie." He was like a gift from the gods to the hard-pressed Yankees. They got to him for three runs in the very first inning, which was all they scored that day, but it was enough to win, 3 to 1. That was all for Ferguson, and Pennock came in and pitched superbly. In seven effective innings Herb gave up only two hits. He eventually went out for a pinch hitter, and Benny Karr blanked the Yankees in the last two frames.

Naturally, everyone said if Pennock had started, he would have won. The Yankees badly needed that game, as they lost to Washington, 6 to 1, on the final Sunday, and as the Browns won their last four, the Saturday victory in Boston gave the New Yorkers the flag by a scant six-point lead over St. Louis.

The Yankees then had a disastrous time with the Giants in the 1922 World Series; despite the fact that Huggins now had all of the former crack Boston right-handers, Mays, Hoyt, Bush, and Jones, the best Miller got in five games with McGraw's scrappy crew was a ten-inning 3-to-3 draw.

"Our staff is top-heavy with right-handers. What we need is a good left-hander I can put in to stop left-handed hitters," little Miller Huggins told Ruppert.

Colonel Jake knew the answer—his old friend "Frazz," of Fenway Park and Forty-second Street. Frazee didn't have much left that the Yankees wanted, but he had that southpaw Huggins craved in Herb Pennock. So after that tail-end season, the Red Sox were stripped of their remaining left-handed ace. Herb was traded to New York for Norman McMillan, an infielder-outfielder, outfielder Camp Skinner, and another Ruppert-autographed check. With the Yankees behind him, Pennock developed into one of the all-time southpaw stars of the American League.

A promising young right-handed pitcher, George Pipgras, drafted by the Red Sox from Madison, South Dakota, in 1921 and farmed to Charleston, South Carolina, in 1922, also was sold to the omnivorous Yankees. The rape of the Red Sox now was complete!

The 1922 season finished Hughie Duffy as manager; his "crime" was that he tumbled into the cellar with the humpty dumpties Frazee turned over to him. They were tough years after 1920, but they had their laughs, especially the Red Sox's fistically inclined trainers. Tommy Murray, the 1921 trainer, spent much of his time in the Hot Springs, Arkansas, clubhouse during the training season teaching the boys left jabs and how to throw punches. "I see we are going to have a fighting ball club," said Hughie Duffy.

A year later, Duffy engaged another trainer, Dinny Harrington, and Dinny quickly won fame at a little party given at a Boston brewery that winter. "I can lick anybody on your ball club, but Joe Bush," Dinny told Duffy with much pride and satisfaction.

"Cripes, I didn't engage you to lick 'em, but to train 'em," said Hughie.

Then there was the little bout in the Fenway clubhouse, involving Win Green, the present-day trainer, then a general clubhouse assistant, and "Leaping Mike" Menosky. Joe Cronin and the present-day Red Sox still enjoy hearing Win's graphic blow-by-blow account of the battle.

Jimmy Burke, Duffy's coach, asked Win in belligerent tones what he had done with the drinking cup.

"If I'm not mistaken, I saw it on the bench," Green replied quietly.

"Well, go and get it," snapped Jimmy.

"You're the guy who wants the drink; get it yourself," said Green.

"You're pretty fresh; aren't you?" said Jimmy, and then giving a wink to Mike Menosky, added, "Here's a young fellow who would like to box with you."

Leaping Mike was standing near by dressed in nothing but a pair of trunks, and somebody fetched in two pairs of gloves which Joe Bush had brought into the clubhouse.

"I'm too busy," protested Green. "I got things to do."

"Oh, you're too busy to fight," chided Burke.

Egged on by Burke's taunts, Win agreed to put on the gloves. Sam Jones was the official timekeeper and kept track of the passing seconds by whacking a bucket with a bat. In the third round, Green gave Mike a one-two punch which caught Menosky flush on the nose and mouth, starting a flow of claret.

"I guess it's gone far enough," said Hugh Duffy.

"Gosh," said Win, "I've just begun to fight."

4

Having wrecked the Red Sox, Frazee tried to restore favor with his fans in 1923 with a managerial name. He lured Frank Chance, the former great Cub first baseman–manager, out of retirement to lead his hopeless misfits. Chance, formerly known as the Peerless Leader, had been the inspiring manager of the Cub pennant winners of 1906,

1907, 1908, and 1910, Chicago's greatest all-time team. As manager of the New York Yankees in 1913 and 1914, Chance had shown that his former managerial renown was of little help if he didn't have the players.

Chance's 1923 Red Sox slid home in the cellar with a percentage of .401, five points better than Duffy's 1922 effort. Yet oddly enough, the Boston boys could make a pretty good showing against the top teams. Chance's team managed to win eight games from the strong Yankee champions and lost their season series to the second-place Tigers and third-place Indians, each by the scant margin of ten to twelve. They were suckers for the club they almost hoisted into the pennant in 1922, the St. Louis Browns. The great Sisler was out that year with eye trouble, and the team plunged to fifth, but for some reason the St. Louisans took out their woe on their 1922 friends, the Red Sox, beating them down to the ground, eighteen defeats in twenty-two games.

Chance had one break, a Frazee trade with Detroit in the fall of 1922, which in Detroit still is called "Ty Cobb's worst deal." Ty didn't think he got enough victories out of the tall angular Howard Ehmke and traded the lanky right-hander; Carl Holling, another pitcher; and a slugging kid first baseman, Babe Herman, to Boston for second baseman Del Pratt and pitcher Rip Collins.

Frazee, the showman, who had sold Babe Ruth, also let this other picturesque Babe—Herman—pass through his fingers. Herman never was a gazelle around either first base or the outfield, but he later was good enough to hit .393 for Brooklyn and bang out thirty-five home runs in one lusty season.

But Chance got a mighty sweet pitcher out of the deal in Howard Ehmke, who performed something of a minor miracle by winning twenty games for that 1923 Boston tailender. The author remembers well how good Ehmke was that year, and through giving Howard the worst of a scoring decision, prevented him from beating Johnny Vander Meer, Cincinnati southpaw, to double no-hit glory by fifteen years. Howard pitched a no-hitter in Philadelphia, September 7. However, here he got a break, as his Philadelphia pitching rival, Slim Harriss, slapped a ball against the right-field wall for an apparent double but lost it by failing to touch first base as he ran by. On another play, Bill Brandt, the Philadelphia scorer, scored an error for Menosky on a smoking liner from Frank Welch's bat which Mike failed to hold.

In Howard's next game, September 11, he opposed the biffing

Yankees at Yankee Stadium with this scribe in the scorer's box. The first New York hitter, Whitey Witt, hit a little hopper which went through the hands of Howard Shanks, the Boston third baseman, and bounced up and struck Shanks on the chest. I took into consideration that Shanks, an outfielder by trade, had played the ball clumsily, but also that Witt, a left-handed batsman was a streak of lightning going down to first base; Whitey was given the benefit of the doubt and the play scored as a scratch hit.

Not only was this the only Yankee hit, but Witt was the only New Yorker to reach base in the full nine innings; Howard retired the next twenty-seven hitters as fast as they came up. In the late innings, considerable pressure was brought on me to change the Witt play to an error for Shanks. However, I held to my original decision. Ehmke was much disappointed with the loss of this second no-hitter; umpire Tommy Connolly said he believed the play should have been scored as an error, and some friends of Ehmke petitioned Ban Johnson to change the verdict, but Ban upheld the scorer. However, several years later when Shanks came to the Yankees, he said to me, "Fred, I think it should have been called an error," and ever since I've had the play on my conscience.

There was another historic play three days later, September 14, when George Burns, Red Sox first sacker, really pulled one for the book at Fenway Park, an unassisted triple play by a first baseman. In a 1946 Quiz Kids program, Jim Enright of the Chicago *Herald-American,* and Cubs Stan Hack and Peanuts Lowrey were guests on Joe Kelley's popular program. One of the kids asked the baseball delegation a vexing question: "How did that first baseman Burns make an unassisted triple play?" No one could exactly figure out the answer.

This is how George did it. With the Red Sox playing Tris Speaker's Indians and Jack Quinn pitching for Boston, Riggs Stephenson opened the second inning with a single and Rube Lutzke walked. On a hit and run play, Brower, the Indians' first baseman, lined a drive smack at Burns, who caught the ball and then reached out and tagged Lutzke for the second out. Seeing Stephenson had run almost to third base, Burns sprinted for second with the ball. Riggs tried to get back, and both players slid into the bag from opposite directions, but Burns won the race by several feet for the third out. As Quinn eventually won the game, 4 to 3, in twelve innings, Burns's play failed to provide any thrill for Spoke. "The lucky sons of guns," the Gray Eagle exclaimed.

Frank "Lefty" O'Doul, the man in the green suit and now the popular and capable manager of the San Francisco Seals, was a member of Chance's second-string pitching staff, also one of the gay blades of the 1923 Red Sox. Chance had warned "the O'Doodle," as he also was called, several times about observing the club's midnight curfew. However, there always are ways for breaking rules, and carefree young players always will try to find them. O'Doul and Mike Menosky, another gay young blade, thought they could outwit the Peerless Leader, and it was 3 A.M. before they returned to the hotel where the club was quartered.

The next morning Chance stormed at O'Doul: "I was up to your room at twelve o'clock, and you weren't there. That will cost you a hundred dollars. I was up there again at two, and you still weren't in, and that will cost you a second hundred. If you want to work for Frazee all season for nothing, that's all right with me."

Shortly afterward, Menosky came into the lobby, fresh as a daisy, and seeing the discomfited O'Doul slumped in a leather chair, asked breezily, "Anything wrong, Frank?" In tracking down O'Doul, Chance never knew that Leaping Mike had been Lefty's pal on the party.

During the club's stay in Cleveland, Chance went to the hotel barbershop, and in an adjoining chair the shop was giving the O'Doodle everything it had in the works—haircut, shampoo, shave, manicure, and shine. After the operation was over, Lefty took several good looks at himself in the big barbershop mirror and apparently was quite pleased with what he saw.

In the afternoon game of the same day, Bill Piercey, the coast right-hander, had a leg bruised by a line drive from Speaker's bat and was forced to limp out of the game with a runner on third and two out. Chance had to get a pitcher ready in a hurry, and called on O'Doul, who had little opportunity to warm up. Hits rattled off the League Park fences like machine-gun bullets, and before the Indians had finished batting they scored thirteen runs. During the height of the carnage, Chance exclaimed on the bench, "I'm going to leave that looking-glass so-and-so in there, if he don't get them out all afternoon."

Late in the season, in a Red Sox game at Yankee Stadium, Ruth hit a tremendously high fly to center field some three hundred feet from the plate. Dick Reichle, the young Boston center fielder, now a St. Louis businessman, settled under it, but the ball did tricks in the air and finally fell a few feet behind Reichle. Ruth was almost on third base when the ball hit the ground, and then beat Reichle's throw to the plate for an inside-the-park home run, a rare feat for the big Bambino.

When Reichle returned to the bench, Chance greeted him with his best irony: "Pretty smart, Dick! It's late in the season, and I wouldn't get hit on the head, either."

16

⊗

BOB QUINN FLOUNDERS IN THE CELLAR

I

AFTER seven and a half unfortunate years the Frazee regime finally ran out its unhappy course. Ban Johnson had been trying to get Harry out of the league, and out of his hair, for some time, and his efforts eventually were crowned with success in July 1923. Ban induced J. A. Robert "Bob" Quinn, live-wire vice-president and business manager of the St. Louis Browns and a baseball man of long experience, to buy the club. Bobbie headed a Columbus, Ohio, syndicate, and his biggest backer was Palmer Winslow, a glassworks millionaire from Indiana.

For a while the deal was held up as a force of auditors went over Frazee's tangled baseball books, and Gus Rooney wrote rather sadly in his letter to the *Sporting News*: "Meanwhile Boston fans are fearful lest there be a mix-up that will prevent the deal going through. The Red Sox have been 'sold' so often that naturally Boston won't be convinced the thing actually has come to pass until the final papers are signed and the new owners take possession."

No good Boston fan wanted a catch in it that would prevent Frazee from getting out. What really held up the deal was a matter of a few unpaid hot-dog bills. Harry Stevens, the famous caterer, had a judgment against Frazee, and when the club was about to be sold, the members of the syndicate learned the property couldn't be transferred to Quinn and Winslow, until the hot-dog king had been paid his money.

Harry Stevens eventually was paid, and Ban Johnson drank a toast to Frazee's departure: "Harry Frazee was a grand old soul; yes, he was in————"

Quinn made Ban's man Friday, Jim Price, the club's new secretary. Price had been serving at the time as Johnson's eastern representative; he was a former president of the Newark club and the famous sports editor of the old New York *Press*, when the author was a member of his fine staff. Bob Quinn is a devout religious man, and one of his early blows as president of the Red Sox came when Price committed suicide by slashing his wrists with a razor blade on January 29, 1929.

"I've been quoted as saying that the big mistake of my career was when I left the Browns in 1923 to go to the Red Sox as president and part owner. I don't remember ever having said that, but perhaps it is true, the way things turned out," the venerable Quinn, now the septuagenarian promotional director for the Wilson Sporting Goods Company, told me.

"I was well situated in St. Louis. Phil Ball practically left me alone in the operation of the club. I drew a good salary and a share of the profits. And the Browns at the time were the club in St. Louis. But Ban wanted Frazee out, and I guess every man in baseball has an ambition to head his own club.

"Eventually, I lost all my money in the Red Sox, but it was due to a combination of poor breaks. Less than two years after we bought the Red Sox, my associate and backer, Palmer Winslow, died. We had some big plans, but his death forced me to go it alone, and I ran smack into the big depression."

Quinn still likes to recall how he met Palmer Winslow, his wealthy associate. "When I had the Columbus club, we played an exhibition game in Matthews, Indiana, where Winslow had his glassworks. We were playing the Matthews team, and eventually had to call the game because it was getting dark. The millionaire who owned the Matthews team and the glassworks was most indignant about this; he said there should be no ties in baseball, and that all ball games should be decided one way or another. He owned the town, and even owned the railroad running into it, and he refused to give us a train to run us to our next stop. My Irish dander was up, but I knew we were on the spot, so I had to be diplomatic, and finally talked him into furnishing us a train. Later I helped him buy tickets for the Tiger-Pittsburgh World Series the same year (1909) and it started a lifelong friendship."

Quinn and Winslow paid $1,150,000 for the property, with Bob putting the savings of a baseball lifetime into the venture. After taking over, Bobbie permitted Chance to finish the season as manager, but the next year, 1924, he brought his former St. Louis manager, Lee Fohl, to Boston as Red Sox director, and for about two months in the 1924 season, Bob and Lee were the new "miracle men" of Boston, and their praises were shouted from the housetops.

During the winter of 1923–24, Quinn pulled what looked like a most astute deal with the Cleveland Indians, obtaining catcher Steve O'Neill, the present Detroit manager; second baseman Bill Wambsganss, hero of the unassisted World Series triple play; Joe Donnelly, an outfielder; and pitcher A. J. "Dan" Boone, for first baseman George Burns, second baseman Chick Fewster, and catcher Al Walters. To replace Burns at first, Quinn enticed Joe Harris, a former Cleveland first sacker, out of semiretirement, and he spent $30,000 of the syndicate's money for shortstop Dudley Lee of Tulsa, then supposedly the number one shortstop of the minors.

Everything worked perfectly for two months; the new Cleveland acquisitions played inspired ball; the hitters hit, the pitchers pitched, and the new shortstop clicked. During May and half of June, the Red Sox were runners-up to the Yankees, 1923 world champions. On both June 4 and June 9, the Red Sox actually were on top. Shades of Jimmy Collins' team of 1903 and 1904 and Bill Carrigan's world champions of 1915 and 1916! Happy days surely were here again!

It was the high tide of Bob Quinn's unfortunate ten-year tenure as boss man of the Red Sox. The bubble soon burst; by June 13, the Red Sox slipped quietly into third place, and by July 1, they had skidded through the standing and landed in seventh place. They eventually staggered home in that position, defeating the White Sox, managed by Chance and Johnny Evers, by four points.

After the spring flurry, the Boston team again was weighed down by weak hitting; Joe Harris had to take a long layoff because of a stubborn case of neuritis; the young shortstop, Lee, suffered from a bone splinter in his elbow, the result of being hit by a pitched ball, and among the pitchers, only Ehmke, with a nineteen-and-seventeen record, could win more games than he lost.

2

Boston had looked forward to the coming of Bob Quinn as the herald of better days. But the Red Sox were soon to explore the very subterranean caverns of the American League. They fell even deeper into the pit than under the ownership of Harry Frazee, as from 1925 to 1932, inclusive, the Red Sox had seven tailenders in eight years, getting a brief glimpse of sunlight in 1931, when they emerged as high as sixth. In each 1925, 1926, 1927, 1930 and 1932, the club lost over a hundred games, reaching the pitiable mark of .279, with 43 wins and 111 defeats in 1932. Games in Boston's Twilight League, especially those in Cambridge, frequently exceeded the slim turnouts at Fenway Park.

It was the dreariest period in the history of the Boston fans, one similar to the dark days in Philadelphia when Connie Mack spent seven successive years in the American League cellar after he broke up his great champions of 1910, '11, '13, and '14. In fact as Quinn's Red Sox were sinking lower and lower, Mack was staging his great comeback which put him in the World Series in 1929, 1930, and 1931. "What did we do to deserve this?" Boston fans asked bitterly as they watched the misfits and class-C pickups in their sorry attempts to fill the uniforms formerly worn by Tris Speaker, Babe Ruth, Harry Hooper, Duffy Lewis, and Everett Scott.

Quinn probably was licked from the very start. Less than a year after he purchased the Red Sox from Frazee, Palmer Winslow was stricken with a lingering illness. Palmer's health soon became so bad that Bob couldn't speak to him of baseball matters, let alone put the bee on him for ready cash to carry on the club's operations. Winslow then passed out of this life early in 1926.

Bob then was beset with a new problem. Should he dispose of Mrs. Winslow's share and clear out, at a profit to both? But Quinn always had a great faith in himself and disliked the idea of quitting on a situation. He had built up the Columbus American Association club and the St. Louis Browns from nothing with no great outlay of cash. He decided to carry on—with an empty till, which he now knows was his big mistake. Quinn's friend and sponsor, Ban Johnson, also left the American League in 1927, partly as the result of illness and partly from inside pressure. Had Ban remained active, it is doubtful if he would have permitted the Red Sox, one of his favorite clubs, to fall into the bottomless pit.

Quinn ran into the depression a little over two years after Winslow's death. His troubles multiplied like the woes of Job. His third-base bleachers at Fenway Park burned down on May 8, 1926. Massachusetts legalized Sunday baseball in 1929, which helped, though the Red Sox lost their first Sunday game at Fenway Park to the

Philadelphia Athletics, April 28, 1929, by a score of 7 to 3. When Bob was president of the Columbus club, he went through a five-year period when he didn't lose a single Sunday date by rain. He had a stretch in Boston when he lost almost as many in succession. Whenever there was a chance for a crowd on a Sunday or a holiday, the floodgates in the sky opened.

Jim Price, the club's secretary, committed suicide, and big Ed Morris, a hefty pitcher from Alabama, was stabbed to death at a fish fry at Century, Florida, March 3, 1932, as his friends were giving him a final going-away party before he was to leave for the Red Sox training camp at Savannah, Georgia. Morris, with a smoking fast ball, had shown great promise. With the 1928 Boston tailender, the big Alabamian won nineteen games and lost fifteen, while he broke even in twenty-eight games in 1929. Ed slumped off in his next two years, but still was considered a fine prospect when his tragic death shocked the nation.

3

Quinn also was beset with managerial problems, and there was a parade of skippers during his ten unhappy years. Lee Fohl had worked well with him in St. Louis and had been the Brown manager when the 1922 club lost the pennant by a game. Lee ran the Boston club three years, 1924, 1925, and 1926, and by the latter year Bobbie got the idea that Lee was too easy with his men. Anyway, the 1926 percentage had shriveled to .301, just one hundred points under Chance's .401 of 1923—the year Quinn took over, and a change seemed desirable.

Back in 1916, when Bill Carrigan left the club after two straight world championships, he gave Boston fans the promise that "if they really need me, I'll be back." That time surely had come. All New England felt a thrill of hope and excitement when announcement was made in the winter of 1926–27, that Quinn had lured old Rough out of retirement and that Holy Cross Bill again would direct the Red Sox. This looked like the first return trip up the ladder. No one could conceive of the aggressive, fighting Carrigan, by this time forty-six years old, having any patience with a tailender.

"It's the best news that Boston fans have read for many, many years," wrote Paul Shannon. Such Red Sox partisans among the writers as Johnny Drohan and Joe Cashman started to write with a new spirit of optimism; life again was worth living. Yes, things definitely were on the upgrade. But were they?

It is difficult to eliminate the personality and the coaching ability of Carrigan from talk about the 1927 Red Sox [wrote Burt Whitman from the New Orleans training camp]. He is a natural baseball teacher. Bill has his own methods of teaching. He does not yell loudly, and he does not wave his arms and call down the wrath of heaven on the stupidity of this generation of pitchers. And it is in the pitching corps where the Sox should show the biggest and quickest improvement.

One of Bill's first moves was to bring his old friend Heinie Wagner back to the club as coach. Bill and Heinie had a fair bunch of pitchers to work with, too, in Charley Ruffing, Danny MacFayden, Jack Russell, Bryan Harriss, and Hal Wiltse. But these hurlers were raw and inexperienced, and Carrigan surrounded them with a team which was a bad last in club batting and seventh in team fielding. In an era of slugging, the champion Yankees of 1927 hit 158 home runs; Carrigan's tailend Red Sox, 28. What a story that told in games won and lost arithmetic! The cards were stacked against Holy Cross Bill just as they were against Chance four years before. Connie Mack has demonstrated most convincingly that a managerial reputation avails little if the manager doesn't have the players.

The improvement wrought by Carrigan was slight, especially between his second and third years. His three tailenders of 1927, 1928, and 1929 had percentages of .331, .373, and .377, respectively. The stock market crash came shortly after the latter season, and the chap who was running Bill's Lewiston bank got out on a limb, and Carrigan had financial worries in addition to fretting over the Red Sox. Like the sturdy soul he is, Rough was willing to carry on and see things through with Quinn, but Bobbie, knowing how much of Bill's lifetime savings were tied up in the bank, told him to remain at home and straighten things out.

Heinie Wagner, Bill's coach, then took a crack at it; he ran the club for a year, dropped the Red Sox a little deeper into the mire, and was followed by Shano Collins, the man from Charlestown. Some Boston fans thought that might be a pretty good omen. They thought of Jimmy Collins and remarked, "Shano's got a good managerial name; maybe, it'll bring luck."

It did. The Red Sox won ten more games under Shano in 1931 than under Heinie in 1930, and had that sixth placer with a .408 percentage. Imagine a team with the background and heritage of the Red Sox getting steamed up over a sixth-place finish!

Poor Shano! That .408 finish left him in no frame of mind for what followed in 1932. Collins was an aggressive ballplayer, and a manager who dearly loved to win. He confidently expected to pick up where he left off in 1931, and possibly fight into the first division. Instead, the club backfired and became the sorriest tailender in Red Sox history. The club almost drove Collins nuts, and he quit on a gloomy Saturday in Cleveland, June 18, after his hapless crew had won only eleven games and lost forty-seven for a hideous percentage of .190.

In desperation, Quinn telephoned infielder Marty McManus, who had been Bob's second baseman on the Browns, to take over the club. Marty incidentally was in church when he was appointed manager. It was a good place to be; he needed all the prayers he could get for the balance of the season. When he returned to the hotel, there was a message to call up Boston, and when he contacted Quinn, the Red Sox president said, "Beginning with today, you're the manager." Marty stayed until the end of the 1933 season.

4

From time to time, Quinn had to borrow from somebody—wherever he could get it to keep his ship afloat. Times were getting worse and worse, and his crowds were getting skimpier and skimpier. Bob had no affiliation with clubs in the larger minor leagues, and he had to obtain his new players from class B down. He dreamed wistfully of picking up more nuggets such as Speaker, Lewis, Hooper, Gardner, Wood, and Ray Collins, but the depression years were poor ones for miracles.

Quinn didn't sell many players, having few to sell, but two good pitchers, Charley Ruffing and Danny MacFayden, followed that familiar old journey from Fenway Park to Yankee Stadium. Ruffing was the first to go, on May 6, 1930, ostensibly in a trade for outfielder Cedric Durst, who had played for Quinn in St. Louis. But those in the know knew that Ruppert helped Bob meet several pressing obligations, and he received one check for $10,000 and another for $7,500, but big Ruffing was a steal at the price.

Ruff, the Red, was a big former miner from the south Illinois coal fields, who had a few toes missing as the result of a mine explosion. Quinn first procured him from Danville in the Three-I League in 1923, sending him to Dover, Delaware, for experience in 1924. Red was the losin'est pitcher in the two majors in his five full seasons in Boston, showing ninety-one losses against only thirty-nine wins.

He dropped twenty-five games in 1928 and twenty-two more in 1929. But smart baseball men knew Ruffing had the stuff to make a great pitcher, and New York was his oyster. With the Yankees, Red became one of the really great pitchers of baseball, with a World Series record of seven victories in nine games.

MacFayden had a better record in Boston than did Ruffing. He was more or less of a home bred, being born in North Truro, Massachusetts, and first attracted attention pitching for Somerville High School and Hebron Academy. Danny wore spectacles, often was called the Deacon, and Quinn picked him off Boston's semipro diamonds. With the need for pitchers so urgent, the spectacled Deacon quickly made the front-line staff. He won a good share of victories from the start, and contributed sixteen wins against twelve defeats to Collins' sixth-place club of 1931. When the harassed Quinn finally sold Danny to the Yankees for $50,000 on June 5, 1932, Collins knew it was the last straw, and he threw up the sponge a fortnight later. But Bob needed the money badly, and got a pair of pretty fair pitchers, Henry Johnson and Ivy Andrews, from the Yankees in addition to the cash.

Barrow, the former Red Sox manager, beamed from ear to ear when he announced the acquisition of MacFayden by the Yankees. "We've got a pitcher who will win twenty games for us for the next ten years," he said proudly. But, for some reason or other, MacFayden couldn't pitch as well with Ruth, Gehrig, and Lazzeri behind him as with the old Boston misfits. He couldn't win in New York, eventually passed to Cincinnati in the National League, and then came to the Braves, where he pitched some brilliant ball under Stengel. Danny was essentially a Boston pitcher.

Before the fatal 1932 stabbing which snuffed out the life of Ed Morris, Quinn was said to be contemplating an offer from the Yankees for the big right-hander which was close to $100,000.

While the Boston clubs were occupants of the cellar, they came up with a few good players. Tom Oliver, the center fielder, was only a fair hitter, but what a fielder! Even Tris Speaker never covered any greater acreage at Fenway Park. Following the 1931 season, the writer took a team of All-Stars to the Orient, headlined by such luminaries as Lou Gehrig, Al Simmons, Mickey Cochrane, Lefty Grove, Frank Frisch, Lefty O'Doul, Rabbit Maranville, Willie Kamm, Larry French, Muddy Ruel, and George Kelly. Oliver, the team's center fielder, was the "green pea" in this galaxy of stars, but Tom had the eyes of the Japs popping out with his fielding. No Jap ever hit anything that Tom couldn't reach.

A few, who were mediocrities in Boston during these distressing years, later made good with other clubs; Jack Rothrock, who divided his time in "the Fens" between second base and right field, later was the right fielder of the Gas House Cardinal world champions of 1934. Playing shortstop for the Tigers against Rothrock in the World Series of that year was Billy Rogell, who had fizzled at third, short, and second in Boston. Now a Detroit councilman, Rogell held down the shortstop post for the Tigers for some ten years.

Doc Prothro, one of the many Red Sox third basemen, later managed the Phillies and now is a power in the Southern Association. Ira Flagstead, a refugee from the Tigers, enjoyed several fine seasons in the Back Bay ball yard, while Charlie Berry, the former Lafayette all-round star and present American League umpire, frequently caught inspired ball. Bostonians still recall the time he blocked off Babe Ruth at the plate late in the Bam's career, and George went hurtling through the air and was rushed off to the hospital.

Boston fans and writers were given their share of laughs as some of the heavy-thighed, slow-footed sluggers from other clubs drifted to Boston. Bob Fothergill, the Massillon fat boy, wound up with the Red Sox after fattening up in Detroit and Chicago, and by the time he arrived at Fenway Park, he looked and bounced around like a rubber ball. Smead Jolley, a .400 hitter from the Coast League, but with no defense against a fly ball but his cap, also performed his late American League acrobatics in "the Fens." One of Quinn's last deals was to acquire Smead, Johnny Watwood, another outfielder, and catcher Benny Tate from the White Sox for catcher Charlie Berry early in the 1932 season. Jolley hit .312 that season, smacked eighteen home runs, and actually stole a base, but it still is a question whether he drove in as many with his bat as he let in with his defense.

In the same unhappy season that saw the Red Sox percentage kerplunk to .279, the Boston Americans had their first batting champion, big Dale Alexander, a Tennessee farmer, and as agile around first base as Smead Jolley was in right field. Dale beat out Jimmy Foxx for the title, .367 to .364, which was rather tough on the Maryland strong boy—later a Red Sox, as it was the season Jimmy hit 438 total bases for Connie Mack, smote 58 homers, coming within two of tying Ruth's record, and drove in 169 runs. Alexander came to the Red Sox in a June trade with the Tigers for outfielder Earl Webb. The Tigers had gone high for the big first baseman in 1929, giving Toronto $100,000 and three players for Alexander and pitcher Johnny Prudhomme—most of it for the big slugger. But Dale was essentially of the type known as "Good Hit! No Field!"

17

⊖

RESCUER YAWKEY SPENDS
HIS MILLIONS

I

BY the start of the 1933 training season, Bob Quinn was practically at the end of his string. The bank holiday had descended on the nation, and Bob had to borrow on some life insurance to be sure there would be enough in the till to pay the bills of his hungry athletes at their Sarasota, Florida, camp.

However, on the eve of the departure of the club for Florida, February 25, Quinn, who by this time owed $350,000, saw his chance to get out. Thomas Austin Yawkey, foster son and nephew of the late Bill Yawkey, flamboyant owner of the early Detroit Tigers, bought the property, though the deal wasn't actually consummated until April 20. With baseball blood trickling in his veins, Tom had had a yen for some years to own a big league ball club—just like his dad, but he did not come into the bulk of his estate until his thirtieth birthday on February 21, 1933. Four days later he was a major league club owner.

Yawkey received a $500,000 trust fund when he became of age—about the time he was graduated from Yale; later he inherited $4,000,000 from his mother (Bill Yawkey's sister) and $3,408,650 from his foster father, but this was only part of the big fortune built up in lumber and ore lands by Tom's grandfather, a thrifty Pennsylvanian of German ancestry.

Baseball values then were at a depressed state, and Bob Quinn, with his habitual tailender, got out at the bottom of a bear market. He used his purchase money to liquidate his $350,000 indebtedness, and came out of his Boston venture as broke as when he started in baseball as a class B minor league catcher thirty-nine years before. "I was broke and out of a job," said Bob. "But I was free—free of debt and free of the cares of the ten years in which I tried to run the club to the best of my ability, with my limited resources. I actually breathed a sigh of relief when it was over."

One of Yawkey's early comforting statements to Boston fans was, "I don't intend to mess around with a loser," and he made good on that statement. With the exception of 1933, the season he took the club over from Bob Quinn, and a few years when most of the Red Sox stars marched off to war, his Red Sox clubs have been fairly consistently in the first division.

Like the late Jake Ruppert, William Wrigley, Jr., and Walter Briggs, Sr., Yawkey is a millionaire sportsman who wants a winner in the games won and lost column first, and if the club makes money, that also is desirable, but secondary. In that way, he followed the pattern of his foster father, Bill Yawkey, who used to vex the late Frank Navin by wanting to spend money on the Tigers faster than it came in at the early Detroit gate. Perhaps as Tom grew older, the business end of the game assumed greater importance, but for the millionaire, living in his luxurious New York apartment, his ball club in Boston is fun and diversion, just as is his shooting lodge and hunting preserve at South Island, South Carolina.

During the 1946 season, Ralph Cannon, executive sports director of the Chicago *Herald-American,* penned a column on Yawkey which fits the man so well that I have obtained Ralph's permission to reprint part of it:

Before a Sunday game several years ago the Red Sox were having a buffet luncheon at Fenway Park for the writers and announcers. It was all very genial and informal. Everybody simply milled around gabbing.

There was a young fellow there in brown twill suit, a rather plump and amiable young fellow who talked easily and unostentatiously with everybody. He was the least obtrusive man there. I myself thought he was a radio announcer for some local station, for those fellows are as a type affable, good-mixers.

It was not until later that I learned that the genial fellow in the brown twill suit was Tom Yawkey. That buffet luncheon convinced me that he is "One of Ours," our kind of people, the kind that belongs in sport, and the kind that deserves to win and enjoy the fruits of this always-hard competition.

As a prep-school youngster attending the Irving School at Tarry-town, New York, Tom Yawkey's great idol was Eddie Collins, the Hall of Fame second baseman of the Athletics and White Sox and the greatest athlete in Irving's history. Tom was only three when Eddie played his first game with the Athletics in 1906, and by the time young Yawkey went to Irving, the name of Edward Trowbridge Collins was as hallowed a tradition as those of Brickley and Grant at Harvard and Hinkey and Shevlin at Yale. The highest athletic honor at Irving is the annual Edward T. Collins trophy, and when Yawkey won it one year, he was the happiest kid in nine states.

Up to the time that Tom played with the idea of buying the Red Sox, he knew his hero only by reputation but decided that he only wanted a part of big league baseball if the great Eddie would run the club for him. Collins, who played his last ball with the Athletics in 1930, then was coach of the club and first assistant to Connie Mack, the venerable Philadelphia baseball patriarch, whom Eddie worshiped. He regarded Mack as his guardian angel, and there was a general belief in the Quaker City that when the "Grand Old Man of Baseball" stepped down, Eddie would be his managerial successor.

"One of the toughest decisions I've had to make in my life was when I met Tom Yawkey at our old school principal's funeral at Irving," related Collins. "And following the funeral Tom asked me if I wanted to go with him as vice-president and general manager of the Red Sox if he bought the club.

"I had come to regard Mr. Mack as I would my own father, and even the thoughts of leaving him were terrifying. But after I had a difficult time breaking the news to Connie, and asking him what I should do, he put me at ease by saying, 'Eddie, if you don't take that job, I'll fire you anyway,' with a twinkle in those kindly blue eyes."

That little quip by Connie clinched it, and Collins told Yawkey, "You can count on me to help when you take over."

Tom Yawkey has counted on Eddie Collins ever since, and for fourteen years the former great infielder has run the Red Sox ably and profitably.

2

"The first thing we've got to do is to get this club out of the cellar," Yawkey told Collins. "I realize the Red Sox are horribly run-down, and we've got to spend money, lots of it, to get the club back to its former strong position in the league. But I've got the money to spend, and I intend to spend it."

Eddie immediately got in touch with other clubs and proceeded to put a dent in Tom's bank roll. On May 9, the Red Sox obtained catcher Rick Ferrell, one of the best then in the game, and southpaw hurler Lloyd Brown from the St. Louis Browns for $50,000 and catcher Mervyn Shea. Three days later, Boston fans heard even more pleasing news: the Red Sox were buying players from the Yankees. That was a news story like the man biting the dog. George Pipgras, the big Dakota pitcher who was drafted by Frazee from Madison in 1921 and won twenty-four games for the 1928 Yankee world champions, and Billy Werber, a Duke University star, who had gone through the Yankee farm system, were the New York players involved. The pair stood Yawkey around $100,000.

Pipgras, until recently an American League umpire and now back with the Red Sox as a scout, doesn't know to this day why Ed Barrow sold him. George had one brilliant stretch of games with the 1933 Red Sox, was looked upon for a spell as the savior of the staff, but he injured his arm, and though he lasted in Boston until 1935, Pipgras never was the same pitcher thereafter. Werber, a fellow of outspoken views, probably early talked himself out of his job with the well-oiled Yankees of Barrow and McCarthy. A shortstop in college and the minors, Werber was converted into a third baseman by manager Marty McManus, who held over from the Quinn regime. Billy, a speed boy and player of initiative, early endeared himself to Boston fans by taking two bases on a base on balls to the amazement and vexation of the Detroit Tigers. Joe Judge, the old Washington first baseman, was engaged, after Joe had a brief fling in the National League with Brooklyn.

While the 1933 Red Sox advanced only one position, finishing seventh, they made the biggest gain of any club in the league, picking up twenty-two and one-half games and .144 points on the miserable tailender of 1932. The 1933 club would have fared better but for its impotence against the new Washington champions, piloted by the twenty-six-year-old shortstop, Joe Cronin. Against Washington, the Red Sox won only four games and lost seventeen, while Cronin was a ball of fire whenever his team played Boston. It made quite an impression on Yawkey.

Many of the club's most amusing stories continued to deal with the team's trainers. While Quinn still was responsible for the bills in the early spring, and everything was being done to cut down expenses, the club's physical welfare was in the care of Moe Gottlieb, a clubhouse attendant and former bat boy. On Easter Sunday morning the club ran into a train accident at Wyoming, Delaware, and while none of the Red Sox were injured, several other persons were hurt, and there was a call for doctors and persons who could administer first aid. But Moe slept all through the wreck, and when he awakened, he asked, "What's all the excitement about?"

Later the club engaged Doc Woods, a chiropractor who had been Yankee trainer under Miller Huggins. Dale Alexander, the clubbing first baseman, was suffering from a leg injury, and Woods gave it heat therapy. While big Dale was in the clubhouse, intently reading a book with a heat lamp over his injured leg, Doc Woods was on the bench looking at the ball game. He became so interested in a Red Sox rally that he forgot all about his Tennessee patient, and by the time he rescued Alexander, Dale's leg was exceedingly "well done." "It was roasted like a leg of lamb," was John Drohan's realistic report. It prevented Dale from playing for weeks, and at one time he contemplated taking legal action for the harm done his baseball career. Gallagher, another Red Sox, also was "well done" in another heat treatment.

Doc Woods and Mrs. Woods had a white poodle of which they were most fond. As far back as Doc's Yankee days, the animal was quite a spoiled pooch, but it passed from this earth during Woods's service in Boston. The grief-stricken owners were too fond of the dog to destroy the carcass, but they couldn't leave it around the apartment. So they stuffed it in the bottom of the refrigerator, later bringing it out as they held a wake. Eventually it was stuffed by a taxidermist and kept for posterity.

3

Even though the club improved only one position in 1933, the crowds started swarming back into Fenway Park. Grateful Boston fans saw that Yawkey and Collins were trying to do something and gave them loyal, fullhearted support. And Tom decided to do something for his fans, give them one of the finest ball parks in the country.

When Tom Yawkey took over the Red Sox, he cleared up all of the club's old obligations with the Taylor estate, and he owns the park and ball club, lock, stock, and barrel. Though the seating capacity of Fenway Park was only moderately increased from the original ball yard of 1912, Tom rebuilt the entire park at a cost of $750,000. A second fire had broken out in the center-field bleachers,

burning them to charred embers, after the 1933 season, and Yawkey
had his engineers, the Osborne Engineering Company, tear down all
the wooden stands and replace everything with steel and concrete.

The grandstand was extended on both sides to the extreme limits
of the field, replacing the old right-field pavilion and the third-base
bleachers destroyed by the 1926 fire. The new enlarged grandstand,
with many additional box seats, swung well around into right field.
Only the newly constructed center-field bleachers were uncovered,
and the only fence left was in left field, where Duffy's cliff had been
cut away and leveled. In place of the old wooden fence there was a
new thirty-six-foot wall of sheet metal and steel. Some six thousand
new grandstand seats had been added, and today Fenway Park is
the only ball yard in the big leagues which still has only a single-
deck stand. A half-dozen years later, Yawkey did a little more
remodeling. The bull pens were placed in front of the right-field
bleachers, and the entire thing was moved in, making it easier for
left-handed home-run hitters.

The rebuilt park was opened April 17, 1934, and oddly enough it
produced an eleven-inning game just as when the lid was pried off
the original Fenway Park in 1912. However, where the Red Sox
defeated the Yankees, 7 to 6, on the earlier occasion, Joe Cronin's
Senators ruined Yawkey's festivities, winning by almost the same
score—6 to 5.

Having a pretty up-to-date park, young Yawkey now needed
something to decorate it. He had replaced Marty McManus, a Quinn
holdover, as manager and entrusted the team's fortunes in 1934 to
Bucky Harris, Clark Griffith's former "boy wonder" who won Washington pennants in 1924 and 1925. Bucky had run the Detroit club
six years before his Boston adventure with no outstanding success,
but Harris was known as a crafty, substantial baseball man, who
played smart, heads-up baseball. During Eddie Collins' several years
as White Sox manager, he frequently matched wits with Harris and
gave him strong endorsement.

Tom again took all the rubber bands off his roll and tossed money
around like a well-heeled sailor on the loose. Connie Mack again was
selling, and Yawkey was his best customer. The crack left-hander of
the Athletics, Robert Moses Grove, Rube Walberg, another southpaw
considerable ability, and Max Bishop, second baseman of Mack's
champions, came to the Red Sox for $125,000, infielder Hal
stler and pitcher Bob Klein.

esley Cheek Ferrell was having one of his periodic flare-ups with
leveland club; he refused to report to the Indians, and in May,

Billy Evans, the Indians' general manager, handed over the temperamental right-hander and infielder Dick Porter to Eddie Collins for pitcher Bob Weiland, outfielder Bob Seeds, and $25,000. Wes gave a few headaches to his Boston managers but also won a lot of ball games, and with Yawkey spending freely, the Red Sox acquired the pitching Ferrell at a bargain-basement figure. Wesley and Rick, his easygoing brother, made up one of the few brother batteries seen in the majors. Shortstop Lynn Lary was purchased from the Yankees after the season was a few weeks old, while Fritz Ostermueller, a sturdy left-hander, was acquired from Rochester, in the Cardinal chain, at a fancy price. And the Red Sox searching everywhere for pitchers had a potential $100,000 twirler, right on their own roster in Bucky Walters, then a second-string third baseman.

Herb Pennock, pitching in his twenty-second year, returned to Boston in 1934, took part in thirty games, mostly in relief, and ranked fourth in earned runs. Herb, a close friend of Collins, then remained in the Red Sox organization as minor league manager, coach, and farm director until he was elevated to the vice-presidency of the Phillies in 1945. In a real baseball romance, Herb's daughter Janet married Eddie's son, Edward Trowbridge, Jr., and now there is Eddie III, who looks like a promising Red Sox of the future.

With his new acquisitions, Harris managed to lift the club to fourth place with a .500 percentage, the 1934 Red Sox winning seventy-six games and losing as many. It was the first first-division team in sixteen years—since Barrow's pennant of 1918. The club won its season's series from the Senators, Browns, Athletics, and White Sox. They completely reversed the 1933 order with Washington, defeating Cronin's team fourteen games to nine. Billy Werber was the shining light of the advance; he was proving a brilliant lead-off man, hitting .321 and stealing forty bases.

There were many disappointments, especially Lefty Grove, who in 1933 had won twenty-four games and lost only eight for the Athletics. Up to this season, tall Bob had had a rubber arm, and never knew what it was to have a lame wing. But the Sarasota training season was only a few days old when the lanky Cumberland mountaineer developed a misery in his expensive left arm, which he used to snap like a snake whip. Almost overnight, Mose learned he had lost his famous speed, and the expression, "he couldn't break a pane of glass," was no figure of speech. The arm became even "deader" as the season advanced, and Lefty pitched only 109 innings in 22 games, being credited with eight victories and as many defeats. With the Athletics, Grove had led the league six times in low earned runs, but it now zoomed to 6.52, and a Grove with such an earned-run average wasn't the most pleasant person to have around.

Good sportsman that Connie Mack is, he wrote to Yawkey: "Bob Grove isn't delivering for you. We believed you were getting a sound pitcher. Under the circumstances, the Athletic club will be glad to take Grove back and refund your money."

But Yawkey was just as good a sportsman, replying: "We also made the deal in good faith; we knew we were acquiring a veteran pitcher, and it is no fault of yours that Grove has developed a sore arm. The Boston club is willing to go through with the deal."

Bishop failed to provide the expected strength at second base, and was beaten out for the position by Chalmer Cissell, a former hard-riding, hard-drinking ex-cavalryman. Walberg was no better than Grove, with only six wins and seven defeats. From the start, Ostermueller looked as though he should be a big winner, but he closed with a ten-and-13 record. Ferrell alone saved the situation and made the fourth-place finish possible, winning fourteen games and losing five.

And the 1934 Red Sox won a 2-to-1 game from Buck Newsom in St. Louis which still makes ol' Bobo see red. He didn't give up a hit until two were out in the tenth, and then a single by Roy Johnson, which hopped by shortstop Alan Strange, cost him the decision. Boston had scored an early hitless run in the second on a walk, a boot by Oscar Melillo, an out, and a fielder's choice at the plate. While Johnson recorded the lone Red Sox hit off Bobo, the Browns tagged Ferrell and Walberg for ten.

4

Yawkey pulled his most sensational deal following the close of the 1934 season. The millionaire got himself a shortstop and a new manager at the same time, when he purchased Joe Cronin, Washington's playing manager and then the game's number one shortstop, from Clark Griffith for $250,000, with the Boston club tossing in shortstop Lyn Lary, another $20,000 player, to sweeten the deal. With the exception of the Babe Ruth transactions, which included a mortgage on Fenway Park, the Cronin purchase was the biggest of all baseball deals.

Cronin was just twenty-eight at the time of the quarter-million transaction, and it made additional headlines from the fact that old Griff actually sold his son-in-law. In September 1934, the fine-looking San Francisco boy married Miss Mildred Robertson, adopted daughter and niece of the Washington owner. Griffith, selling his son-in-law, brought concern to some editorial writers, one of whom termed the Washington owner a "baseball Simon Legree." A columnist complimented Griff, writing: "Maybe old Griffith has something. I wish I could sell my son-in-law for $250,000. Any bidders?"

Joe arrived in San Francisco on Columbus Day, 1906, the son of Irish-born parents who were just then digging themselves out from the ruins of the great earthquake and fire of that year. A slim kid in his youth, Joe Cronin was as good a tennis player as he was a ballplayer. But baseball was his number one sport, and he was picked up early by a Pittsburgh scout, and Joe was farmed to Johnstown, Pennsylvania, and New Haven.

Pittsburgh then had one of the National League's greatest shortstops in Glenn Wright, and though Cronin showed promise when he played briefly with the Pirates in 1926 and 1927, Barney Dreyfuss, the Pittsburgh owner, didn't realize the young prize he had in his hands. Anyway, Donie Bush, Barney's manager, didn't think the coast kid would hit much, and Joe was sold to Kansas City in 1928. Cronin was there only half a season, when he was snatched up by Washington.

Joe's progress from there on was meteoric. In 1930, his second complete season with Washington, he hit .346 and played such a dazzling brand of shortstop that he was voted the American League's most valuable player. There has been a little tendency to belittle Joe's shortstop play, but the writers of his day gave him full acclaim. He won the shortstop position on the *Sporting News*'s annual All-Star team in 1930, '31, '32, '33, '34, '38, and '39 and played shortstop for the American League in all the All-Star games from 1933 to 1941, inclusive, with the exception of 1940. To make the *Sporting News* team, he had to get a majority of the votes of some 250 baseball writers; for the All-Star squads he was the shortstop choice of the American League managers.

Though his judgment frequently has been criticized, Cronin, over the years, has made a successful, aggressive manager for the Red Sox. Once he gets an idea into his head, he doesn't often change. His critics say his mind is not flexible, that Joe is obstinate and doesn't like subordinates to question his moves or judgment. But perhaps that's the Irish in him. Who can imagine a Giant coach having said to John McGraw: "Now, Mac, I wouldn't do so and so." Cronin has his faults, but he is loyal, likable, a sportsman and gentleman. The writer once had occasion to call on Cronin after he had lost two successive double-headers to the Browns, then an easy

quest in the American League. Joe was burning up inside, but he
kept it inside and outwardly remained calm, cordial, and friendly.

Joe's immediate contribution to the Red Sox was only a gain of
a game and a half over Harris' .500 season of 1934. Cronin's 1935
team, by now called the "Millionaires" and "Gold Sox," again finished fourth, winning seventy-eight games and losing seventy-five for
a percentage of .510. Cronin seemed to feel the tension of managing
Yawkey's expensive team, as his batting average dropped to .284, the
first time it was under .300 in five seasons. He didn't click too well
with his young Coast League first baseman, Babe Dahlgren, later
the first-base nomad of the big leagues. Babe was later quoted as
saying he always was scrambling around first base to save Cronin
errors on wild throws.

Grove had a magnificent comeback after his "dead arm" season
of 1934. Much of the old smoke was back in his fast ball; Mose won
twenty games and lost twelve, and regained the lead in earned runs
with 2.70. Wes Ferrell also had a grand season, winning twenty-five
games and losing fourteen. In fact, between them Bob and Wes
contributed forty-five winning games, or nearly fifty-eight per cent
of Boston's seventy-eight victories. Neither was too easy on the
managers, and they were both subject to clubhouse tantrums, when
benches were overturned, uniforms ripped, and gloves and shoes sent
hurtling through the air. Wesley is a believer in astrology, and when
he was under an evil sign, Win Green could post storm warnings in
the clubhouse. But they certainly gave Tom, Eddie, and Joe all they
had in that hectic season.

Grove really mellowed with the years, and when things didn't go
too badly, became a delightful person. Early in his career, he had
a mountaineer's distrust of strangers, and once he remarked, "The
trouble with people [meaning fans] is that they don't leave ballplayers alone." But eventually Mose learned people mostly meant
well, and their enthusiasm over ballplayers made the big baseball
earnings possible.

In case Wesley or Robert Mose wanted to blow off steam in some
tongue other than their own, Cronin added to the club's catching
corps "the man of many languages," the estimable Moe Berg, of
Princeton, Columbia, the Sorbonne, and points east.

The 1935 season can't be dismissed without some reference to the
liner from Joe Cronin's bat which hit Cleveland's third baseman
Odell "Bad News" Hale on the konk and snuffed out one of the Red
Sox's finest rallies. The game took place at Fenway Park in the first
half of a double-header, September 7, and I am indebted to Joe

Cashman for the gory details. "The Sox were trailing by a score of 5 to 1, when they started a big rally in the ninth; they had two runs in and the bases still full when Joe came up. He lined one down the third-base line, which looked like a sure hit until it struck Hale on the head and caromed over to shortstop Knickerbocker, who caught it on the fly. Billy tossed it to Hughes at second before Werber could scramble back, and then darned if Hughes didn't shoot it to Trosky at first in time to complete a triple play on Mel Almeda."

18

⊖

TERRIBLE TED SNARED IN SAN DIEGO

I

IN many respects, the season of 1936 was Tom Yawkey's most disappointing year in Boston. Connie Mack had slipped from fifth to eighth in his latest plunge from the championship heights to the cellar and had tags on his remaining stars and better than run-of-the-mine players. Tom and Eddie Collins made shopping excursions to Mack's Shibe Park emporium all during the winter and stripped the shelves clean.

In the biggest deal they obtained the Philadelphia club's slugging first baseman, Jimmy Foxx, the brawny Maryland home-run king, and John "Footsie" Marcum, an effective Kentucky right-hander with great feet, for $150,000, pitcher Gordon Rhodes, and catcher George Savina. In a lesser deal the Boston shoppers walked off with outfielder Roger "Doc" Cramer and infielder Eric McNair for $75,000, pitcher Henry Johnson, and infielder Al Niemiec. In smaller transactions, outfielder Bing Miller, shortstop Dib Williams, and pitcher Joe Cascarella gravitated from Shibe Park to Fenway Park. "I think this year we really should go places," Tom told Collins and Cronin, and his associates readily agreed.

After two years in fourth place, and the club strengthened with these additional Athletic players, especially Foxx and Cramer, it was reasonable to expect further substantial progress. Many Boston fans could see nothing short of the pennant, but at the finish the club limped home a poor sixth with seventy-four victories and eighty defeats. Clubs with half of the Yawkey pay roll breezed by the gilt-hemmed Red Sox.

It was difficult to put the finger exactly on the 1936 club's failure, even though Cronin was ailing with a lame arm, and played in only eighty-one games. However, Foxx did all that was expected of him. Jimmy of the big biceps hit .338, took a quick fancy to the left-field fence at Fenway Park, and fired an extra-base barrage which included thirty-two doubles, eight triples, and forty-one home runs. He was third in both homers and runs batted in. Cramer dropped from .332, his last average with the Athletics, to .292, but he scored ninety-nine runs and was a fly hawk, another Speaker, in center field. McNair hit .285, and filled in capably wherever Cronin employed him. He proved an able understudy for Joe in eighty-four games at shortstop.

The Red Sox again fared well enough when Lefty Grove or Wesley Ferrell was on the rubber. Mose won seventeen and lost twelve, again headed the list in earned-run effectiveness, and with Wesley it was twenty and fifteen. Ferrell also led in complete games with twenty-eight. But from there on down, Footsie Marcum, Jack Wilson, Walberg, Ostermueller, Jack Russell, and Jack Welch showed Boston fans a lot of pitching mediocrity.

Yawkey had spent well over a million dollars for players, and still he was sixth. It was disconcerting, dismaying, and discouraging, and another man might well have quit.

"Ruppert bought some pennants, when he was able to reach into the Red Sox for players," Tom told Collins and Cronin. "But, it doesn't seem to work for us when we buy Mack's old champions. So we've got to try something else and raise our own. We've got to build up a farm system such as Rickey has built up for Breadon in St. Louis and Barrow and Weiss for Ruppert in New York. That's the only way we can catch the Yankees."

For farm director, Yawkey employed Billy Evans, former famous American League umpire, former general manager of the Cleveland Indians, and now vice-president of the Detroit Tigers. Billy is a sound, experienced baseball man who knows the game from every angle. And it was Yawkey's decision to conduct a farm system, and Billy's spadework in finding and developing young minor league stars, which really started the Red Sox on their way up the ladder of success.

2

The 1937 club showed a seven-game improvement and got up to
.526, its highest percentage after Yawkey took over, but through a
freak in the won-and-lost table, the Red Sox finished in the fifth
slot, thirteen points behind the fourth-place Cleveland Indians.

It was a season for shaking up the club, trades, a general over-
hauling, and trying something different. Before the season, Cronin
swapped Billy Werber to the Athletics for Pinky Higgins, a former
University of Texas star, who had come fast with the Athletics after
Dykes was sold to the White Sox. Werber had played some grand
ball for the Millionaires, but Billy never lasted longer than a few
seasons in any clubhouse.

Then, just before the limit on the trading ban, June 10, Eddie
Collins and Cronin swung a rather odd deal with Washington. They
gave up the Ferrell brothers battery and the Mexican outfielder,
Mel Almeda, for none other than the colorful pitcher, Louis Norman
"Buck" Newsom, and Ben Chapman, the former Yankee outfield
speed boy, now the manager of the Phillies.

The deal brought about the end of Wesley's tantrums in the Fenway Park clubhouse, but Newsom, the new arrival, found it difficult
to pitch with a mentor on the infield. Cronin considered it part of the
manager's job to tell a pitcher what he should pitch under certain
conditions. "I think I know a little bit about this pitching business
myself," Bobo frequently interjected. It was like Dizzy Dean's
famous remark to his former manager, Frankie Frisch: "How come
an infielder like you is telling a great pitcher like me what and how
to pitch?"

Bobo lasted with Joe only for the balance of the 1937 season, when
he moved to the Browns in another pretty big swap, Newsom, infielder Ralph Kress, and Colonel Mills for outfielder Joe Vosmik,
who formerly had swung a mean bat for Cleveland. Chapman has
proved a dynamic, successful manager of the Phillies under Herb
Pennock, but when Ben was a private in the ranks no manager ever
marked his card A-plus for deportment and disposition.

By 1937, the Millionaires were becoming the slugging Red Sox,
with 831 runs scored, third only to the Tigers and Yankees, and an
even hundred homers. It was a clouting year, even though Jimmy
Foxx had an off season, the Marylander slipping to .285, while his
home-run production fell to thirty-six. Cronin's arm mended, and
he again played in 148 games, and hit .307. Cramer hit .305, and
Chapman .297, and Ben was tied with Werber for most steals, thirty-

Bobbie Doerr   Ted Williams, "The Kid"

Cecil "Tex" Hughson   Dom DiMaggio

five. After Rick Ferrell was traded to Washington, Gene Desautels, a former Holy Cross catcher, procured from San Diego, caught most of the club's games. Catcher Johnny Peacock, a North Carolina University graduate and mule trader, an early product of the Evans farm system, was brought up after a finishing course with Mike Kelley in Minneapolis.

Grove as usual was the pitching leader with seventeen games won and nine lost; Jack Wilson helped a lot that year with a sixteen-and-ten performance, while Marcum had a good stretch and wound up with thirteen and eleven. In between Washington and Boston, Newsom won sixteen and lost fourteen.

The pitchers clicked and the batters hit in one magnificent stretch at the Back Bay grounds in late July and early August, when Fenway Park fans saw their best stretch of baseball since the Carrigan days. Starting with a 5-to-4 game which Newsom won from the Browns on July 28, the Red Sox ran off twelve straight, interrupted only by a 2-to-2 tie. The bubble burst in the second game of a double-header with the White Sox on August 8, when Dykes's boys shot up Fenway Park to win, 13 to 0.

3

It was after the 1936 season that Billy Evans' spading in the minor league field began to bear rich fruit. In going after them young, Billy and Eddie Collins, his superior, came up with the two choicest plums of the San Diego club of the Pacific Coast League, a team with which the Red Sox then had a close affiliation. Both acquisitions were just eighteen-year-old kids, a pair of native sons of California, but they were to write brilliant chapters in Boston baseball, Theodore Samuel Williams and Robert Pershing Doerr. Both were born in 1918, the war year in which the Red Sox had won their last pennant. Bobbie arrived in Los Angeles on April 7, exactly a year after the declaration of war, Ted in San Diego, October 30, twelve days before the armistice.

With the exception of Babe Ruth and Ty Cobb, Ted Williams, known as "the Kid," "Terrible Ted," and the "Splendid Splinter," has been the most publicized of ballplayers. Whether Ted goes good, bad, or indifferent, and it frequently has been the latter, he always is a story. And like Ruth and Cobb, he has the natural faculty of making the headlines in activities other than baseball. And Ted is a born showman!

His mother is a Salvation Army worker in San Diego, with as

much zeal for her work in saving souls as Ted has in his sphere of hitting. His father is a rover, who has found it difficult to stay put in any one place. Mrs. Williams has been known as "Salvation May," "The Sweetheart of San Diego," and the "Angel of Tia Juana," but there has been nothing angelic about her oldest son, Teddy. One of the great hitters of all time, he has for years been Joe Cronin's problem child. An introvert, individualist, and lone wolf, Ted is irascible, hot-tempered, unsocial, and easily offended. Suffering from a certain persecution complex, he has had periodic run-ins with fans and sports writers all during his career. He tolerates them, just as a great maestro tolerates the critics who judge his work and the audience which pays to hear him conduct or to play his instrument.

Ballplayers say Ted has what the craft terms, "rabbit ears"; he hears everything. He considers himself an artist of hitting, baseball's outstanding hitter of today—the Babe Ruth of this generation, and he is as sensitive to criticism as would be a great pianist or singer if someone yelled from the gallery, "Who ever told that bum he could play?" One should come to praise and admire, not to criticize.

Yet there is much that is likable and winning about the tall, lithe, loose-swinging Californian. He is so natural and without inhibitions. Ted is like a boy who never grew up; whatever he feels, he portrays. If he has a good stretch, he can be amiable, a good conversationalist, with an intelligent grasp of his own problems, those of his team, his country, the world. He even has a shy sense of humor, which is whimsical, and often delightful. But when things go into reverse, Williams suffers moods when he frequently goes into a blue funk which drives Cronin to distraction. Though Williams dearly loves to hit and is one of baseball's greatest students of hitting, in one of his sullen, morose moods, he has taken halfhearted swings at the ball, failed to run out hits, loafed in going after fly balls. Three times Cronin has had to take Williams out of a game after such displays of petulance; at other times, there have been fines and admonishments.

Ted, tall and lanky, eventually grew up to six feet three inches, and in the vernacular of the diamond, he is "loose as a goose." He has terrific power in his wrists and forearms, and the knack of getting his power with a last-moment flick of his wrists. Along with great strength, he has perhaps the most remarkable pair of eyes ever brought into baseball. During Williams' war years in the Marines, it was disclosed that his eyesight is twice that of the normal person. When driving, he can read the states and license numbers of plates on cars far ahead, while the chap sitting next to him, with average vision, can merely make out the dim outlines of the plate. Ted can identify birds high in the air when they are mere specks in the sky, and enjoys having other persons verify his identifications with binoculars.

He won a student gunnery record in the Marine Corps, is a crack shot with rifle or shotgun. One of his favorite extracurricular activities at Fenway Park was to shoot the pigeons, which had become a nuisance, off the park fence or on the wing. Once when pigeons were scarce, Ted decided not to waste the ammunition in his gun. He shot the lights out of the scoreboard causing four hundred dollars' worth of damage.

In an article in *Life*, John Chamberlain says Williams is almost "monomaniacal" in his attempts to make himself the game's most perfect hitter. Almost since Ted was born, he has swung at everything he could swing against—rag balls, tennis balls, rocks, and he still is swinging. Swinging in front of a mirror at the Hotel Chase in St. Louis, he almost wrecked his bed with one of his powerful thrusts. And though his hands smarted from the impact, he couldn't help but remark pridefully to his roommate, "What power!"

He has talked hitting with every man who ever has hit .350 or better—Cobb, Ruth, Speaker, Hughie Duffy, Hornsby, Cravath, or to persons who knew a .350 hitter. He always feels he may learn something, and at the 1946 All-Star game at Fenway Park, he was observed intently watching Del Ennis, the Philadelphia National freshman star, at batting practice. "Never can tell where you might pick up something new in batting," said Ted.

Originally a southpaw pitcher in the San Diego High School, Ted joined the San Diego club at the early age of seventeen in 1936, when he was converted into an outfielder, hitting .271 in forty-two games. In 1937, he boosted his figures to .291, hitting 23 home runs and driving in 98 runs in 138 games. Billy Evans still is proud of the deal he made for Williams, calling it a steal; San Diego was paid $25,000 and five rather obscure players.

Williams could have gone immediately into the American League in 1938, but he already had shown some of his idiosyncrasies, and Collins and Evans figured a year in Minneapolis under the veteran Mike Kelley would do the young Californian a lot of good. At nineteen, Ted turned the American Association upside down with an average of .366, 43 home runs and 142 runs driven in. And in the outskirts of Minneapolis, Ted met Miss Doris Soule, who now shares Ted's ups and downs as Mrs. Theodore Williams.

Bobbie Doerr, the present Red Sox second-base star and captain, has an even more brilliant Coast League background than Williams. A former west coast American Legion star, Bobbie joined the Hollywood club at the schoolboy age of sixteen. In 1935, at seventeen, he played in 172 games for the Stars, hitting .317. By 1936, he transferred to San Diego and raised his batting average to .342.

By this time, the Red Sox had their working agreement with San Diego, and Eddie Collins made a trip to the coast just to see Doerr. In the first game he saw Bobbie, the kid made four errors. Even so, Collins was sold on the youth, and when he returned east he was bubbling with enthusiasm, saying, "I've just acquired the best second baseman in the minors." And Eddie is something of an authority on second basemen.

4

The triumvirate of Tom, Eddie, and Joe finally felt they were getting somewhere in 1938, when the club leaped from fifth to second. The club finished nine and a half games behind McCarthy's Yankees, but the Red Sox split their twenty-two games with the powerful New Yorkers. They finished with a percentage of .591, the same as Carrigan's championship club of 1916. After what Boston fans had gone through, such a finish was desirable—and most enjoyable. The end of the long drought seemingly was in sight.

Though some of the youngsters developed in the new farm system were coming up, and Bobbie Doerr was a part-time second baseman, it still was a veterans' year, with special emphasis on veteran Jimmy Foxx. The former Maryland plowboy was just about the whole works in the American League that year; he was the batting champion with a .349 percentage, the league's most valuable player, the leader in runs scored (139), runs batted in (175), home runs (50), most total bases (398). It was a pleasure to see him swing, and the ball disappear over the left-field fence.

Jimmy wasn't the only apple-knocker. The Red Sox had a big lead in both major leagues in team batting with .299. They led the New York champions by 25 points in that department, though the Yanks, with 174 homers to 98 for the Red Sox, outscored Boston, 966 to 902. But these two clubs were the only 900-run teams in the two majors.

Foxx had a lot of other guys emulating his fine example. Ben Chapman was fourth in hitting with .340 and second in doubles with forty. With a .325 average, Cronin had his second-best batting year in the majors, while other .300 hitters were Vosmik, .324; Higgins, .303; Cramer, .301. A young Dixie third baseman from Owens Cross

Roads, Alabama, and former Alabama University star, Jim Tabor, joined the club in the fall and showed indications of his batting future with .316 for nineteen games.

Cronin also had reasonably good pitching. Though Grove now worked only once a week, he won fourteen games and lost four, and still led the earned-run parade. Ostermueller finally lived up to some of his early promise with thirteen wins in eighteen games, and Jim Bagby, Jr., son of Sergeant Jim Bagby, thirty-one-game winner with the Gray Eagle's 1920 Cleveland world champions, started in strongly with fifteen victories and eleven defeats. Though Cronin had his tiffs with the headstrong Bagby, Joe won quite a little acclaim in the Fenway Park opening, when he unexpectedly pulled Jim, Jr., out of his cap for his first day pitcher and got away with an 8-to-4 victory over Charley Ruffing, the Yankee ace. Jack Wilson was worked harder than anyone on the staff, but had to divide thirty games, while a handsome lad from Buffalo, Emerson Dickman, who looked like a Hollywood leading man, performed like a real comer.

Joe Heving was picked up from Cleveland early in the season, and as a relief man he had a fine record, nine wins and two losses. There was one game in which the opposition belted tar out of the whole staff—Grove, Wilson, Dickman, Ostermueller, and several others—six in all. In desperation, Cronin put in Heving, making seven. The next morning, the Boston *Herald* used single-column cuts of the first six, and a two-column cut of Heving. And the title over the art read: *"ALL THESE AND HEVING, TOO!"*

One good second-place turn deserved another. The Red Sox, with another powerful line-up, again were the American League runners-up in baseball's centennial year of 1939. The Boston percentage was .589, two points less than in 1938, but this time the Sox trailed a .702-percentage Yankee team by seventeen games. Even so, the Red Sox licked the powerful New Yorkers on the season's series, eleven games to eight.

There was one brilliant fortnight in that 1939 season which Joe Cronin still considers one of the high spots of his career in Boston —in fact, in baseball. During a sensational July twelve-game winning streak, in which the Red Sox were shooting from all barrels, they shot up Yankee Stadium and pinned back the ears of the haughty Yankees in five straight games. It was one of the worst humiliations suffered by the Yanks during the heyday of their success under McCarthy.

Oddly enough, while the winning streak started with a pyrotechnic display in Philadelphia on July 4, when the Red Sox celebrated the nation's natal day with 17-to-7 and 18-to-12 swat fests, and a 6-to-4 victory on the fifth, the New York series was won largely by superior Boston pitching. On July 7, Dickman defeated Ruffing, 4 to 3, and Boston swept a double-header on the eighth with Ostermueller defeating Hildebrand, 3 to 1, and Denny Galehouse getting a 3-to-2 verdict over Gomez. The Sox then rubbed it in by winning a second double-header on the ninth, as Dickman, relieving Grove, was credited with his second 4-to-3 win, and Wilson and Heving triumphed, 5 to 3, in the last game.

The entire winning streak was on the road, but as in 1937, the Red Sox were tripped going after number thirteen. This time they were stopped by Buck Newsom in Detroit, 13 to 6, the Tigers pounding Woody Rich, Heving, and Sayles. By the end of the streak, Boston had clipped New York's big early July lead to six and a half games, but from there on the Yankees drew away.

Despite the fact that the 1938 and '39 clubs wound up with practically the same percentages, the complexion of the team changed materially. Though Foxx was second in American League hitting with .360, there was a much greater accent on youth. Williams, who wasn't twenty-one until after the season, broke in like a prairie fire. He played right field then and hit .327, seventh among regular players. The Kid led in runs driven in with 145, was second in runs scored, 131, and in doubles, 44; and was high up in homers with 31.

Even so, the famous Williams pout manifested itself early. In the blues over a slump, Ted acted as if he just didn't give a hoot in a game in Detroit. Cronin pulled him out of the line-up and sent in Lou Finney to run for him. "Ted, you're a boy playing a man's game," he told his young slugger. "And if you're going to stay in baseball, you've got to be a man."

Doerr, who participated in only 55 games in 1938, played in 145 and hit .289 in 1939. That's exactly where Jim Tabor, the new third baseman, finished in the batting tables. Tabor collected thirty-three doubles, eight triples, and fourteen home runs. In the July 4 double-header with the Athletics, Jim set two records by hitting four home runs, including three in the second game, when he twice cleared the bases with grand slam homers.

The Red Sox board of strategy thought so highly of Tabor in the previous winter that it traded third baseman Pinky Higgins and southpaw Archie McKain to the Detroit Tigers for pitchers Elden Auker and Jake Wade and outfielder Chet Morgan. In another winter trade, Ben Chapman and infielder Tom Irwin were sent to Cleveland for pitcher Denny Galehouse.

On the revamped pitching staff, Grove won fifteen games and lost four, and was the American League's earned-run leader for the last time. There were times when the newcomer, Galehouse, looked like a Joe Wood, but Denny had too many off days, and wound up at nine and ten. Oddly enough, that also was the record of Auker, the former Tiger. Wilson had the same kind of a season with eleven and eleven, though Ostermueller and Dickman won most of their games. Wade flopped completely and was passed along to the Browns.

Joe Cronin ended his five-year $30,000 per annum contract as player-manager, and everybody was greatly pleased. The popular San Franciscan, who had won his way into the hearts of the Boston Irish, was signed to a new document at a tidy increase. The future, indeed, looked bright.

19

⊖

HOPES AND DISAPPOINTMENTS

I

THE season of 1940 should have been the Red Sox's year. In 1938 and 1939, they were chasing super-duper Yankee ball clubs, New York teams so strong that they swept their two World Series with the Cubs and Reds without the loss of a game. Everyone in Boston was praying for them to have an off year. They had it in 1940, dropping to a percentage of .571, but the Red Sox, instead of taking advantage of it, finished tied with the White Sox for fourth place with a percentage of .532. Detroit was the winner with a lowly .584, defeating Cleveland with .578. What made it heartbreaking in Boston was that the .591 and .589 percentages of the Red Sox in 1938 and 1939 would have won in 1940.

Though bitterly disappointed, Tom Yawkey had no stronger criticism than to remark, "Well, I guess we missed the boat again."

There were a number of explanations for the 1940 cave-in. Some pointed to Cronin's supposed inability to get the best out of his pitchers. It was the year Buck Newsom pitched the Tigers into the pennant, winning twenty-one games and losing five, despite missing a month of play with a broken thumb. "If only Cronin had kept Newsom, then we'd have had the pennant instead of Detroit," muttered Joe's detractors.

The truth is that Cronin's entire pitching department bogged down. Bob Grove by now was forty, and the elastic in the great left arm snapped during a vital part of the season. Taking part in only twenty-two games, Lefty brought in only seven victories against six defeats. With Grove fading, there was no bellwether for the pitching flock, and the Red Sox hurlers had their worst season under the Yawkey regime. The 1940 Millionaires again were tops in team batting; they scored 872 runs, but the pitchers gave them back as fast as the sluggers could score them;.825 hostile runs were tallied against Boston. Only the pitchers of the lowly Browns and Athletics took a more harrowing beating.

There was no outstanding twirler; Wilson and Heving won more games than they lost, but Galehouse, Bagby, Ostermueller, Bob Harris, and Herb Hash, a newcomer from Boston, Virginia, were all mediocre. Mickey Harris, freckled Long Island southpaw, moved up from the Scranton farm that year; he won four games and lost two. In beating the bushes for pitchers, Billy Evans came across a tall bean pole, Bill Voiselle, of Ninety Six, South Carolina. Bill was so thin that Evans bought him a cow, so he would have a winter to fatten up. Voiselle was in the Red Sox Rocky Mount farm in 1940, but somehow got shuffled out of the Boston deck, only to bob up in 1944 as a twenty-one-game winner with the New York Giants.

Old Mr. Time also started edging up on several of Tom Yawkey's expensive player investments. Cronin, himself, was starting to put on weight; his batting average slipped to .285, and he wasn't covering the ground he did in former years. Joe finished tied with Berardino of the Browns for most shortstop errors.

Foxx dropped from .360 to .297, but still was able to bash out 36 homers. For a spell, Cronin got a hunch to use Jimmy behind the bat, his original Athletic position, and Foxx caught 42 games, as Lew Finney, another Athletic pickup, and later Tony Lupien, a Harvard graduate who hit .474 in ten games, filled in at first base.

Like a good trouper, Jimmy put on his catching harness but pointed out he was using entirely different muscles in squatting behind the plate, and he didn't think the shift helped his batting. Jim still would get in his murderous clouts, and after he hit a game-winning homer off Red Ruffing of the Yanks, a joy-crazed fan dashed out of the stands, with a quart bottle in his hand, and tried to induce Foxx to celebrate the occasion with a drink at the plate. Of course, the tippler was shooed away, as the crowd rocked with laughter.

If the 1940 season was a disappointment, it had its bright spots, one of them the introduction of a new budding outfield star, Dominic DiMaggio, youngest of baseball's so-called "Royal Family," to the fans of the Fens. Dom's oldest brother, Vince, had played with the Braves, and most of the other National League clubs, while Joe was the famous center fielder of the New York Yankees. Wearing a studious look under his strong glasses, and considerably smaller than the other DiMaggios, Dom looked like an assistant professor of biology at Smith or Harvard, and promptly was dubbed "the Little Professor."

He was purchased from San Francisco, his home-town team, for $30,000. Some scouts had stayed off him because of his thick glasses. His record on the Seals was good, though his marks were not as high as those of brother Joe in the same circuit. With Cramer still playing center field for the Red Sox, Williams was moved to left field, and young DiMaggio assigned to right. Injuries confined his activity to 108 games in his first Boston season, but he hit .301 and gave every indication of possessing the same uncanny defense skill as Joe. Not much of a mixer, and inclined to be a little shy, Dominic has the keenest mind of the DiMaggio boys. He showed just a trace of resentment at being known merely as "Joe DiMaggio's kid brother," and once remarked, half in jest and half seriously, "Maybe, the time will come when he will be known as Dom's brother."

In the development of the Red Sox farm system, Yawkey acquired controlling interest in the Louisville Colonels of the American Association. "We bought the Louisville club largely to get Peewee Reese, their shortstop," Billy Evans says. However, he and Joe Cronin didn't see eye to eye on Reese, who in 1940 was sold to the Brooklyn club and today is that team's star shortstop. Cronin personally scouted Reese and thought he was too light for big league purposes. The club also thought it had an even greater shortstop prospect than Reese in the Oregonian, John Michael Paveskovich (Johnny Pesky), browsing that year in the Rocky Mount farm. In the same summer, the Red Sox moved up a Kentucky-bred outfielder, Stan Spence, from the Louisville club; he hit .279 in fifty-one games for Cronin.

Ted Williams' second year in the American League saw a 17-point gain in his batting average to .344, but his home run-crop receded to 23 and runs batted in to 113. Shifted to left field in Boston, he soon found himself in a feud with the fans who inhabit the left-field stands. Ted never had the knack of kidding back with the fans, a practice which such outfielders as Babe Ruth and Casey Stengel enjoyed and recognized as part of their daily chores. Though a dead right-field hitter, he even tried to drive his wicked liners into the left-field stands so as to make the Williams-baiters duck for safety.

And once, in an inadvertent moment, he remarked, "Anyway, I'd rather be a fireman." Apparently, on a fire ladder there are no riding fans or critical reporters. Ted has an uncle who is the head of a fire

Dave Ferriss, His Sister, Ann, and Mother, Mrs. W. P. Ferriss

Johnny Pesky   Rudy York

company in Mt. Vernon, New York, and while playing in New York, Williams frequently visits his fire-fighting relative. He'll probably never live down the remark, and it has become part of baseball's legend, like Schoolboy Rowe's, "Are you listening, Edna?"

Fans began to chide Ted about wanting to be a fireman all around the circuit, and that clown, Jimmy Dykes, then the Chicago manager, always thinking up things to rile the Kid, made an act of it. He equipped some of his bench hands with five-and-ten-cent store firemen's hats; wore a chief's hat himself, and when Ted went to bat somebody started off a siren. Actually, Ted took it in better grace than when fans have yelled, "Fireman, save my chee-ild."

2

The Yankees shook off their lethargy in 1941, regaining the championship, and the Red Sox snapped right back with them and regained second place. However, the Bostonians couldn't make it very close and trailed McCarthy's club at the finish by seventeen games. A few trades had been made at the start of the season, which were expected to strengthen both catching and pitching. Even though Cramer was the only American Leaguer in 1940 with two hundred hits, he was traded to Washington for outfielder Gee Walker. Gee, the colorful Mississippian, never was given a locker at Fenway Park; he promptly was packed off with pitcher Jim Bagby and catcher Gene Desautels and sent to Cleveland for pitcher Joe Dobson, catcher Frankie Pytlak, and infielder Odell Hale, whose dome figured in the freak triple play. Cronin weakened on both pitchers Ostermueller and Denny Galehouse and sold them to the Browns. Charley Wagner, brought up from Louisville, took up some of the pitching slack with twelve victories and eight defeats.

The high spot of the 1941 season was Ted Williams' .406 batting average, the first .400 in the majors since Bill Terry hit .401 for the 1930 Giants and first in the American League since the mighty Tiger, Harry Heilmann, smote .403 in 1923. That season Williams really was the "Splendid Splinter," as he led the American League hitters from here to Christmas; the second hitter, Cecil Travis of Washington, was forty-seven points away. He won his .406 average by closing in high, getting six hits, including a homer and two-bagger, in Philadelphia in a double-header on the last day of the season. The double smashed one of the horns on the loud-speaker on the right-field fence.

Yet Ted told one and all, there wasn't too much to his feat. "If

Yawkey gave you ten things to do and you did only four of them, you would be fired," he said. "I do four of them by getting four hits out of ten and I am a hero. Heck, I should be hitting .750 by right."

The Kid also won his league home-run leadership with 37, scored the most runs, 135, but was walked so often in the pinch (he drew 145 passes), that he could drive in only 120 runs, five behind Joe DiMaggio, the loop leader. In the 1941 All-Star game in Detroit on July 8, Ted knocked the bottom out of the National League's hope chest with the most dramatic homer in the history of the midseason classic. With the National League All-Stars leading by 5 to 4, two out in the ninth, and the Yankee Joes, DiMaggio and Gordon, on base, Terrible Ted unlimbered his artillery and sent one of Claude Passeau's fast pitches deep into the upper right-field stands at Briggs Stadium, giving the joyous American Leaguers the game, 7 to 5. Ted wasn't unsocial when Del Baker, the American League manager, and all the players who could reach him kissed him in the club-house. However, even though the *Sporting News* designated him as the Player of the Year, the American League's most valuable player award went to Joe DiMaggio.

With a .406 average, and things going rather smoothly, there were only a few flare-ups. One came in a game in Detroit when Lefty Grove was trying for his three-hundredth major league victory; Joe Cronin thought Ted loafed on a hit and admonished him in a Detroit lobby. Ted didn't resent the rebuke, but he resented a reporter putting the incident into print.

Grove finally made his three-hundredth victory on his third attempt on a hot blistering day, July 25. It wasn't one of Grove's best-pitched games, but was another of the unforgettable contests which high-light Fenway Park history. The Cleveland Indians were the victims as Grove staggered home by a score of 10 to 6, with Jimmy Foxx, Mose's old Athletic buddy, supplying the TNT charge which broke up the game in the eighth. Grove was hammered hard in the early innings, and each team scored two runs in the seventh, making the score 6 to 6.

Dom DiMaggio walked to start the Red Sox eighth, and was sacrificed to second by Finney. Roger Peckinpaugh, the Indians' chief, then used an odd bit of strategy; he had Lefty Al Milnar, his third pitcher, walk Cronin to get at .400-hitting Williams, a left-handed hitter, who already had smacked a homer and single. For a moment it looked as if he might get away with it, as the disgusted Ted went out on a pop foul.

But Milnar still had Foxx, a right-handed hitter, to reckon with.

Jimmy sent a terrific line drive crashing off the center-field fence, scoring Dom and Joe, and puffed around to third, trying for a triple. When the relayed throw from the outfield bounced into the dugout, Foxx completed the journey to the plate. And just to make it doubly safe for Mose, Jim Tabor followed with his second homer of the day.

Grove lasted just long enough to register number three hundred— he and Eddie Plank, the old Athletic southpaw, being the only left-handers ever to turn the trick. Grove never won another big league game, closing his last season in Boston with seven victories and as many defeats. However, as the light of the forty-one-year-old southpaw star flickered out, a new Red Sox pitching luminary, a right-hander, Cecil Carlton "Tex" Hughson, a former University of Texas ace, appeared in the baseball heavens. Tex, six feet three, tall, dark, and handsome, had a world of stuff and the savvy to know how to use it. Almost immediately he had the hearts of the Ladies' Day fans aflutter. Developed on the new Louisville farm, Tex won five games and lost three after reporting to manager Cronin in August.

Billy Evans' splendid labors as head of the new Boston farm system ended with the 1941 season, when Herb Pennock, the old Red Sox left-hander, succeeded him as Eddie Collins' right-hand man.

3

For the fourth time in five seasons, the Red Sox ran second to the Yankees in 1942. "What the hell; can't we ever pull out in front of those guys?" asked many a disappointed Boston fan. But it was a year in which the Fenway Park denizens felt they were rooting for a real ball club, and actually it was one of their best. The 1942 club finished with ninety-three victories, fifty-nine defeats, and a percentage of .612, Boston's highest since Bill Carrigan won 101 games to beat out that hundred-victory Tiger team in 1915. So happy were the Boston fans over their club, that they established a new turnstile record for Fenway Park—730,340 paid admissions.

Cronin's club had a good fighting chance for the flag for the greater part of the season. When the clubs paused for their All-Star holiday after the July 4 games, the Red Sox trailed New York by four games. The Yanks then had a percentage of .658 to Boston's .605. About the same relative difference separated the two clubs at the finish in October, .669 to .612, Boston then trailing by nine games. But it was a satisfying campaign. Though held to an eleven-to-eleven even break by Luke Sewell's troublesome third-place Browns, the Red

Sox won the season's series from everyone else, including the champion Yanks. They shaded the New Yorkers, twelve to ten.

It was the season after Pearl Harbor, when Uncle Sam still was getting ready and before the great world holocaust had taken its heavy toll on the big league personnel. About the only important loss Cronin suffered to the services that year was pitcher Mickey Harris, who flew up from Panama in his army khaki to pitch an inning for the service All-Stars against the American League winners of the All-Star game in Cleveland, July 7.

For the first time Cronin tried his hand as a bench manager, and it worked out quite satisfactorily. The Californian did get into forty-five games as utility infielder and pinch hitter, hitting .304, but Joe's place at shortstop was taken by the brilliant Yugoslav from the northwest, Johnny Pesky, who was an immediate sensation. Pesky played shortstop like a Scott or Barry, and the brash kid, in his first season in the majors, hit .331, runner-up among the players in a hundred games or more to the leader, who again was Ted Williams. Tall Theodore again won the marbles in almost everything his league had to offer, the batting crown with .356; most runs, 141; most runs batted in, 137; and most homers, 36. But the lads in the press boxes again were looking the other way when they voted for the American League's most valuable player, and they gave it to Joe Gordon, the Yankee, who hit .322 and had exactly half of Ted's home runs. No wonder Ted concluded, "Those guys don't like me."

While Cronin sat this season out, Jimmy Foxx also reached the end of his string as a full-time regular. The sturdy Maryland boy had slowed up considerably, and to make matters worse, Tony Lupien, his eventual first-base successor, broke several of Jimmy's ribs with a line drive, while James was helping out by pitching in batting practice. One way of getting rid of a rival! Foxx wasn't the kind of a player one could bench, so on June 1 he was sold to the Chicago Cubs for something in excess of the interleague waiver price. At the time, "Double X" was hitting .270 for thirty games, in which he had hit five home runs. He closed his American League career with 524 round-trippers, 222 of them in Yawkey's gilt-trimmed knickers. Foxx picked up ten more home runs in the National League, giving him 534, more than ever were hit by a right-handed batsman and second only to Ruth's majestic total of 714.

Jimmy groused a bit about his departure from Boston and was quoted as taking a few digs at Joe Cronin and his old manager's handling of pitchers, in the Chicago press. But Jimmy denied saying it. Another quote came in answer to a question why Connie Mack won pennants with stars who couldn't produce for Cronin. "Double X's" alleged reply was, "One manager knew what he was doing; the other didn't."

Perhaps the outstanding thing about the .612-percentage season was the improved pitching situation, especially when contrasted with 1940. Collins and Cronin had made over the entire staff, and it came up with a new pitching bellwether in Tex Hughson, who in his first full season won twenty-two games and lost only six. Butland had a brilliant stretch in which he won seven games out of eight. Charley Wagner was listed at fourteen and eleven, and Joe Dobson at eleven and nine. Oscar Judd, a left-hander, was unlucky and could win only eight out of eighteen. Dominic Ryba, the one-man ball team who could pitch, catch, or play any position, was procured from the Cardinal chain in exchange for Alpha Brazle, who later did some fine work for the St. Louis Redbirds.

One of the few sour notes of the 1942 season was the backwash of the Stan Spence deal the winter before. Clark Griffith, wily old fox of Washington, inveigled Collins into giving up Spence and pitcher Jack Wilson for pitcher Ken Chase and outfielder Welaj. Spence was topped in hitting in 1942 by only Williams and Pesky, while southpaw Chase promptly bobbed up with a sore arm as soon as he put on Yawkey regalia.

4

From a highly respectable second in 1942, the Red Sox tumbled down the percentage ladder to seventh in 1943. This time it was not old age creeping up on the club as in 1906, nor the depredations of a Frazee as in 1921 and 1922. Uncle Sam beckoned to Yawkey's young men, and some of the brightest Red Sox stars, along with lesser Boston lights—Ted Williams, Dom DiMaggio, Johnny Pesky, Frankie Pytlak, the new catcher; Tom Carey, Eddie Pellagrini, and pitchers Joe Dobson, Charley Wagner, Bill Butland, and Earl Johnson, exchanged Millionaire Tom's gilt-edged flannels for the khaki, blue, and olive green of the Army, Navy, and Marines. Williams and Pesky both started as cadets in naval aviation, Ted came out a second lieutenant in the Marines, and Johnny an ensign in the Navy. DiMaggio put in three years in the Coast Guard.

Tom Yawkey gave more time and attention to his lumber and ore interests, which were closely tied up with the war effort, and less to baseball. Collins, Pennock, and Cronin scurried around digging up whatever talent was available—4-F's, players not yet called up, those who were too old, or too young, and rookies from the farm. A raft of new outfielders were acquired, Bob Johnson from the Senators, Pete Fox from the Tigers, and George Metkovich, a former Brave farm hand who also played first base, from San Francisco. Johnson, a part Cherokee, was the former Athletic hitter and brother of Roy Johnson, a Red Sox fly-chaser under Quinn. A whole quartet of outfielders, Leon Culberson, Tom McBride, Johnny Lazor, and Floyd Garrison, were advanced from Louisville.

The infield was patched up by the purchase of Skeeter Newsome from the Athletics, and shortstop Eddie Lake from Sacramento, then a Cardinal farm. At one time Eddie fought Marty Marion, Mr. Shortstop himself, for the St. Louis shortstop job. New pitchers included Heber Newsome, Clem Hausmann, Lou Lucier, Yank Terry, and the 225-pound George Woods, a man with a ravenous appetite. Even Joe Wood, Jr., son of the 1912 ace, was given a chance to make the staff, after being nurtured under Mike McNally in Scranton.

Cronin jumped in, hit .312 in fifty-nine games, and hung up a pinch-hitting record that they'll be shooting at for a long time. He established an American League record with five home runs as a pinch hitter, three of them coming within two days of each other at Fenway Park against the Athletics in four times at bat, for a major league mark. Joe let out all of his pent-up fury at Connie Mack's pitchers and made Connie inquire, "What's got into Joe? We just can't get him out."

All three pinch homers in this three-day barrage came with two men on. In the seventh inning of the first game of a June 15 double-header in Boston, Joe batted for Mace Brown in the seventh, prodded a productive homer, but couldn't prevent his team losing by 7 to 4. Something went wrong when he tried it in the second game; he flied out. But two days later, he was at it again, hitting three-run round-trippers in each game of a second double-header while batting for his pitchers. The first won the first event for Boston, 5 to 4, the second missed by one run of tying the score in the eighth inning of the nightcap—a game the Red Sox lost, 8 to 7.

5

By 1944, the club again gave a fairly good account of itself, though it had a terrible late September, in which the Red Sox lost ten straight and were rolled over twelve times in fifteen games on their last western trip, sending the war Red Hose reeling to a .500 finish. They wound up fourth, with seventy-seven victories and seventy-seven defeats, which oddly enough was Bucky Harris' position and percentage ten years before, in the second year of Yawkey's ownership.

It was the year the Browns won their first and only American League pennant with the low percentage of .578, but the Red Sox were a spirited contender as late as Labor Day, when only three games separated the first four clubs. On Tuesday, September 6, the day following the holiday, New York led St. Louis by a half game; Detroit was two and a half games out of first place, and the Red Sox trailed the Tigers by a half game.

For a good part of the season, the Red Sox were in their familiar second-place notch, and though the Boston club still had to make a western trip, many observers gave them the best chance of the four contenders. However, Uncle Sam had a war on, and couldn't hold off a month before stripping the Red Sox of their remaining stars.

Tex Hughson was having a brilliant season and had won eighteen games and lost five up to August 24, when he was called into the Army. The Red Sox withstood that shock until Bobbie Doerr's draft board gave him his induction notice a fortnight later. Bob also was having a phenomenal year; a homer from his bat had won the midseason All-Star game for the American League; he was nosed out for the batting championship by Lou Boudreau by two points, and was selected by the *Sporting News* as the American League's most valuable player. After Bobbie left, the backbone of the club was broken, and the team went on its late September nose dive.

Next to Doerr, the club's outstanding performer in the drive for the 1944 pennant was the veteran Bob Johnson, who hit .324, third among the regulars, and banged out seventeen home runs. Cronin made a smart deal with the Athletics, obtaining catcher Hal Wagner for Floyd Garrison. Hal hit .330 for seventy-one games and caught superbly before he, too, was called into service.

Bob Carpenter, a wealthy young chap from Wilmington, Delaware, purchased the Phillies, and when he offered Herb Pennock the job of general manager, Eddie Collins refused to stand in the way of his son's father-in-law. He advised Herb to take it, and George Toporcer, a former Cardinal infielder and Red Sox farm team manager, succeeded the able Pennock as the Boston club's farm director. Phil Troy, for years the Red Sox road secretary, was advanced to the post of assistant to the general manager, and Tom Dowd, a Bostonian with a fund of Irish stories, took over Phil's former duties.

During the winter of 1944–45, Uncle Sam scanned the Red Sox roster again to see whether he had overlooked anyone who might be of use, and he called up another pair of regulars, third baseman Jim Tabor and Tony Lupien, the new first sacker, and relief pitcher Mace Brown. Cronin, by now in his thirty-ninth year, was as big as a Boston alderman, but he trained faithfully to take over at third base. The Red Sox opened in New York, and in three games Joe had three hits in eight times up for an average of .375.

In the third game, Joe made a really phenomenal play in tossing out a Yankee, and he yelled happily at Art Fletcher, the former New York third-base coach, "Hey, Art, who was that guy Jimmy Collins they used to talk about?"

But in the very next inning, in rounding second base Cronin's spikes caught in the bag, and he pitched forward with a fractured right leg. Everyone knew it was the end of a great playing career, but Joe was comforted by good-will messages which came streaming in from all corners of the country.

In addition to Cronin's injury, it was a gloomy April for the Red Sox. The Millionaires now wore more patches than Huckleberry Finn, and they started out like a Frazee or Quinn team at its worst. Eight games were lost before the Sox rewarded the long-suffering Boston fans with an 8-to-4 victory over the Athletics in Philadelphia on a Saturday, April 28.

A double-header was scheduled the following Sunday, and in the first game, Cronin, managing the club on crutches, started a young G.I. from Shaw, Mississippi, recently discharged from the Army because of an asthma condition. The name of the newcomer was quite similar to that of the early Boston second baseman, Hobe Ferris; this young chap was David Meadow "Boo" Ferriss, and when he blanked the A's with two hits by a score of 2 to 0, he started a new chapter in Red Sox baseball. A week later, when Boo shut out the stronger Yankees, 7 to 0, Boston fans began to realize a new star had arrived in the Back Bay firmament. Dave set an American League record for a freshman pitcher by dealing out twenty-two goose eggs before he was scored upon. Ferriss didn't stop there but won his first ten games, four of them shutouts.

But for those eight straight spring losses by the 1945 Red Sox, Dave probably would not have had this early chance in the majors. A former Mississippi State college star, he had had little prewar professional experience except as a class B Red Sox farm hand. In 1942 he won seven games and lost seven for Greensboro, North Carolina in the Piedmont League. Inducted into the Army, he served as a corporal, physical instructor, and pitcher for Bib Falk's Air Corps team at Randolph Field. In army games, Boo not only distinguished himself as a pitcher but as a hitter. With a .417 average, he outhit Enos Slaughter, the Cardinals' slugger.

Discharged on February 24, 1945, he was ordered by Eddie Collins to join the Louisville Colonels and trained with Nemo Leibold's club. When the Red Sox got off to their woeful start and were desperate for pitchers, Leibold wrote Cronin, saying, "I think this young fellow Ferriss can help you." And what help the young fellow rendered!

Despite the fact that the 1945 Red Sox floundered in seventh place, Boo Ferriss kept interest alive all season with his great pitching feats, and in his freshman year he compiled the remarkable record of twenty-one victories and ten defeats. Dave was the first American League freshman since Wes Ferrell in 1929 to win twenty games, and the first for the Red Sox since Hugh Bedient in 1912. Even so, at midseason it looked as if Boo would approach thirty victories. He scored his nineteenth win on August 12, when his old bugaboo, asthma, slowed him down. He won his twentieth on August 26 and didn't get his twenty-first until September 10. Four of his ten defeats were suffered in September.

Boston took the near two-hundred-pound Mississippian to its heart. Dave not only was a great pitcher, but everyone voted him a "swell kid." In fact, Jack Malaney, veteran Boston scribbler, wrote: "Ferriss had a personality which was infectious; everybody fell in love with the guy. He was brand new. He was a babe-in-arms, but grand to talk with. He was frank, but earnest, and braggadocio never had occurred to him. He was so grand to talk to that everybody fell in line."

Despite the seventh placer, the 1945 Red Sox drew 603,784 at home, and made around $50,000. Much of it was due to Boo; on Sunday, September 23, with nothing at stake, a 28,743 crowd invaded Fenway Park just to let Ferriss know of Boston's affection for the modest son of Mississippi. Boo was presented with a new Lincoln Zephyr, with all gadgets, originally built for Mrs. Edsel Ford, a wrist watch, and gold key chain. The Red Sox players gave their pitching star a radio, and his home town, Shaw, Mississippi, sent a great floral piece. His mother and sister, up from Shaw for Boston's Ferriss Day, were presented with flowers and fountain pen sets. Then the unsympathetic Yankees defeated Boo, 2 to 1.

And the Fenway Park pigeons had multiplied while the great Nimrod, Ted Williams, was off to war. In throwing in a ball from the outfield to second base, outfielder Hal Peck of the Athletics killed a pigeon on the wing. Had the ball not hit the pigeon, the throw would have been wild and the Red Sox runner would have been safe.

However, when the ball killed the bird, it deflected the sphere into the hands of the second baseman, who caught it and tagged out the Boston runner coming in. In another game with the Athletics at Fenway Park, Tom McBride, playing center field for Boston, chased a pigeon instead of Sam Chapman's line drive.

20

⊖

BACK IN THE PENNANT SWIM AGAIN

WITH the end of the war, there was a great parade of Red Sox stars back to Fenway Park: Ted Williams, Johnny Pesky, Bobbie Doerr, Dom DiMaggio, Tex Hughson, Mickey Harris, Joe Dobson, Hal Wagner, and lesser lights. Baseball addicts recognized that Cronin's "pros" were back, that Joe again would have a good team, but few suspected how good.

In New York, Joe McCarthy also had a lot of baseball warriors back in Joe DiMaggio, Charley Keller, Red Ruffing, Bill Dickey, Spud Chandler, Joe Gordon, Rizzuto, Henrich, and others, and the majority of critics believed the Yankees would start right in where they left off in 1943. The Tigers, the 1945 world champions, also with a lot of good men back, had their enthusiastic boosters and were given strong pennant consideration. There were other brave souls who were willing to climb out on a limb and pick the Red Sox, but they "if'd" more than Iffy, the Detroit Dopester.

On the eve of the season, the Boston *Globe's* erudite Harold Kaese wrote one of his able pieces for the *Saturday Evening Post*, "What's the Matter with the Red Sox?" It carried an added box head: "One of baseball's major mysteries is the annual flop of the star-rich, pennant-poor Boston club. Could Manager Joe Cronin be the answer?"

Well, that article didn't sit too well with Cronin and more or less put him on the spot. In Boston, they argued the article back and forth, with the Irisher from San Francisco having more boosters than detractors. Many felt that what had been wrong with the Red Sox was that in the past the Yankees simply had been too good. But in 1946 it was the Red Sox who were too good for the field. They were so good that despite a weak stretch around pennant-clinching time, they led the second-place Tigers at the finish by twelve games, and the third-place Yanks, their main contenders most of the season, by seventeen.

There is a turning in every lane, and this was it for the patient, long-suffering Red Sox fan, after the tortuous road he had trod since the war pennant of 1918. And when the Red Sox rode safely into Pennant Haven for their seventh flag after that lapse of twenty-eight years, the race was won with almost ridiculous ease. With the exception of two days in April, when the Yanks and Tigers each led for a day, and a few first-place tie days, the Red Sox held undisputed possession of the front seat all season. Propped up by early winning streaks of seventeen and twelve straight, they had money piled in the pennant bank, which took care of late-season lapses. After middle July, Cronin's lead never was less than ten games, and as the Red Sox approached the stretch in early September they led by sixteen games.

By winning 104 games and losing 50 for a percentage of .675, the 1946 club had the second-highest mark in the long history of the Red Sox, being topped only by the .691 of the colorful world champions of 1912. In fact, at one time it looked as if excelling the record of Jake Stahl's team would be a breeze. The sights once were leveled at the 110-victory performance of the 1927 Yankees, but they had to be lowered. The 1946 champions won the year's series from every club, defeating the second-place Tigers, fifteen to seven, and the third place Yankees, fourteen to eight.

The club went safely through its big early test in April. With a record of six victories in their first eight games, they met the Yankees for the first time at Fenway Park since Cronin and McCarthy regained their stars. It was an unhappy occasion for Boston, as the New Yorkers clubbed Hughson, Bagby, Butland, and Brown into submission, to win easily—12 to 5. Many shook their heads sorrowfully and muttered, "Well, it's still the same old story when they play the Yankees." But the very next day, April 25, the Red Sox reversed the score, and won, 12 to 5, behind Dobson. That game, more than any other, put starch in the 1946 club, and from then on, the Yankees held no terrors for them.

For weeks, the Sox were unbeatable at home, and the western clubs actually looked silly in their futile efforts to win a game at Fenway Park. The Red Sox threatened to break all records for winning at home, but eventually closed with sixty Fenway Park victories to seventeen defeats, against the record of the 1932 Yankees —sixty-two wins and fifteen reverses at Yankee Stadium. It wasn't until the western clubs made their second invasion of Fenway Park that the Red Sox finally lost a home game to a western team. That was June 12, when Bobbie Feller stopped the twelve-game winning streak with a 7-to-2 victory. In fact up to July 20, the Sox had lost only two games in Back Bay to a western club, and both were to Feller.

However, if they were tough hombres at home, the Red Sox were terrible on the road in night games, especially in the early season. "I've got a great day-time ball club, but we surely can louse things up at night," said Cronin. "Even a team of nine pitchers would be ashamed of the batting averages our hitters have compiled after dark." They had one stretch in St. Louis, when they scored one unearned run and made thirteen hits in twenty-seven night innings against the Browns.

Never pressed at any time, the club had a heck of a time scoring its clinching victory on its last western trip in September. The Yankees, with managerial troubles, were receding fast in early September, and after the games of September 4, the Red Sox led by sixteen and a half games. It looked as if the Red Sox would clinch the flag by the week end of September 6, 7, 8, but Boston lost one to Washington and two to the lowly Athletics.

Everything then was set for the clinching of the pennant in Detroit; road secretary Tom Dowd had the champagne on ice, and all plans made for a joyous victory celebration. But the Tigers, who had been the easiest kind of pickings up to then, smacked down the Red Sox twice and moved into second place, ahead of the Yankees. The Red Sox then took their champagne and ice to Cleveland, where Bob Feller turned them back for their sixth straight loss, September 12. That business of pennant clinching was getting to be a decided pain in the neck.

Finally, on Friday, September 13, they made it. With Tex Hughson pitching, the Red Sox won a low-hitting game from Red Embree, Cleveland right-hander, by a score of 1 to 0. Tex gave up only three hits, and Red, two, but one of the latter was Ted Williams' inside-the-park first-inning home run, his thirty-eighth of the season. Lou Boudreau had played his famous shift for Ted, with the infield shifted far to the right, and the left fielder, Pat Seerey, playing behind shortstop. Ted punched the ball over Seerey's head, and by the time the Indians ran it down, the Kid stretched it into a homer. This was the first inside-the-field home run that Williams made in the American League. The Yanks defeated Detroit at the same time, making everything perfect, and it was a night for celebration. All club rules were suspended, and the new American League champions sang, drank champagne, and frolicked far into the night. After his long pennant wait, owner Tom Yawkey was especially playful. Ted Williams was the only absentee; supposedly he visited a wounded war veteran.

And among the telegrams of congratulations received by Cronin was one from Harold Kaese: "Congratulations to a champ who made me a chump."

2

A winter deal with the Detroit Tigers had done much to make the 1946 pennant possible. In their efforts to strengthen at short-stop, the Tigers gave up Rudy York, their hefty 215-pound Georgia first baseman, to land Eddie Lake, the Boston club's war shortstop. The deal helped both clubs, but York was an especial tower of strength for Cronin. While big Rudy hit only .275, he pounded in 119 runs and smacked 16 homers. In one hectic game in St. Louis, York hit two grand slams. Pitcher Jim Bagby was regained from Cleveland in another trade for Pitcher Vic Johnson.

Williams had an odd year. For half of the season, it looked as if Ted would knock most of the records out of the book. They didn't give him much chance to hit, and Arch Ward, sports editor of the Chicago *Tribune*, wrote: "Ted Williams walks so much Joe Cronin has to slip car-fare into Teddy's uniform pocket before every game." For a spell, it appeared as if even Ruth's record of 170 bases on balls might topple, but Ted walked less in September and closed the season with 156 passes.

When the pitchers got the ball anywhere near the plate, he literally murdered "the pill." In justice to National League pitchers, they gave Ted every opportunity to hit in the 1946 All-Star game played at Fenway Park, July 9, which was a Boston picnic, a Williams circus, and a 12-to-0 rout of the National League. Never was Teddy more magnificent. In five times at bat, he hit two home runs, two singles, and drew one walk; he scored four runs and drove in five. His last home run was made off the famous blooper ball of Rip

Sewell of the Pirates, a pitch against which the hitter must supply his own power.

"That's the greatest exhibition of hitting I've ever seen," said Charley Grimm, the National League manager, in openmouthed awe.

Yet it was shortly after the All-Star game that Lou Boudreau began shifting his club around to the right for Ted, practically leaving the left side of the field unprotected. It made Williams try harder to hit one out of the lot against Cleveland. "I wanted to hit a homer more than ever," he said, "so I could tell Boudreau, 'You put them in the right position all right, Lou, but you should have had taller men.' "

However, Ted, a pull hitter who sends twenty-four out of twenty-five balls to right field or right center, found it more difficult to hit 'em "where they ain't." He pressed, and admitted later in the season that he became very tired as the campaign progressed. "It seems odd a fellow should become tired, just from playing a ball game every afternoon, but that's just what happened," he said.

He was out of the line-up for several days with a fever, and on August 27, while traveling to an exhibition game, Ted and Mrs. Williams were severely shaken up when his car skidded on a wet Massachusetts highway and crashed into another car.

At the start of the 1946 season, it was said that Ted was a changed Williams. He now was twenty-seven, and three years in service supposedly had sobered him. But as Ted experienced several mediocre weeks, and other players were pressing him for leadership in various departments, his prewar feuds with fans and writers again broke into the open. Even Bobo Newsom volunteered his services as a public relations counselor and advised Ted how to get along better with his public and press.

In an article on Williams in *Collier's,* Kyle Crichton quoted Ted as saying he liked only four sports writers in the whole country, and the quartet included Grant Rice and Frankie Graham of New York.

Taylor Spink, enterprising publisher of the *Sporting News,* wired Jack Malaney, his Boston correspondent, for the identity of the other two. Jack wired back: "Joshua and John."

Williams engaged Fred Corcoran, of the Professional Golfers' Association, to handle his side lines and by-products, one of which was a daily Williams-signed column in the Boston *Globe.* One day Ted said quite petulantly to Hy Hurwitz, his little ghost writer: "I get tired looking at a little squirt like you."

"That makes us even, for I get tired looking at a big galoot like you," was the ghost's snappy rejoinder.

At a time when it looked as if Johnny Pesky would pass Williams in the American League hit parade, it was reported in the Boston press that Ted wasn't speaking to Paveskovich. However, the players went out of their way to speak on the ball field, and Ted remarked: "A lot of guys work in an office, and they get along all right. When the day's work is over, the men have their own interests and scatter in different directions. It's the same way with me on a ball club."

Williams eventually lost the batting championship to Mickey Vernon of Washington, .353 to .342. Hank Greenberg outdistanced the Kid in home runs in September, 44 to 38, and beat him in the stretch in runs batted in, 126 to 123. Ted never hit another home run after the pennant-clinching game of September 13.

Despite his falling off in the latter part of the season, Ted romped off with the annual Kenesaw Mountain Landis plaque, winning the American League's most valuable player prize for the first time. He finished with 224 points. The Red Sox did especially well in the balloting, placing five in the first ten, Williams, Doerr, Pesky, Ferriss, and DiMaggio. Bobbie finished third with 158 votes, and Johnny fourth with 141.

Pesky, thanks to a great spring, followed Williams in the batting averages with .335. On May 3 and 4, against Cleveland at Fenway Park, Johnny ran off eleven straight hits; he just missed tying Pinky Higgins' record of twelve straight with the 1938 Red Sox. Dom DiMaggio hit .317, and while Doerr finished with .271, Bobbie did terrific damage with 34 doubles, 9 triples, 18 homers, and 117 runs batted in. Hal Wagner, the former Athletic catcher, took part in 116 games, caught superbly until September, but he tired perceptibly at the finish and wound up with an anemic .225 batting average.

Oddly enough, Cronin had the same third-base trouble that Barrow had experienced with the last Red Sox winner twenty-eight years before. Jim Tabor frequently had taken Cronin's training regulations lightly, and when Jim was released from service, he was passed along to Pennock and the Phillies. It left quite a gap at Boston's hot corner, as Ernie Andres, Eddie Pellagrini, Leon Culberson, Rip Russell, and Pinky Higgins participated in Cronin's third-base parade. Higgins, the 1937–38 Red Sox third baseman, was regained from Detroit by purchase, May 19, and carefully nurtured until the World Series. Right field was another season-long concern for Cronin, as George Metkovich, Tom McBride, Leon Culberson, and Wallie Moses, a midseason pickup from the White Sox, took turns at playing the position.

However, there would have been no 1946 Boston pennant but

1946 Red Sox American League Champions

Thomas Austin Yawkey

© Sporting News

Joe Cronin, Manager 1946 Champions

© Sporting News

for the development of a crack "Big Pitching Four," all former G.I.'s—Boo Ferriss, Tex Hughson, Mickey Harris, and Joe Dobson. Defying the superstition that a star freshman usually experiences a second year letdown, the brilliant Ferriss finished with twenty-five victories against six defeats. The popular Mississippian again won his first ten games, and then had a later streak of twelve straight.

Hughson came back brilliantly after the war; somehow the boys couldn't score for the handsome Texan as they did for Boo, and Tex seemed to catch the most doughty opponents on the opposition. Even so, Hughson won twenty games, lost eleven, many of them heart-breakers, pitched twenty-one complete games and six shutouts. Harris (seventeen and nine) and Dobson (thirteen and seven) were better pitchers than before the war. Bob Klinger, a former Pirate, was acquired on waivers and did some strong relief pitching, as did left-hander Earl Johnson, wounded in the Battle of the Bulge. Cronin found spots for Bill Zuber, a Yankee waiver pickup, and Bagby. A batch of other pitchers, Clem Dreisewerd, Charley Wagner, Mace Brown, and Mike Ryba completed Joe's motley staff.

No manager ever went into a pennant race with more coaching brains at his elbow than Joe Cronin—Del Baker, leader of the 1940 Tiger champions; Larry Woodall, former Detroit catcher; and the popular Tom Daly, a Boston coach since 1933. When Don Gutteridge was obtained from the Browns for infield insurance, Tom Carey, the former infielder and Joe's particular pal, was shifted from the playing ranks and made a fourth coach. And behind this quartet, Cronin had the wise heads of Eddie Collins and chief scout Hughie Duffy to advise him.

And what support the 1946 Red Sox fans accorded their pets after the years of pennantless ball in Boston! In a season in which baseball attendance records were broken right and left, as were home-run records when Babe Ruth started wholesale blasting in 1920, the Red Sox fans almost doubled the former Boston American attendance record, the turnstile count at Fenway Park soaring to 1,416,944. And on the road the Red Sox also played to around 1,250,000. The twenty-two games with the Yankees in Boston and New York attracted around 600,000. The 1946 attendance mark at Fenway Park would have been even higher if Yawkey and Collins could have found room for their many customers. Time after time Fenway Park was a sellout with thousands turned away.

"We had to turn away over twenty-five thousand on a dozen occasions," said Red Sox publicity director Ed Doherty. "On several Sundays, and when Feller pitched his first two games against us, we had to stop people as far away as Kenmore Square if they didn't have tickets. There were as many people heading back for the subways an hour before game time as there were coming to the ball park."

The famous Lolly Hopkins, with her megaphone, never missed a contest. She lives in Providence, forty-two miles away, but buys the same reserved seat for every game. And she really gives the visiting players a going over! But Lollie says she is getting old and couldn't stand another season like 1946.

3

When the Red Sox were smearing all opponents before their September slump, and the Cardinals and Dodgers were in their dragdown fight in the National League, many sighed for the poor Frick leaguers. They feared the 1946 World Series would be the same kind of a massacre as the July All-Star game. Many predicted a four-straight clean-up for the Sox, while others said, "If the National League club is lucky, it will win one game."

When it became necessary for the National League to play a play-off series to settle the pennant, Cronin chafed at the idleness. "Why don't they play one game, and have it over with, so that we can get on with the series?" he asked. The Cardinals, coming fast, won the right to play the Red Sox by downing the Dodgers in two straight games.

The start of the World Series, originally scheduled for the National League city on Wednesday, October 2, was postponed until Sunday, the sixth, and in order to keep the Boston club from getting stale, Collins and Cronin decided to put in the time by playing a three-game series with a team of American League stars, headed by Steve O'Neill, and including such stars as Joe DiMaggio, Hank Greenberg, Luke Appling, Stan Spence, Hal Newhouser, and Dizzy Trout.

There are many who believe that the National League play-offs and the series with O'Neill's All-Stars cost the Red Sox the first World Series defeat in their history, a series which eventually hinged on the final play of the seventh game.

In the fifth inning of the first game of the practice series, October 1, little Mickey Haefner, Washington's pony southpaw, threw an inside pitch which hit Ted Williams a sharp blow on the right elbow. After the first twinges of acute pain, the bruised elbow became numb and badly swollen. Williams immediately left the game and missed the remaining contests with the O'Neill stars, while Win Green treated the elbow with heat and electric therapy. Williams later had a terrible World Series record, five singles, one run batted in, and a batting average of .200 in seven games, and generally was voted the goat of the series.

Ted was too much of a man to alibi himself, but ballplayers close to him say that pitch by Haefner cost the American League the Worlds Series. Ted's timing was off; he couldn't regain it, and with the exception of a few long flys in the last game, he couldn't swing with his customary power.

Even though it was known that Williams was not in good condition, betting commissioners made the Red Sox favorites at odds that later proved to be fantastic—six to twenty. For every individual game, the Bostons were the favorites. The theory was that a well-rested club would run down a jaded, tired team, worn out from its furious battling for the National League pennant. Instead the Red Sox, who had loafed for weeks, played a club which was whetted to the keenest edge by the furious late-season competition it had participated in.

Yet in the very first game, played in St. Louis on a beautiful Sunday, October 6, before 36,218, it looked as if the "smart money" was on the right horse. Howie Pollet, St. Louis' twenty-one-game winning southpaw, who pitched most courageously despite a pulled muscle in his back, weakened in the final innings, and with the score tied at 2 to 2 in the tenth, big Rudy York broke up the game with a terrific home run into a refreshment stand on top of the left-field bleachers. It sent Cronin and his players chuckling back to the Chase Hotel in possession of a 3-to-2 victory.

Eddie Dyer, Cardinal manager and an old college football man from Rice Institute, used an even more exaggerated form of the Boudreau shift for Williams. He had the third base side of the field entirely unprotected, with shortstop Marion playing a little to the right of his normal position, and third baseman Kurowski on the right field side of second base. Ted's first series game was his best; he got out of it with a single and two walks in five attempts.

The Red Sox were within one pitch of losing the game, but it was a contest in which the breaks fairly balanced each other. Tex Hughson started for Cronin and pitched fine ball, though he eventually went out for a pinch hitter with the score 2 to 1 against him. Earl Johnson, the left-hander, pitched the last two innings, took credit for the victory, and the only Cardinal to reach base on him got there on a fumble by Pesky. "What do you think of my Battle of the Bulge boy?" chirped Cronin happily.

Boston drew first blood, scoring in the second inning, when York was hit, took second when Doerr walked, and crossed the plate when Higgins stabbed a long single to right. Tex held that 1-to-0 lead until the sixth, when St. Louis tied the score. Red Schoendienst scratched an infield single with one out, and Doerr fumbled on Terry Moore long enough to lose a force play at second, but got Terry at first. Musial brought in Schoendienst with a double to right. The Redbirds then filled the bases when Slaughter walked and Kurowski was hit, but Tex poured it in and fanned young Garagiola.

The Cardinals took the lead in the eighth, when with two out, Kurowski singled, and the near-perfect outfielder, Dom DiMaggio, lost Garagiola's fly in the sun. The ball dropped in back of Dom for a long double, but Garagiola, the Italian kid, was nailed trying for three bases. It looked as if "Little Joe" was retired before Kurowski crossed the plate, but umpire Lee Ballanfant allowed Whitey's run. Cronin leaped out of his dugout, and other Red Sox surged around the umpire, when Lee explained he had permitted the run because Higgins had interfered with Kurowski while the Pole was rounding third base.

The Red Sox tied it by the very skin of their teeth in the ninth. After Doerr fanned, Higgins hit a grounder at Marion, which instead of taking the usual hop, skidded on the ground through Mr. Shortstop for a gift hit. Little Gutteridge ran for Pinky and sprinted to third on a single by pinch hitter Glen Russell. Roy Partee fanned for the second out, and the count was two strikes and three balls on McBride, when Tom hit a high bouncer which jumped past Kurowski, and Gutteridge ran home with the tying run.

Harry Brecheen, the Cardinals' sinewy 160-pound left-hander, known in St. Louis as "Harry, the Cat," first started to get into the hair of Cronin and the Red Sox in the second game played at Sportsman's Park, October 7. A fifteen and fifteen pitcher in the National League, Brecheen's specialty all season was winning clutch games for Dyer, and he tied up the series by winning a four-hit 3-to-0 shutout. The Cat was especially effective against Williams, and the tall slugger couldn't get a ball out of the infield, was once called out on strikes, and when he tried to push a ball into left field in the ninth, raised a sickly foul which Marion settled under.

Cronin also called on a left-hander, Mickey Harris, who pitched well enough to win the ordinary game, and a costly error was responsible for two of the St. Louis runs. Del Rice, the Cardinals' sophomore right-handed hitting catcher, was the Boston left-hander's nemesis. Del opened the third with a solid double to left, and darned if that pestiferous Cat, a .133 National League hitter, didn't bring Rice home with a torrid single to right.

Rice again opened the fifth with a clean single to left. This time Brecheen tried to sacrifice, but Higgins pounced on the bunt, and a good throw to second would have resulted in an easy force play. But Pinky hurled the ball with so much Texas beef behind it that the sphere landed in right center; Rice pulled up at third and Brecheen at second. The catcher scored on Schoendienst's infield out, and the Cat came in when Moore smacked one so hard at Doerr that it was ruled an infield hit.

4

After two games in St. Louis, there was a one-day lapse as the two clubs made the long hop to Boston. The series was resumed at Fenway Park on Wednesday, October 9. It was the day Boston fans had been looking forward to for years, the return of baseball's great late-season carnival to the scene of so many of the Red Sox's early triumphs. In an effort to give as many of their fans as was possible a chance to see the series, the Red Sox sold single-game tickets, in place of the strip tickets for three games, which for years has been the usual procedure. Even so, thousands were sorely disappointed when they received their rejection slips. One was so put out that he sent Eddie Dyer the family's lucky penny of 1826 to give him luck in the series, luck which the fan had intended bringing to the Red Sox.

The third game was a real Boston holiday. Rudy York, hero of the first game, promptly put the game on ice with a second homer in the very first inning, and Boo Ferriss, the likable Mississippian, pitched up to the fondest expectations of his many admirers. Boo again put the Red Sox ahead in the series, two games to one, by pitching a 4-to-0 shutout. It was the fiftieth World Series shutout, and the first pitched by a Boston pitcher since Babe Ruth won his 1-to-0 decision over Jim Vaughn in the first game of the 1918 series. The six hits yielded by Ferriss and his lone pass were scattered through seven innings, and St. Louis never advanced a runner past second until Musial tripled with two out in the ninth. Stan was left when Boo whipped a third strike over on the dangerous Slaughter for the final out.

Murry Dickson, Dyer's pint-sized right-hander, pitched well, but one pitch beat him in the first inning. After Pesky had gone hitless nine times, Johnny slapped his first hit of the series, a single to left field, and advanced to second on DiMaggio's roller to Musial, the second out of the inning. At this juncture, Dyer paid Williams an unexpected compliment. He ordered Dickson to give Ted a walk, preferring to gamble on York. It proved a poor gamble, for with the count two strikes and three balls, Rudy rifled the ball against the screen on top of the left-field wall, driving in Pesky and Williams ahead of him.

A fourth Boston run was tallied at the expense of Ted Wilks in the eighth on York's single, Doerr's double, and Hal Wagner's infield out.

One of the kicks of the third game for Boston fans was Ted Williams' finally taking advantage of the unprotected left side of the diamond. The Kid punched a safe bunt down the line in the third inning, and the fans received it as joyously as York's homer. After the bunt, Dyer reshifted his Williams defense. He kept Kurowski on third, and Marion, the shortstop, went to the right side of the second-base bag.

With Tex Hughson well rested since the first game, Yawkey, Cronin, the Boston fans, and most of the assembled writers confidently expected the Red Sox to enjoy a three-to-one margin by the time the fourth game of October 10 was over. For a pitching choice, Dyer was down to George Munger, who only returned from military service in August, and whose late-season pitching with the Redbirds was spotted.

The result of the game was one of the World Series' greatest upsets. All through the nine innings, the Cardinals were hitting fools; they smashed out twenty hits for twenty-nine bases and won with silly ease, 12 to 3. Three consecutive batters in the St. Louis line-up, Enos Slaughter, George Kurowski, and young Joe Garagiola, each came out of the melee with four hits. Slaughter started the carnage in the second inning, when he opened on Hughson with a 380-foot homer, and he scored after each of his hits. Enos had a chance to be the first World Series player to get five hits, but was stopped by Clem Dreisewerd in the ninth inning. Marty Marion hit two doubles and a single and groused, "Ted Williams beats out a bunt and makes the headlines; Marion gets three hits and nobody notices it." As for National League cohorts, they joyfully cried, "That wipes out the sting of that 12-to-0 All-Star beating."

Hughson pitched his poorest game since his return from service. After being bumped for three runs in the second inning, he went out during a second three-run St. Louis offensive in the third. In desperation, Cronin trotted out Bagby, Zuber, Brown, Ryba, and Dreisewerd in an effort to halt the slaughter—and Slaughter.

The Red Sox banged out nine sturdy hits themselves, including Bobbie Doerr's two-run homer off Munger, but from the second inning on, Big Red always had that comfortable feeling of the big St. Louis lead propping him up. Following Doerr's home run in the eighth, he left the game, suffering from a migraine headache.

That 12-to-3 defeat had a sobering effect on the Red Sox. The Cardinal team surely was proving no pushover, and the Boston players began to realize there was a real task ahead of them. But when Joe Dobson put them ahead for the third time by winning the fifth game, 6 to 3, at Boston, October 11, the Red Sox felt Oklahoma Joe had given them the game "we had to win." Cronin was delighted and said, "This is the game I had planned for Joe from the very start." Dobson pitched even better than the final score indicated, as the Cardinal attack simmered down from twenty hits to four, and their three runs were made possible by two untimely boots by Johnny Pesky, who had a mediocre series both at bat and in the field.

Howie Pollet, St. Louis' frail left-hander, tried it a second time, even though he still was in poor condition to pitch. The Red Sox demonstrated that early, and after Gutteridge, substituting for Doerr, Pesky, and Williams, three of the first four Boston batters up, lashed out singles, Dyer promptly lifted Pollet and put in another southpaw, Alpha Brazle, formerly of the Red Sox organization. Williams had driven in Pesky with a hard single down the right-field foul line, Ted's only run batted in of the series.

Brazle was continually in hot water, but the Red Sox had a difficult time scoring on the tall redhead. Dyer had Alpha present three intentional walks to York and a fourth to Culberson in his effort to hold the score down, but eventually the gifts caught up with him.

Boston scored a second run in the second inning when Partee led off with a single—the only hit by a Red Sox catcher in the series; Culberson banged out a homer in the sixth, and the Red Sox finally put the game on ice with three in the seventh. After DiMaggio doubled, Brazle fanned Williams, and Dyer ordered that third intentional pass to York. It didn't work as well as the two earlier ones, as Higgins doubled to left, scoring DiMaggio and sending York to third. This time Culberson was given a walk. It might have worked, but as Marion tried for a force play at second on Partee's grounder, he threw the ball into center field, and both York and Higgins scored. It left red-socked runners on third and first, but Brazle fanned Dobson and retired Gutteridge on a fly to Moore.

The three games at Fenway Park drew respective crowds of 34,500, 35,645, and 35,982, according to the amount of standing room which was sold, little above the average Red Sox–Giant games at old Fenway Park in 1912 and well behind the 42,000 Boston crowds of 1916, when the Red Sox played their World Series home games with Brooklyn at Braves Field.

5

It became necessary to go back to St. Louis to finish the series. The Cardinals returned on their special train, but Cronin decided to fly his boys to the Mound City, so they would have that extra night of sleep at the Chase Hotel. The Red Sox had a three-to-two jump, but Joe knew the Cardinals had proved tough competitors in the past, pulling out both the 1926 and 1934 series when their opponents had them down by a similar margin. He tried not to slip up on a single move which might give him a slight percentage.

The general belief was that the two shutout pitchers, Dave Ferriss and Harry Brecheen, would battle each other when the series was resumed at Sportsman's Park on the thirteenth. Pitching Brecheen was an absolute "must" with Dyer, but Cronin felt he was in a position where he could gamble. He thought it smarter to pitch Harris and hold back Ferriss as his "ace in the hole," if a seventh game was necessary. Inasmuch as Harris had done well in the second game, the logic was sound.

It was a month from the day the Red Sox clinched the pennant in Cleveland, and most of the Boston players considered it a good sign that they also would end the World Series on the thirteenth. But that vexatious Harry the Cat had other ideas, and Joe just couldn't comb him out of his hair. While Brecheen was hit harder than in his earlier game, he again tied up the series for Dyer as the Cardinals won the sixth game, 4 to 1.

Great support helped Brecheen in the early frames. In the first inning, the Red Sox filled the bases with one out on singles by Pesky and DiMaggio and Williams' walk. York had a glorious chance to break it up, but slapped a grounder down to Kurowski which the Pennsylvania Slav converted into a double play. Doerr and Higgins opened the second with singles, but Bobbie's hit was nullified when the Redbird left fielder, Erv Dusak, shot down Doerr at third. York scored the lone run on the Cat in eighteen innings, when he boomed a long triple to the wall in left center and cantered home on Doerr's fly. Had Rudy hit that triple in the first inning, it would have been a different story.

The Cardinals leaped out in front with a 3-to-o lead in the third. Harris pitched two strong innings, and then he was routed with a barrage of five rousing hits. Mickey's "debbil man," Del Rice, started it again with a single, and was forced by Brecheen. Then Schoendienst's double and Moore's long fly scored the Cat. Two more runs followed on successive hits by Musial, Kurowski, and Slaughter. Hughson relieved Harris, and Dom DiMaggio prevented more runs when he made a lunging catch of Walker's low line drive. A fourth St. Louis run was scored on Earl Johnson in the eighth on a walk to Slaughter, a force by Walker, and Marion's double.

Sam Breadon was so confident that the sixth game was in the bag, that an announcement was made over the public address system in the eighth inning, giving full details for obtaining tickets for the seventh and final game, to be played on Tuesday, October 15. "Hell, he's sure taking a lot for granted," muttered DiMaggio, Doerr, and other Red Sox, while the Cardinals were afraid their boss was putting a whammy on them. No club ever wanted to pull out a game with a ninth-inning rally as badly as did the Red Sox, but it was not to be.

The betters again made the Red Sox strong favorites for the seventh game. In fact, Cronin was congratulated for having so jockeyed his pitchers that he had his ace, Dave Ferriss, fresh and primed for the all-important contest. Dyer was forced to employ Murry Dickson, flattened in the third game by York's homer. The cards seemed all in Cronin's favor, but it was the Cards who won a soul-stirring, never-to-be-forgotten battle, 4 to 3. Up to then the Red Sox had won all the odd-numbered games, one, three, and five, and the Cardinals the even-numbered ones, two, four, and six, but the Redbirds now broke the order and also won number seven. They again proved themselves the National League's greatest money team.

Williams finally got some "wood" on the ball, but Terry Moore, despite his aching knees, pulled down Ted's terrific drive in the first inning, and Harry Walker brought down another powerful Williams blast in the fourth. Moore then made an even greater catch on Pinky Higgins off the wall in deepest left center in the fifth.

The Red Sox started in as if little Dickson would be a pleasing dish, and scored a quick run in the first inning. Moses and Pesky opened the game with singles, Wally taking third, from where he romped home on Dom DiMaggio's fly. Moore stopped further scoring with his circus catch on Terrible Ted.

Ferriss showed early that this wasn't likely to be another shutout day, as Schoendienst singled in the Cardinal half and Musial doubled, but the Redbirds lost a run when the former was out trying for a two-bagger. St. Louis tied it up in the second, when Kurowski opened with a double to left and got around on Garagiola's infield out and Walker's long fly.

To the horror and amazement of American league partisans, the great Ferriss met the same kind of fate in the fifth inning that Harris had encountered in the third two days before. The Cards teed off, knocked out Boo with four solid hits, and took the lead, 3 to 1. Walker led off with a single to center, was sacrificed to second by Marion, and scored when Dickson slammed a double to left. Schoendienst's single scored the pony pitcher, and Moore's single sent Ferriss to the showers. Dobson came in and did a swell relief job. After retiring Musial, he walked Slaughter, filling the bases, and then got rid of Kurowski.

From the time Doerr opened the second with a scratch hit, the Red Sox put only one runner on base until the eighth inning, DiMaggio drawing a pass in the sixth. But without warning, two pinch hitters, Rip Russell and George Metkovich, came through with clean hits to start the eighth, and the Sox were back in the ball game. Russell, first hitter of the inning, banged a single to center, and "Catfish" sent him racing to third with a steaming double to left. The Red Sox bench was in an uproar. "This is it! This is the big inning!" everybody shouted.

Dyer stopped the game and motioned in his hard-worked Cat, Harry Brecheen, from the bull pen. Cronin elected to permit Moses, a left-handed hitter, to bat against the southpaw, and Wally watched a screw ball break over the plate for a called third strike. Then Pesky sent a short fly to Slaughter.

There were curses and mutterings on the Red Sox bench. Was the rally to perish like that? It was a sickening thought, but DiMaggio brought life to the dugout with a double off the right-field wall, driving in the two tying runs. Then came another bad break, as Dom sprang a charley horse on the base lines and limped painfully into second base. It was necessary for Cronin to send in Culberson to run for Dom. Williams again had a great chance but popped weakly to Schoendienst.

Cronin had Hughson, Klinger, and Johnson warming up, and there were murmurs of surprise when Klinger came in, with the outcome of the series riding on every pitch. Joe's thought was that Klinger, the old Pirate would know just what to pitch at this stage, but the hunch was a poor one, and the Cardinals regained the lead in the second half.

Slaughter greeted Klinger with a single, and Kurowski popped to the pitcher, trying to sacrifice. Walker then hit a double, little more than a long single, to left center, starting the most discussed play of the series. Culberson didn't field the ball as cleanly as DiMaggio might have done, but he got it to Pesky in time to shoot down Slaughter, if Country attempted to score. But Johnny didn't think Enos would be so daring as to try to come in. Pesky paused a moment to look around, and that moment was fatal. Slaughter, running faster than he ever ran in his life, never paused at third, but came tearing in for the plate. Pesky's throw pulled Partee some ten feet up the base line, and Slaughter slid safely over the dish with the gold-encrusted run. The scoreboard now read, Cardinals, 4; Red Sox, 3.

The Red Sox fought to the very last ditch, and for a few minutes it seemed as if they again would tie or win in the ninth when York and Doerr opened on Brecheen with singles. The Cat then made his greatest stand. Higgins' attempted sacrifice bunt resulted in a force play on Doerr at second, but Campbell, York's pinch runner, reached third with one out. But the Red Sox catchers remained futile to the end, as Partee fouled to Musial.

With two out there was a momentary flicker of hope when pinch hitter McBride grounded to Schoendienst near second base. The redhead experienced difficulty in finding the "handle," and the ball ran up his arm like a mouse. Red finally got hold of it and made the short throw to Marion for a force play on Higgins on a close decision. Had Pinky been a half step faster, he would have beaten the force, and Campbell would have scored the tying run.

As the score had been tied after DiMaggio's eighth inning double, the game was Brecheen's to win or lose, and the victory was chalked up as the Cat's third of the series. He was the first left-hander ever to win three World Series games, and the first pitcher to perform the feat since Stan Coveleskie of Cleveland won three games from the Dodgers in 1920.

As yells of uninhibited joy came out of the Cardinals' clubhouse, the gloom in the Red Sox dressing room was so thick one could cut it with a knife. Cronin praised the Cardinal outfielders, asking, "How does anyone get anything past those guys?" and when some reporters questioned Pesky, Joe called over, "Leave him alone." Cronin then went into the Cardinal clubhouse, and though his heart felt like a lump of lead, he tried his best to smile as he grabbed Dyer's hand. "You have a fine team, Eddie, and you did a great job leading it," he said with his usual sincerity.

Long after the other Red Sox dressed and left the clubhouse, Ted Williams sat on the bench in front of his locker, still in uniform and staring grimly at the floor. Failure to hit the Cardinal pitchers was his most harrowing experience since he embarked on his baseball career with San Diego ten years before.

A public reception, which Mayor James Curley had planned for the Red Sox in Boston, October 17, win or lose, hastily was called off. And for the gilt-edged members of the Red Sox, the series didn't run into important money. The parks of the two contending clubs were comparatively small. Despite a big postwar roster, the Red Sox were most generous with their series melon, and by the time they divided their loser's portion into forty-one shares, there was only $2,077.06 left for each man.

21

⊝

LOOKING FORWARD

AFTER twenty-eight years of effort, the Red Sox regained the top spot in the American League, but baseball's highest honor, the world championship, evaded them. So there remains another goal for the hard-hitting, star-studded postwar Red Sox—an emphatic victory over the champions of the National League, such as was scored by the old Carrigan teams.

But with the 1946 Red Sox winners by a twelve-game margin, the future is bright, and many see a cycle for the club similar to the one which started in 1912, when the Red Sox won four league pennants and four world championships, and had two runners-up, in a seven-year stretch. A World Series at Fenway Park won't be the strange, almost-forgotten rite that it was in 1946. Many more will be played there in the next decade.

Though many of the Red Sox stars spent what might have been their best years in service, the club still is young and in its prime. A manager who has two pitching aces such as Dave Ferriss and Tex Hughson for the nucleus of his pitching staff is envied by his fellow managers. And Joe Cronin has a lot of additional pitching strength besides his two big right-handers.

Williams' World Series debacle should merely whet Ted's ambition for bigger and better hits in some future World Series, and even may have a salubrious effect on the "Splendid Splinter's" psychology. Hans Wagner, Ty Cobb, Babe Ruth, and Rogers Hornsby all went through bad or mediocre series without affecting their reputations as great batsmen. They sprang back strongly after their

World Series failures. Prior to the 1946 World Series, Dave Egan of the Boston *Record* ran the story that Williams would make his last appearance in a Red Sox uniform in the games with the Cardinals. He believed Ted would figure in a big trade. Many Boston fans thought Dave had the right hunch. Ted thought so himself and was willing to bet teammates and New York sports columnist, Jimmy Cannon, a hundred dollars that he would be traded ten days after the series. One reported trade was that Ted to go to the Yankees for Joe DiMaggio, catcher Aaron Robinson, and third baseman Bill Johnson. Williams expressed a preference for Briggs Stadium, which would be a home-run haven for him.

There probably were persons in the Boston organization who would have countenanced a Williams trade, if suitable material were procured in exchange. But owner Tom Yawkey always has been strongly pro-Williams, and likes to see Ted play in his spangles. Tom said, "I haven't even considered a Williams deal."

The Louisville Colonels, the Red Sox's class AAA farm, had a 1946 season similar to the team at the top of the Yawkey-Collins chain. The Colonels won their American Association pennant, successfully fought their way through the A. A. play-offs, but lost the junior World Series to the Dodgers' farm team in Montreal. But there is plenty of good material on Nemo Leibold's team if the Red Sox need quick replacements.

After the close of the 1946 season, pitcher Charley Wagner was named assistant to George Toporcer in the Red Sox farm system, and it was announced that Tom Carey, Mace Brown, and Mike Ryba would be placed elsewhere in the organization.

To fill their places on the roster came a batch of newcomers, mostly pippins raised on the Red Sox farms. From the great Mike McNally's Scranton pasture came Sam Mele, leading hitter of the Eastern League, a big fellow with lots of power and a great arm. Sam was scheduled to get first crack at the right field position on the 1947 Red Sox. Mele's Scranton pitching teammate, Tommy Fine, with twenty-three victories, seventeen of them in succession, against only three defeats, looked like important help for the mound department. Fine had the distinction of being the unanimous choice of Eastern League writers for the most valuable pitcher award of that circuit.

Louisville graduated to the Boston varsity pitchers Harry Dorish and Al Widmar, third baseman Jack Albright, second baseman Chuck Koney, and shortstop Strick Shofner; while Scranton sent up another third-base candidate in Sam Dente. From New Orleans came still another third baseman, George Strickland, and an outfielder, Peter Layden, before the war a great pro football player.

In 1946, the Red Sox were one of the three clubs which didn't play night ball at home, along with the Detroit Tigers and Chicago Cubs. The 1,416,944 attendance mark of 1946 was compiled entirely in daylight games. But a certain amount of night ball seems desirable in present-day baseball, and though the wealthy Yawkey prefers day ball and has bucked the night trend for years, he has put in what has been termed the last word in a lighting system since the end of the 1946 season. A specified number of after-dark games will be played in 1947.

There also has been talk that the Red Sox will double-deck their grandstand, but that seems something for the future. At present Tom says, "I like my ball park as it is."

There has been a glorious past for the Red Sox, some cruel intervening years, a satisfying present, but the greatest Red Sox years still are ahead.

INDEX

Jack Carlson of the Society for American Baseball Research prepared this index. Corrections of spelling errors in the original text are from John Thorn and Pete Palmer, eds., *Total Baseball: The Ultimate Encyclopedia of Baseball,* 3d ed. (n.p.: Harper Perennial, 1993).

Acosta, Jose, 185
Adams, Merle, 30
Agnew, Sam, 164, 167, 171, 172, 175
Ainsmith, Ed, 183
Albright, Jack, 256
Alexander, Dale, 201, 202, 207
Alexander, Grover Cleveland, 15, 124–26, 128–32, 135, 143, 164
Almeda, Mel, 213, 216
Altrock, Nick, 31, 35, 54
Ames, Red, 103, 104
Andres, Ernie, 242
Andrews, Ivy, 200
Anson, Adrian, 5, 16
Appling, Luke, 244
Armbruster, Charlie, 66
Armour, Bill, 65
Arrelanes, Frank, 84, 89
Auker, Eldon, 222, 223

Bagby, Jim, 221
Bagby, Jim, Jr., 221, 225, 227, 238, 240, 243, 249
Baker, Del, 228, 243
Baker, Frank, 95
Baker, Newton, 159, 163
Baker, William, 125, 134, 144
Ball, Phil, 181, 194

Ballanfant, Lee, 246
Bancroft, Dave, 125, 127–33, 135, 136, 137
Barber, Turner, 172
Barnes, Ross, 5
Barnes, Walter, 27, 63
Barrow, Ed, 118, 159, 161, 162, 164, 167, 171, 173, 175, 176, 179, 181, 183, 184, 200, 206, 209, 215, 242
Barry, Jack, 122, 126–28, 130, 131, 133, 135, 142, 144, 156, 157–61, 230
Beaumont, Ginger, 40, 43–45
Becker, Beals, 99, 100
Bedlent, Hugh, 89, 93, 100, 104, 105, 109–11, 235
Beebe, Fred, 72
Bender, Chief, 36, 64, 95, 96, 122
Berardino, John, 225
Berg, Moe, 212
Bernhard, Bill, 14, 15, 22, 29, 31
Berry, Charlie, 201
Beville, Charlie, 25
Birmingham, Joe, 86
Birtwell, Roger, xxii
Bishop, Max, 208, 210
Boland, Bernie, 121
Boone, Dan, 195
Boudreau, Lou, 233, 239, 241, 245

259

Bowerman, Frank, 34
Bradley, Hugh, 88, 93
Braggins, Dick, 25
Brandt, Bill, 189
Bransfield, William, 41, 45
Brazle, Alpha, 231, 249, 250
Breadon, Sam, 179, 215, 251
Brecheen, Harry, 246, 247, 250
Briggs, Walter, 10, 204
Brower, Frank, 190
Brown, Lloyd, 206
Brown, Mace, 232, 234, 238, 243, 249, 256
Brush, John, 34, 38, 52, 60–62, 96
Burchell, Fred, 79, 80
Burke, Jimmy, 188
Burkett, Jess, 12, 28, 66
Burns, George, 186, 190, 195
Bush, Donie, 141, 211
Bush, Joe, 160, 162, 164, 166–68, 171, 179,
    184–86
Butland, Bill, 231, 238
Byrne, Bob, 134

Cady, Forrest, 93, 97, 103, 104, 109, 111, 127,
    133, 136, 145, 151, 160
Caldwell, Ray, 179
Callahan, Jim, 78, 155
Callahan, Joe, 27, 87
Campbell, Paul, 253
Cannon, Jimmy, 256
Cannon, Ralph, 204
Cantillon, Joe, 24, 74
Carey, Max, 75
Carey, Tom, 231, 243
Carnes, George, xxii
Carpenter, Bob, 233
Carrigan, Bill, 79, 88, 100, 103, 113, 115, 116,
    118–21, 123–32, 134–38, 140, 141–52,
    156, 157, 165, 179, 195, 197, 198, 217, 220,
    229, 255
Cascarella, Joe, 214
Cashman, Joe, 197, 213
Chalmers, George, 124, 132–43
Chamberlain, John, 219
Chance, Frank, 161, 188, 189, 191, 192, 195,
    197, 198
Chapman, Ben, 216, 220, 223

Chapman, Ray, 159
Chapman, Sam, 236
Chase, Ken, 231
Chech, Charles, 82–84
Cheney, Larry, 143, 150
Chesbro, Jack, 39, 53, 56–60, 67, 164
Cicotte, Ed, 79, 80, 84, 88, 93, 141
Cissell, Chalmer, 210
Clark, Dean, 72
Clarke, Fred, 39–41, 43–46
Clarkson, Walter, 54
Coakley, Andy, 64
Cobb, Ty, 68, 75, 76, 79, 84, 93, 115, 122,
    137, 138, 140, 141, 159, 171, 189, 217, 219,
    255
Cochran, George, 172
Cochrane, Mickey, 200
Coffey, Jack, 162
Collier, Willie, 155
Collins, Eddie, 122, 205, 206, 208, 209, 214–
    17, 219, 220, 229, 231, 233, 235, 244
Collins, Eddie, Jr., 209
Collins, Eddie, III, 209
Collins, Jimmy, 12–15, 17–38, 42, 43, 46, 47,
    50, 52–54, 57–60, 62, 70, 73, 74, 78, 153,
    164, 195, 234
Collins, Ray, 84, 88, 93, 99, 106, 122, 199
Collins, Shano, 186, 189, 198, 200
Collins, Warren, 185, 186
Combs, Earl, 76, 86
Comiskey, Charles, 6, 9, 11, 14, 23, 34, 55, 78,
    86, 116, 117, 140, 181
Conant, William, 13, 26, 31, 47
Congalton, Bill, 74, 77
Connolly, Tom, 41, 190
Conroy, W. D., 34, 39
Coombs, Jack, 69, 70, 95, 143, 148
Corcoran, Fred, 241
Corcoran, Larry, 80
Coumbe, Fritz, 119, 180
Coveleskle, Harry, 101, 122, 141
Covelskie, Stan, 253
Covington, Tex, 93
Cramer, Roger, 214, 215, 220, 226, 227
Crandell, Otey, 98
Craveth, Gavvy, 79, 124, 126–28, 130–33,
    135–38, 219

Crawford, Sam, 33, 37, 117, 141, 171
Crichton, Kyle, 241
Criger, Lou, 15, 17, 20, 34–36, 42, 44, 47, 52, 53, 58, 59, 63
Cronin, Joe, 188, 206, 208–16, 218, 220–32, 235, 237–40, 242–46, 248–53, 255
Crosley, Powell, 10
Cross, Monte, 54
Crowder, Enoch, 159, 163
Culberson, Leon, 232, 242, 249, 252, 253
Cuppy, George, 15, 20, 22, 25
Curley, James, 138, 152, 254
Cutshaw, George, 143, 145, 146, 148, 149, 151

Dahgren, Babe, 212
Dahlen, Bill, 143
Daley, Tom, 243
Daubert, Jake, 143, 145, 146, 149, 151, 166
Dauss, George, 122
Davis, George, 35, 38
Davis, Harry, 36, 65, 160, 161
Davis, Ralph, 42
Deal, Chuck, 165–68, 172
Dean, Dizzy, 165, 216
Delehanty, Ed, 28, 31, 33
Dente, Sam, 256
Desautels, Gene, 217, 227
Devery, Bill, 60, 61
Devore, Josh, 97, 103, 105–8, 109–11, 117
Dickey, Bill, 237
Dickman, Emerson, 221–23
Dickson, Murray, 247, 248, 251
DiMaggio, Dominic, 76, 225, 226, 228, 229, 231, 237, 242, 246, 248, 249–53
DiMaggio, Joe, 76, 225, 226, 228, 237, 244, 256
DiMaggio, Vince, 225
Dineen, Bill, 15, 21, 31, 32, 42–45
Dobson, Joe, 227, 231, 237, 238, 243, 249, 250, 252
Doe, Fred, 63
Doerr, Bobby, 217, 220, 222, 233, 237, 242, 246–49
Doheny, Ed, 41
Doherty, Ed, 243
Dolan, Harry, 71

Donlin, Mike, 20
Donnelly, Joe, 195
Donohue, Frank, 28
Donohue, Pat, 79
Donovan, Bill, 33, 119, 141
Donovan, Patsy, 84–86, 88
Doolan, Mickey, 117
Doran, Tom, 52
Dorish, Harry, 256
Dougherty, Pat, 18, 29, 31, 37, 44, 47, 52, 53, 58, 73
Douglas, Phil, 164, 168, 172
Dowd, Tom, 18, 20, 21, 233, 239
Doyle, Jack, 12
Doyle, Larry, 97, 99, 104, 105, 108–11, 117
Dreisward, Clem, 243, 248, 249
Dreyfuss, Barney, 39, 45–47, 61, 160, 211
Drohan, John, xxii, 178, 180, 197, 207
Dubuc, Jean, 168
Duffy, Hugh, 10–12, 14, 26, 31, 34, 65, 72, 184, 185, 187–89, 219–43
Dugan, Joe, 185
Dugey, Oscar, 133, 136
Duggleby, Bill, 28, 29
Dunkle, Davey, 51
Dunn, Jack, 119
Dunn, Jim, 140, 180, 181
Durst, Cedric, 199
Dusak, Erv, 250
Dwyer, Frank, 24
Dyer, Ed, 245–52, 254
Dykes, Jimmy, 216, 217, 227

Eaton, Francis, 116
Ebbetts, Charles, 144, 147, 149, 152, 153
Edgren, Bob, 62
Egan, Ben, 119
Egan, Dave, 256
Ehmke, Howard, 159, 189, 190, 195
Elberfield, Kid, 34, 38, 58, 59, 78
Embree, Red, 239
Engle, Clyde, 86, 88, 107, 112–14, 118
Ennis, Del, 219
Enright, Jim, 190
Evans, Billy, 115, 116, 133, 209, 215, 217, 219, 225, 226
Evers, Johnny, 195

Falk, Bib, 234
Falkenburg, Cy, 86
Farrell, Charles, 35, 37
Farrell, Duke, 52, 66
Farrell, Frank, 56, 60, 61, 67, 78
Feller, Bob, 79, 94, 239, 243
Ferguson, Alex, 187
Ferrell, Rick, 206, 209, 216, 217
Ferrell, Wes, 208–10, 212, 215, 216, 235
Ferriss, Dave, 234, 242, 243, 247, 250–52, 255
Ferriss, Hobe, 17, 20, 21, 32, 42, 45, 46, 53, 57–59, 65, 69, 78, 234
Fewster, Chick, 185, 195
Fine, Tommy, 256
Finn, Mickey, 78
Finnegan, Herb, xxii
Finney, Lou, 222, 225, 228
Fitzgerald, John, 50, 96, 98, 99, 112, 116, 171, 173, 174
Flack, Max, 165, 167, 172, 175, 176
Flagstead, Ira, 201
Flatley, Nick, 120
Fletcher, Art, 97–102, 104, 105, 107, 109, 111, 113, 234
Fogel, Horace, 85, 86
Fohl, Lee, 180, 195, 197
Ford, Edsel, Mrs., 235
Foreman, Frank, 18
Foss, Governor, 96
Foster, George, 118, 122, 123, 128, 129, 134–37, 142, 148, 149, 152, 157, 159, 161
Foster, John, 111
Fothergill, Bob, 17, 91, 201
Fox, Pete, 232
Foxx, Jimmy, 201, 214–16, 220, 222, 225, 228–31
Franklin, James, 9
Fraser, Chick, 14, 22, 29
Frazee, Harry, 52, 66, 154–57, 159–61, 165, 177–91, 193, 194, 196, 206, 231, 234
Freeman, Buck, 14, 20, 22, 25, 26, 29, 31, 37, 42, 53, 63, 66, 78, 179
French, Larry, 200
Frisch, Frank, 200, 216
Fullerton, Hugh, 133
Fultz, Dave, 34

Gaffney, Jim, 120, 129
Gainer, Del, 116, 136, 137, 147, 159
Galehouse, Denny, 222, 223, 225, 227
Gallagher, Ed, 207
Gandil, Chick, 157
Garagiola, Joe, 246, 248, 252
Gardner, Larry, 84, 88, 93, 97, 99–100, 102, 104–9, 128–30, 132–36, 141, 142, 145, 148, 150–52, 160, 199
Garrison, Floyd, 232, 233
Gavin, Joe, 27, 31, 34
Gehrig, Lou, 142, 200
Gessler, Harry, 79
Gibson, Norwood, 38, 53, 56, 64, 65, 67
Gilhooley, Frank, 179
Gilmore, Jim, 95
Goldsmith, Wallace, 63
Gomez, Lefty, 222
Goodrich, Edna, 87
Goodwin, Nat, 87
Gordan, Joe, 60, 228, 230, 237
Gottlieb, Moe, 206, 207
Gould, Charley, 4
Graber, Larry, 155
Graham, Frank, 179, 241
Green, Carl, 49, 51, 66
Green, Charles, 92, 153
Green, William, xxii
Green, Win, 188, 212, 245
Greenburg, Hank, 242, 244
Gregg, Sylvanus, 119
Gregg, Vean, 153, 160
Griffith, Clark, 14, 23, 24–26, 29, 30, 52, 55–59, 61, 64, 74, 78, 181, 183, 185, 208, 210, 211, 231
Grillo, Jed, 47, 48
Grimm, Charley, 241
Grimshaw, Myron, 66
Grove, Lefty, 200, 208–10, 212, 215, 217, 221–25, 228, 229
Gruber, John, 41
Grutteridge, Don, 243, 246, 249, 250

Hack, Stan, 190
Haefner, Mickey, 244, 245
Hale, Odell, 212, 213, 227
Hall, Charles, 84, 86, 89, 94, 98–100, 104

Hallahan, John, 52, 57
Hamilton, Earl, 93
Hanlon, Ned, 41, 53
Harmon, Julia, 70
Harper, Charles, 28
Harper, Harry, 183, 184
Harrington, Dinny, 158
Harris, Bob, 225
Harris, Bucky, 208, 209, 211, 233
Harris, Joe, 69, 148, 195
Harris, Mickey, 225, 230, 237, 243, 246, 250–52
Harriss, Slim, 189, 198
Hart, Juley, 10
Hash, Herb, 225
Haskell, John, 22
Hausman, Clem, 232
Hawley, Davis, 15
Hayden, Mike, 69
Heidrick, Emmet, 28
Heilmann, Harry, 227
Hemphill, Charles, 18, 20
Hendrix, Claude, 164, 168, 169, 172
Henley, Weldon, 64
Henrich, Tom, 237
Henriksen, Olaf, 111, 127, 148
Herman, Babe, 189
Herrmann, Garry, 33, 96, 101, 110, 161, 163, 170, 173, 174, 176, 182
Herzog, Buck, 98–100, 102, 104–8, 111
Heving, Joe, 221, 222, 225
Heydler, John, 173, 174
Higgins, Pinky, 216, 220, 222, 242, 246, 247, 249–51, 253
Hildebrand, George, 168, 169
Hildebrand, Orel, 222
Hilligan, Earl, xxii
Hoblitzel, Dick, 118, 122, 126, 128, 130–33, 135–37, 144, 145, 150, 162
Hoey, Jack, 69
Hoffman, Danny, 54
Hogg, Bradley, 67
Holling, Carl, 189
Hollocher, Charles, 165, 168, 172, 174–76
Hooper, Harry, 85, 86, 88, 89, 93, 97–99, 102, 104, 105, 107, 108, 110–13, 122, 125–28, 130–37, 144, 145, 147, 150, 159, 162

Hopkins, Lolly, 244
Hornsby, Rogers, 219, 255
Hoyt, Waite, 184, 185, 187
Huff, George, 72–74, 77
Huggins, Miller, 92, 184, 186, 187, 207
Hughes, Roy, 213
Hughes, Tom, 29, 31, 38, 42, 52
Hughson, Tex, 229, 231, 233, 237–39, 243, 245, 246, 248, 251, 252, 255
Hulbert, William, 5, 6
Hulswitt, Rudy, 34
Hurwitz, Hy, 241
Hustings, Bert, 29, 30
Huston, Tillinghast, 140, 178, 179, 185

Irwin, Arthur, 9–12, 28
Irwin, Tom, 223
Isaminger, Jimmy, 27

Jackson, Joe, 93, 115, 118, 159
Jacobson, Albert, 73
James, Bill, 121
Janurin, Hal, 118, 128, 138, 142, 144–52
Jasper, Hi, 180
Jennings, Hugh, 12, 13, 75, 120, 122
Johnson, Ban, 8, 10, 12, 14, 19, 22, 24, 25, 28, 29, 31–34, 36, 39–41, 43, 49, 50, 52, 53, 60, 61, 66, 68, 69, 74, 78, 91, 92, 96, 115, 116, 137, 140, 145, 154, 155, 158, 173, 174, 181, 182, 190, 193, 194, 196
Johnson, Bill, 256
Johnson, Bob, 232, 233
Johnson, Earl, 231, 243, 245, 251, 252
Johnson, Henry, 200, 214
Johnson, Jack, 155, 156
Johnson, Rankin, 119
Johnson, Roy, 210, 232
Johnson, Vic, 240
Johnson, Walter, 15, 16, 93, 94, 155, 159
Johnston, Jim, 143, 149
Jolley, Smead, 20
Jones, Charles, 22
Jones, Sam, 139, 162, 166, 174, 175, 184–88
Jordan, Rip, 180
Judd, Oscar, 231
Judge, Joe, 206

INDEX

Kaese, Harold, 237, 240

Kamm, Willie, 200

Karger, Ed, 89

Karr, Benny, 187

Keeler, Willie, 12, 33, 55, 58

Keller, Charles, 237

Kelley, George, 200

Kelley, Joe, 190

Kelley, Mike, 217, 219

Kelley, Peter (Hi Hi), 6, 10, 11, 19, 22–24, 25, 29, 31, 32, 34, 35, 47, 49, 52, 70, 91

Kellum, Winford, 20, 25

Kennedy, Bill, 41, 44

Kennedy, Joseph, 50

Killefer, Bill, 125, 137, 164, 165, 167, 171, 172

Killilea, Henry, 9, 34, 39, 45, 47, 49, 50

Killilea, Matthew, 34

Klein, Bob, 208

Kleinow, Jack, 58–59

Klem, Bill, 106, 136, 146, 147, 168, 170

Klinger, Bob, 243, 252, 253

Knabe, Otto, 117, 168

Knickerbocker, Bill, 213

Knight, Jack, 65, 74, 75

Koney, Chuck, 256

Kopp, Merlin, 160

Kurowski, Whitey, 245, 246, 248, 250–53

LaChance, George, 29, 46, 53, 58, 59, 66

Lajoie, Napoleon, 14, 17, 25, 29, 33, 37, 55

Lake, Austen, xxii

Lake, Eddie, 232, 240

Lake, Fred, 81–85, 93

Landis, Kennesaw, 41, 157, 182, 185, 242

Lanigan, Ernest, xxii

Lannin, Joe, 116–20, 122, 123, 142, 144, 147, 152–55, 182

Lannin, Paul, 117

Lannin, Tom, 17, 139, 140

Lardner, Ring, 120

Lary, Lynn, 209, 210

Lavener, Jimmy, 102

Lavis, Charles, 60

Layden, Peter, 257

Lazor, John, 232

Lazzeri, Tony, 200

Leach, Tommy, 34, 39, 41, 43–45, 47

Lee, Dudley, 195

Leever, Sam, 39, 41, 42, 44

Leonard, Hubert (Dutch), 118, 121, 123, 129, 130, 137, 142, 149, 150, 152, 153, 157, 159, 162, 179

Lewis, Duffy, 86–89, 91, 93, 94, 97, 99, 100, 102, 112, 113, 122, 125, 126, 129–34, 136–38, 144, 147, 149, 152, 157, 159, 161, 179, 196, 199

Lewis, Ed, 14

Lewis, Parson, 22, 24–26

Liebold, Nemo, 186, 235, 256

Lobert, Hans, 117

London, Jack, 87

Long, Dan, 87

Long, Herman, 14, 17

Lord, Harry, 78, 79, 83, 86, 88

Love, Slim, 179, 183

Lowe, Bobby, 14

Lowery, Peanuts, 190

Lucier, Lou, 232

Lundgren, Carl, 72

Lupien, Tony, 225, 230, 234

Lutzke, Rube, 190

Lynch, Tom, 96, 103, 114

MacFayden, Dan, 198–200

Mack, Connie, 9–12, 14, 15, 17, 18, 20, 22, 25, 26, 29, 30, 33, 36, 37, 49, 54, 55, 64, 73, 92, 114, 118, 119, 122, 148, 160, 161, 181, 185, 196, 198, 205, 210, 214, 215, 230, 232

Mack, Gene, xxii

Magee, Lee, 117

Mahony, Steve, 10

Malaneey, Jack, 235, 241

Mann, Les, 165–68, 170, 172–76

Manning, Tom, 9

Maranville, Rabbit, 158, 200

Marcum, John, 214, 215, 217

Marion, Marty, 118, 232, 245, 246, 249, 251–53

Marquard, Rube, 95, 102, 106, 109, 143–45, 147, 149, 150

Mathewson, Christy, 15, 16, 34, 60, 84, 96, 109–13, 140, 171

Mathias, Brother, 119

Mayer, Erskine, 124, 128–30, 135, 136

Mays, Carl, 122, 123, 142, 146–48, 152, 156, 157, 162, 164, 166, 169, 175, 180–82, 185, 187

McAleer, Jim, 14, 15, 30, 81, 91, 92, 105, 107–10, 115, 116

McBreen, Hugh, 14, 66, 70, 91

McBrice, Tom, 232, 236, 242, 246, 253

McCabe, Bill, 172

McCarthy, Joe, 206, 220, 221, 227, 237–38

McCarthy, Tom, 10, 11

McConnell, Anby, 78, 79, 83, 86

McCormich, Harry, 100, 104, 105

McGinnity, Joe, 20, 22, 25, 60

McGlone, Joe, xxii

McGraw, Bob, 181, 183

McGraw, John, 8, 9, 12, 14, 18, 20, 22–24, 26, 32, 35, 38, 39, 52, 53, 60–62, 77, 84, 95, 96, 98–102, 104, 105–10, 112, 113, 114, 116, 117, 143, 144, 187, 211

McGreevey, Nuf Sed, 40

McGuire, Jim, 74, 76, 77, 81, 87

McInnis, Stuffy, 160, 162, 166, 169, 171, 172, 175, 176, 179

McKain, Archie, 222

McLean, Larry, 17, 18, 20

McLin, Shoney, 27

McManus, Marty, 199, 206, 208

McMillan, Norman, 187

McMillan, Ralph, 120, 157, 158

McNair, Eric, 214, 215

McNally, Mike, 118, 141, 147, 158, 159, 184, 232, 256

McRoy, Robert, 91, 92, 107, 108, 110, 116

McVey, Cal, 4, 5

Mele, Sam, 256

Mellio, Oscar, 210

Menosky, Mike, 183, 188, 189, 191

Mercer, Sid, 113

Merkle, Fred, 98, 100, 102, 105, 106–8, 111–13, 117, 143, 145, 149, 164, 166, 167, 169, 172, 176

Mertes, Sam, 34

Metkovich, George, 232, 242, 252

Meusel, Bob, 86, 186

Meyers, Chief, 98–100, 102, 105–8, 111–13, 143, 145, 150, 151

Miller, Bing, 185, 214

Miller, Elmer, 185

Miller, Otto, 148

Milligan, Bill, 21

Mills, Colonel, 216

Milnar, Al, 228

Mitchell, Fred, 20, 25, 29, 30, 164, 166, 168, 169, 171, 172, 174

Mitchell, John, 185

Moore, Terry, 76, 246, 247, 250–52

Moran, John, 120

Moran, Pat, 124, 126, 128–33, 135–37, 142

Morgan, Cy, 74, 80, 84

Moriarty, George, 141

Morrell, John, 6

Morris, Ed, 197, 200

Morse, Jake, 27, 63

Moses, Wally, 242, 251, 253

Mowry, Mike, 143, 145, 146, 148, 150–51

Mullin, Jim, 64

Mundy, Bill, 114

Munger, George, 248, 249

Murnane, Tim, 6, 7, 27, 28, 41, 51, 57, 63, 85, 86, 91, 92, 121, 122, 137, 156, 158

Murphy, Dan, 29–31, 54, 70

Murphy, Ed, 122

Murray, Red, 97–99, 102, 105, 106, 108, 110, 111

Murray, Tom, 187

Musial, Stan, 246–48, 251–53

Mutrie, Jim, xix

Myers, Elmer, 183

Myers, Hi, 143, 146, 148, 149, 151, 172

Myers, Ralph, 88

Navin, Frank, 181, 204

Newhouse, Hal, 94, 244

Newsom, Buck, 210, 216, 217, 222, 224, 241

Newsome, Heber, 232

Newsome, Skeeter, 232

Nickerson, Herman, 91, 154, 155

Niehoff, Bert, 125, 126, 132, 133, 134, 136, 137

Niemlec, Al, 214

Niles, Harry, 83

O'Brien, Jack, 37, 38

O'Brien, Thomas, 92, 93, 102, 106, 107, 114

O'Connell, Dan, 72
O'Connell, Frederick, 63–67, 71, 72
O'Connell, James, 72, 73, 80–82
O'Connell, Joe, 72
O'Connor, Jack, 39
O'Day, Hank, 41, 168
O'Doul, Lefty, 185, 191, 200
O'Leary, Jim, 120
Oliver, Tom, 200, 201
O'Loughlin, Silk, 100, 126, 131, 135, 136
Olson, Ivan, 143, 145, 148–51
O'Neill, Jack, 53
O'Neill, Steve, 159, 195, 244, 245
O'Rourke, Jim, 6, 7
Orth, Al, 28, 56
Osborne, Wilfred, 72
Ostermueller, Fritz, 209, 210, 215, 221–23, 225, 227
Owens, Brick, 158, 168, 171

Padden, Dick, 28
Pape, Larry, 88, 92, 93
Parent, Fred, 17, 20, 21, 25, 37, 53, 57–59, 74, 78
Partee, Roy, 246, 249, 253
Paskert, Dode, 125–31, 133, 135–37, 165, 166, 169, 172, 175, 176
Passeau, Claude, 228
Patten, Case, 51
Peacock, Johnny, 217
Peck, Hal, 235
Peckinpaugh, Roger, 185, 228
Pellagrini, Ed, 231, 242
Pennock, Herb, 23, 153, 159, 183, 184, 186, 187, 209, 216, 229, 231, 233, 242
Pennock, Janet, 209
Pesky, Johnny, 226, 230, 231, 237, 242, 246, 248–53
Peterson, Bob, 67–69
Pfeffer, Jeff, 143, 145, 148, 151
Phelps, Eddie, 41, 45
Phillippe, Deacon, 39, 41–47
Pick, Charles, 165–67, 169, 172, 175, 178
Piercy, Bill, 185, 191
Pipgras, George, 187, 206
Plank, Eddie, 18, 37, 54, 64, 95, 122, 229
Pollet, Howie, 245, 249

Porter, Dick, 209
Powell, Jack, 28, 56, 57, 60
Powers, Mike, 54
Pratt, Derrell, 184, 189
Prentiss, George, 30
Preston, Walter, 13
Price, Jim, 194, 197
Prothro, Doc, 201
Prudhomme, Johnny, 202
Pulliam, Harry, 61
Purtell, Bill, 86, 88
Putman, Ambrose, 59
Pytlak, Frank, 227, 231

Quinn, Bob, 193–201, 203, 204, 206, 208, 232, 234
Quinn, Jack, 185, 186, 190
Quirk, Joe, 92

Reach, Al, 4, 5
Reese, Peewee, 226
Regan, Mike, 40, 63
Reichle, Dick, 191, 192
Rhodes, Gordon, 214
Rice, Del, 246, 247, 251
Rice, Grantland, 241
Rich, Woody, 222
Richey, Claude, 41, 45
Rickey, Branch, 215
Rigler, Cy, 127, 129, 133
Riley, Charles, 173
Riley, Eddie, 91, 120, 153
Risberg, Swede, 157
Rixey, Eppa, 124, 135–37
Rizzuto, Phil, 237
Robertson, Mildred, 210
Robinson, Aaron, 256
Robinson, Wilbert, 20, 96, 112, 143, 144, 146–52
Robison, Frank, 16, 28
Rogell, Bill, 201
Rooney, Gus, 193
Roth, Bobbie, 183
Rothrock, Jack, 201
Rowe, Schoolboy, 227
Rucker, Hap, 143, 150, 152
Ruel, Muddy, 184, 186, 200

Ruffing, Charles, 198–200, 221, 222, 225, 237
Runyon, Damon, 120
Ruppert, Jake, 140, 178, 179, 182, 185–87, 199, 204, 215
Rusell, Bob, 181, 183
Russell, Glen, 246
Russell, Governor, 50
Russell, Rip, 242, 252
Ruth, Babe, 76, 86, 119–22, 127, 129, 132, 134, 141, 146, 147, 149, 153, 157–62, 164, 166, 167, 171–73, 176, 179, 180, 182, 183, 185, 186, 189, 191, 192, 196, 200, 201, 210, 217, 219, 230, 240, 243, 247, 255
Ryan, Jack, 82, 83
Ryba, Dominic, 231
Ryba, Mike, 243, 249, 256

Salsinger, Harry, 121
Savino, George, 214
Sayles, Bill, 222
Schaefer, Herman, 101
Schafer, Harry, 6
Schang, Wally, 160, 167–70, 172, 175, 176, 179, 184
Schlitzert, Vic, 84
Schoendienst, Red, 246, 247, 251–53
Schreckengost, Ossie, 17, 18, 25, 29, 70
Scott, Everett, 118, 121, 126–28, 131–34, 137, 142, 145–47, 149, 151, 153, 162, 166, 169, 171–73, 180, 185, 186, 196, 230
Sebring, Jimmy, 41, 42, 45, 47
Seeds, Bob, 209
Seerey, Pat, 240
Selback, Albert, 53, 59, 63
Sewell, Luke, 229
Sewell, Rip, 240, 241
Seybold, Socks, 70, 179
Shafer, Art, 100, 101
Shanks, Howard, 190
Shannon, Maurice, 183
Shannon, Paul, 40, 72, 91, 120, 179, 197
Shawkey, Bob, 180, 186
Shea, Mervyn, 206
Shean, David, 161, 166, 167, 171, 172, 175, 176, 179
Shelton, Benny, 77
Shibe, Ben, 10, 181

Shocker, Urban, 159
Shofner, Strick, 256
Shore, Ernie, 119–23, 125–27, 132–34, 137, 138, 141, 144, 145, 147, 151, 153, 157–59, 179
Shorten, Charles, 141, 148, 151, 152, 159, 183
Simmons, Al, 200
Sisler, George, 189
Skinner, Camp, 187
Slaughter, Enos, 235, 246–49, 251–53
Smart, Joseph, 34, 36, 40, 41, 45, 47, 49
Smith, Charles, 89
Smith, Elmer, 185
Smith, Frank, 86, 89
Smith, George, 179
Smith, Harry, 34, 41
Smith, Sherry, 143, 146, 147
Snodgrass, Fred, 95, 97, 99, 100, 106, 108, 111–13, 175
Soden, Arthur, 12, 13, 22, 26, 47
Somers, Charles, 9–12, 18, 19, 25, 27–29, 31, 34, 87, 140
Somers, Frank, 82
Soule, Doris, 219
Spalding, Albert, 4, 5
Sparks, Frank, 28, 31
Sparrow, Harry, 113, 184
Speaker, Tris, 76–78, 83, 84, 86, 89, 90, 93, 94, 96–100, 102, 105, 108, 109, 111–13, 115, 117, 118, 122, 125, 126, 128–37, 139–42, 159, 162, 180, 181, 183, 190, 191, 196, 199, 200, 215, 219, 221
Spence, Stan, 226, 231, 244
Spencer, Ed, 81, 83
Spink, J. G., 173, 241
Stahl, Chick, 14, 19, 22, 24–26, 30, 31, 37, 38, 45, 53, 55, 63, 68–72, 74, 81, 82, 103, 104, 108, 109, 113
Stahl, Jake, 35, 52, 72, 78, 79, 88, 91–93, 96–100, 104, 107, 110, 112, 114–16, 118, 134, 142, 238
Stallings, George, 24, 120, 125, 129, 164, 165
Stanage, Oscar, 157
Stansbury, Jack, 162
Steele, Elmer, 79
Stengel, Casey, 143, 145, 148, 149, 200, 226
Stephenson, Riggs, 190

Stevens, Harry, 193, 194
Stock, Milt, 125–27, 129–31, 133, 135–37
Stone, George, 65, 66
Strange, Alan, 210
Strickland, George, 257
Strunk, Amos, 160, 166, 168, 171, 172, 175, 179
Sudhoff, Willie, 28
Sullivan, John L., 18, 35, 179
Sullivan, Mike, 19, 50

Tabor, Jim, 221, 222, 229, 234, 242
Tannenhill, Jesse, 52–55, 64, 65, 67, 69
Tare, Benny, 201
Taylor, Charles, 50, 51, 90–92, 116
Taylor, John I., 49–53, 59, 61, 63, 68–74, 79–87, 89–92, 116, 118, 153, 159, 182
Tener, John, 96, 144, 153, 170
Tenney, Fred, 6, 14, 26, 29
Terry, Bill, 227
Terry, Yank, 232
Tesreau, Jeff, 95–98, 103, 104, 108, 109
Thielman, Jack, 79
Thomas, Chet, 125, 149, 168
Thomas, Fred, 139, 159, 162, 165, 167, 170, 172, 175
Thompson, Jack, 44
Thoney, Jack, 49, 83
Thormalen, Herb, 184
Tinker, Joe, 117, 164
Toporcer, George, 233, 256
Travis, Cecil, 227
Trosky, Hal, 213
Trout, Dizzy, 244
Troy, Phil, 233
Turner, J. H., 91
Tyler, George, 143, 164, 167, 168, 171, 172, 175

Unglaub, Bob, 52, 73, 74, 78

Vail, Fred, 41
Vander Meer, Johnny, 189
Van Ness, Dorothy, 83
Vaughn, Jim, 92, 164, 166–69, 174, 175, 247
Veach, Bobby, 141, 171
Vernon, Mickey, 242

Vick, Sam, 184
Vitt, Oscar, 183
Voiselle, Bill, 225
Von Der Ahe, Chris, 6, 11
Vosmik, Joe, 216, 220

Waddell, Rube, 16–18, 29–30, 36, 53–54, 64, 65
Wade, Jake, 222, 223
Wagner, Hal, 233, 237, 242, 248
Wagner, Heinie, 74, 79, 83, 86, 88, 93, 97–100, 102–4, 106–8, 111, 114, 115, 118, 122, 123, 153, 158, 168, 198, 227, 231, 256
Wagner, Honus, 39, 41, 43–47, 160, 165, 255
Walberg, Rube, 208, 210, 215
Walker, Clarence, 140, 141, 145, 146, 150, 160, 162
Walker, Gee, 227
Walker, Harry, 251–53
Wallace, Rhody, 28
Walsh, Ed, 54, 88, 164
Walsh, Jimmy, 153, 159
Walters, Al, 179, 195
Walters, Bucky, 209
Wambsganss, Bill, 195
Ward, Arch, 240
Ward, Hugh, 154–56
Warner, Jack, 28, 34
Warstler, Hal, 208
Watwood, Johnny, 201
Weaver, Buck, 117, 158, 159
Webb, Earl, 202
Webb, Mel, 19, 51
Weeghman, Charles, 164
Weiland, Bob, 209
Weiss, George, 215
Welaj, John, 231
Welch, Frank, 189
Welch, Jack, 215
Werber, Bill, 206, 209, 213, 216
Wheat, Zack, 143, 145, 147–51
White, Jim, 5–7
Whiteman, George, 77, 161, 166, 168, 169, 171, 172, 175, 176
Whitman, Burt, 120, 165, 168, 176–78, 180, 198
Whitted, George, 125–27, 133–36

Widmar, Al, 256
Wilhelm, Irvin, 41
Wilks, Ted, 248
Willard, Jess, 155
Williams, Alva, 88
Williams, Delores, 241
Williams, Dib, 214
Williams, Jimmy, 58, 59
Williams, May, 218
Williams, Ted, 37, 75, 214, 217–20, 222, 226–
    28, 230, 231, 235, 237, 239–42, 244, 246,
    248, 252, 254–56
Williamson, Ed, 179, 180
Willis, Vic, 15, 21, 33, 34
Wilson, Art, 100, 109
Wilson, Howard, 29
Wilson, Jack, 215, 217, 221–23, 225, 231
Wilson, Woodrow, 127, 129, 163
Wiltse, George, 117
Wiltse, Hal, 198
Winslow, Palmer, 193–96
Winslow, Palmer, Mrs., 196
Winters, George, 18, 25, 30, 31, 36, 38, 51, 53,
    59, 64, 65, 68
Witt, Whitey, 190
Wolast, Ad, 87
Wood, Joe, 79, 84, 88, 93, 94, 96, 97, 98, 103,
    104, 106–15, 118, 122, 123, 134, 139, 142,
    199, 223

Wood, Joe, Jr., 232
Wood, Paul, 107
Woodall, Larry, 243
Woodring, Helen, 159
Woods, Doc, 207
Woods, George, 232
Wortman, Chuck, 172
Wright, George, 3, 4, 6, 7
Wright, Glenn, 211
Wright, Harry, 3, 4, 6, 7
Wright, Orville, 3
Wright, Sam, 5
Wright, Wilbur, 3
Wrigley, Phil, 10
Wrigley, William, Jr., 204
Wyckoff, Weldon, 153

Yawkey, Bill, 203, 204, 208
Yawkey, Tom, 10, 203–6, 214, 216, 220, 224–
    26, 228, 231, 233, 240, 243, 248, 256,
    257
Yerkes, Steve, 88, 93, 97, 99, 100, 103–7, 112
York, Rudy, 240, 245–51, 253
Young, Cy, 15, 16, 18, 20–22, 25–31, 33, 37,
    38, 41–47, 51, 53–55, 57, 60, 62, 64, 65, 71,
    72, 74, 75, 80–84, 88, 158

Zeider, Rollie, 172
Zuber, Bill, 243, 249

Other Books in the Writing Baseball Series

Man on Spikes
ELIOT ASINOF
Foreword by Marvin Miller

Off-Season
ELIOT ASINOF

The American Game: Baseball and Ethnicity
EDITED BY LAWRENCE BALDASSARO AND RICHARD A. JOHNSON
Foreword by Allan H. "Bud" Selig

The Chicago Cubs
WARREN BROWN
Foreword by Jerome Holtzman

My Baseball Diary
JAMES T. FARRELL
Foreword by Joseph Durso

The Brooklyn Dodgers: An Informal History
FRANK GRAHAM
Foreword by Jack Lang

The New York Giants: An Informal History of a Great Baseball Club
FRANK GRAHAM
Foreword by Ray Robinson

The New York Yankees: An Informal History
FRANK GRAHAM
Foreword by Jack Lang

The Best Seat in Baseball, But You Have to Stand!
The Game as Umpires See It
LEE GUTKIND
Foreword by Eric Rolfe Greenberg

Line Drives: 100 Contemporary Baseball Poems
EDITED BY BROOKE HORVATH AND TIM WILES
Foreword by Elinor Nauen

Full Count: Inside Cuban Baseball
MILTON H. JAMAIL
Foreword by Larry Dierker

Owning a Piece of the Minors
JERRY KLINKOWITZ
Foreword by Mike Veeck

The Pittsburgh Pirates
FREDERICK G. LIEB
Foreword by Richard "Pete" Peterson

The St. Louis Cardinals: The Story of a Great Baseball Club
FREDERICK G. LIEB
Foreword by Bob Broeg

Bottom of the Ninth: Great Contemporary Baseball Short Stories
EDITED BY JOHN MCNALLY
Foreword by Richard Russo

The National Game
ALFRED H. SPINK
Foreword by Steven P. Gietschier

Baseball's Natural: The Story of Eddie Waitkus
JOHN THEODORE
Foreword by Ira Berkow